RICHARD III

D1421922

The RSC Shakespeare

Edited by Jonathan Bate and Eric Rasmussen

Chief Associate Editor: Héloïse Sénéchal

Associate Editors: Trey Jansen, Eleanor Lowe, Lucy Munro, Dee Anna Phares, Jan Sewell

Richard III

Textual editing: Eric Rasmussen

Introduction and Shakespeare's Career in the Theatre: Jonathan Bate

Commentary: Charlotte Scott and Héloïse Sénéchal

Scene-by-Scene Analysis: Esme Miskimmin

In Performance: Karin Brown (RSC stagings) and Jan Sewell (overview)

Actor, Director and Designer (interviews by Jonathan Bate and Kevin Wright):
Simon Russell Beale, Bill Alexander and Tom Piper

Reflections: Richard Eyre

Editorial Advisory Board

The RSC Shakespeare

WILLIAM SHAKESPEARE

RICHARD III

Edited by
Jonathan Bate and Eric Rasmussen

Introduced by Jonathan Bate

Macmillan

Published 2008 by
MACMILLAN PUBLISHERS LTD
Houndmills, Basingstoke, Hampshire RG21 6XS
Companies and representatives throughout the world

ISBN-13 978–0–230–22110–9 hardback
ISBN-13 978–0–230–22111–6 paperback

This book is printed on paper suitable for recycling and made from fully managed and sustained forest sources.

A catalogue record for this book is available from the British Library.

10   9   8   7   6   5   4   3   2   1
17 16 15 14 13 12 11 10 09 08

Printed in China

CONTENTS

INTRODUCTION

THE CYCLE OF HISTORY

Shakespeare's first group of historical plays comes to a harmonious conclusion with the defeat of wicked King Richard at the battle of Bosworth Field in 1485. The victorious Henry, Earl of Richmond, belongs to the House of Lancaster. He marries the Princess Elizabeth, of the House of York, thus unifying the nobility and bringing to an end the Wars of the Roses. In the final scene of *Richard the Third*, the Lord Stanley, Earl of Derby, places the crown on Richmond's head and he becomes King Henry VII, inaugurator of the Tudor dynasty. The play closes with a speech in which Henry looks back on the civil strife that has been the subject not just of this play but also of the *Henry the Sixth* sequence. It also looks forward to the golden age over which his wife's namesake, Queen Elizabeth, liked to believe that she reigned:

> England hath long been mad, and scarred herself;
> The brother blindly shed the brother's blood,
> The father rashly slaughtered his own son,
> The son, compelled, been butcher to the sire:
> All this divided York and Lancaster,
> Divided in their dire division.
> O, now let Richmond and Elizabeth,
> The true succeeders of each royal house,
> By God's fair ordinance conjoin together.
> And let thy heirs—God, if thy will be so—
> Enrich the time to come with smooth-faced peace,
> With smiling plenty and fair prosperous days!

On hearing these lines, Shakespeare's audience would themselves have looked both forward and back: back to a bloody period in the nation's history, with relief at how it was providentially ended by the Tudor dispensation; forward to an uncertain future, in the knowledge that the queen was now too old to sustain the line.

Historians still debate the question of how villainous Richard III really was, and in particular whether he personally ordered the slaying of the princes in the Tower. What is not in doubt is that it was convenient for the Tudors to paint him as a villain, in order to make his opponent, the future Henry VII, into a hero and a saint. Sir Thomas More played a major part in the process with his *History of King Richard III*, written at the court of Richmond's son, Henry VIII. Shakespeare finished the work in the public theatre of Henry VIII's younger daughter, immortalizing Richard as the scheming Crookback. The English are notorious for getting their theology from Milton and their history from Shakespeare, rather than from more orthodox sources. The endurance of the image of a Richard who is 'determinèd to prove a villain' is proof of the power of drama to be more memorable than written history. *Richard the Third* is one of those core Shakespearean plays that everybody has heard of, even if they have never read it. The success of two film versions – first Sir Laurence Olivier's and subsequently Sir Ian McKellen's dazzling update to the fascist 1930s – has assured its continuing life.

As in the *Henry the Sixth* plays, the language is frequently elevated and highly rhetorical. The combination of formal language and a sense of symmetry in the events – action leading to reaction, bloody violence to revenge, a slippery rise followed by a crashing fall as the wheel of fortune turns – places the play in the tradition of the Roman tragedian Seneca. The influence on Shakespeare was probably both direct – Seneca had been published in English translation in the 1580s – and indirect, via the multi-authored *Mirror for Magistrates*, a highly Senecan collection of 'complaint' poems, telling of misfortunes and wickedness, written in the voices of the victims of history, including both King Richard's brother George, Duke of Clarence, and King Edward IV's mistress, Jane Shore.

The Senecan symmetry is taken to an extreme in the role of Queen Margaret, the widow of King Henry VI, who had been such a powerful force throughout the Wars of the Roses plays. In Act 1 scene 3, she formally curses Rivers, Dorset, Hastings, Buckingham and Richard himself. All her curses are fulfilled and as each character dies, Richard realizes that this is the case. Senecan tragedy traditionally began with a ghost returning from the underworld and demanding revenge for his or her murder. In an elegant variation, Shakespeare withholds the ghosts for the climax of the play, bringing them on to taunt King Richard in his tent on the eve of the battle that will be his downfall. The scene in which Richard confronts those ghosts would duly become one of the great set-pieces of the English stage: this was the play, and the moment within the play, chosen in the eighteenth century by the actor David Garrick and the painter William Hogarth for the portrait that immortalized Garrick and showed that Shakespeare was a fit subject for art of high moral and historical seriousness.

1. Engraving after William Hogarth's 1745 portrait of the actor David Garrick as Richard facing the ghosts on the night before the battle of Bosworth Field. Executed in the artist's studio, but influenced by the elaborate stage design of the period, this painting inaugurated the tradition of representing great moments in Shakespeare in the style of 'history painting' that had hitherto been reserved for elevated biblical and classical stories. The original portrait is in the Walker Art Gallery, Liverpool.

RICHARD THE PLAYER

Whereas nearly everybody in the *Henry the Sixth* plays appears to be caught up in a maelstrom of historical events that they are not able to control, Richard attempts to take command of his own and his country's destiny. There is little doubt that the part was written for Richard Burbage, just as he was becoming Shakespeare's closest friend in the theatre world. *Richard the Third* is the first of the small group of Shakespearean plays that are not ensemble pieces – as the *Henry the Sixth* plays so clearly were – but star vehicles, in which the leading player has three times as many lines as anybody else. This play was the making of both the writer and the star. It accounts for their nicknames in a well-attested theatrical anecdote that has them as rivals in the bed of a theatre-crazed citizen's wife: Burbage is 'Richard the Third' and Shakespeare 'William the Conqueror'.

The trick that they seem to have worked out together was to make the leading character into the apparent author of his own script. From the very opening soliloquy, Richard takes the audience into his confidence and shares with them the role he will adopt and the plot of the drama that he intends to act out, which might be entitled 'an unlovely but clever man plans his ascent to the throne, not letting anybody – even an innocent child – get in his way'. He is master of the wink and the aside; he rejoices in playing the role of Iniquity, the Vice in the old tradition of morality plays. The audience enjoys his performance exactly because they know it is a performance.

The master actor needs a 'straight man'. For Richard, this role is played by Buckingham, who assists him as he stage-manages his public image for his appearance before the Lord Mayor and citizens of London:

Enter Richard aloft, between two Bishops
MAYOR See, where his grace stands 'tween two clergymen.
BUCKINGHAM Two props of virtue for a Christian prince,
  To stay him from the fall of vanity:
  And, see, a book of prayer in his hand,
  True ornaments to know a holy man.—
  Famous Plantagenet, most gracious prince,

> Lend favourable ear to our requests,
> And pardon us the interruption
> Of thy devotion and right Christian zeal.

In the previous play in the sequence, Henry VI's prayer-book was a sign that he did not want to be king. Richard's is a sign that he is pretending not to want to be king, thus leading the Londoners to beg him to take on the office. 'Will you enforce me to a world of cares?' he says, feigning reluctance – and in the next breath he whispers 'Call them again', ensuring that the offer is renewed so that this time it can be accepted. In all this, he is, as always, the consummate actor.

There are two key turning points for Richard. One is when he contrives to lose his right-hand man, Buckingham. The comedian begins to flounder without his stooge. The other is when the lamenting women who serve as a kind of Greek chorus to the action come together and confront him in the enormously long fourth scene of the fourth act. Richard's bravura seduction of the Lady Anne had revealed his skill with words, but now his verbal power is matched by the combined forces of Queen Margaret and Queen Elizabeth. If one innovation in the writing of *Richard the Third* was the conversion of the ensemble chronicle play into a star vehicle for a single huge theatrical personality, the other was the feminization of this traditionally masculine form. In Shakespeare's earlier history plays, in those of other authors, and indeed in the tragedies of Marlowe, women are bit-part players. Here, however, the boy-actors who play Elizabeth, Margaret and Anne are given larger parts and more richly inflected rhetoric than all of their adult colleagues save the leading three who play Richard, Buckingham and Clarence. Symbolically, given that Richard explains his own lust for power as a consequence of his inadequacy in the arts of love, it is fitting that he meets his match in the form of women and boys.

It is Richard's theatrical self-consciousness that ultimately sets his play above the three parts of *Henry the Sixth*. In *The First Part of Henry the Sixth*, Talbot is a manly hero and Joan an intriguing semi-comic villain; in *The Second Part*, there is splendid energy (Queen Margaret running amok) and variety (Jack Cade and the voice of the discontented commons); in *The Third Part*, we witness a scene of high drama when York is taunted with a paper crown before being stabbed to death. But it is not until Richard of Gloucester gets into his stride that we meet a figure with the compelling theatrical presence of a Falstaff or an Iago. At the climax of his first long soliloquy in Act 3 of *The Third Part of Henry the Sixth* – a speech that the theatrical tradition has often imported into *Richard the Third* – he announces that he will 'play the orator', 'add colours to the chameleon', and 'change shapes with Proteus for advantages'. Each image is of the art of the actor, with his persuasive tongue and power of self-transformation.

BEYOND MARLOWE

Richard adds that he will 'set the murderous Machevil to school'. In his black farce *The Jew of Malta*, Christopher Marlowe had brought on a representation of Machiavelli, the Renaissance archetype of the scheming politician, to speak the prologue. As soon as the Prologue leaves the stage, Barabas the Jew is revealed, speaking his opening soliloquy. The audience thus makes the equation that Barabas is a machiavellian schemer. In *Richard the Third*, Shakespeare made a bold advance on this device. He dispensed with a prologue and began the action with Richard's riveting soliloquy, 'Now is the winter of our discontent'. Where Marlowe had cast Barabas in the role of the machiavel by means of a pointed structural device, Shakespeare's Richard casts himself. He announces that since his crookback prevents him from playing the role of a stage lover, he will self-consciously adopt that of a stage villain. For good measure, he goes on in the second scene to show that he can in fact play the lover – with such accomplishment that he successfully woos Lady Anne over the very corpse of her father-in-law when she knows that he has been responsible for the murder of her first husband. As promised, he plays the orator to supreme effect. By the third act, he is changing shapes with Proteus and, as we have seen, appearing between two bishops in the colour of a holy man. By means of the orator's art of saying the opposite of what he means – 'I cannot, nor

I will not' accept the crown – he wins over the Mayor and the citizens of London.

The character of Richard III is Shakespeare's overstepping of the Marlovian anti-hero. Marlowe's Tamburlaine, Barabas and Dr Faustus fashion their identities by assuming roles – scourge of God, machiavel, conjuror. They do not stop to think that such roles are precisely that: flimsy theatrical impersonations. If they did stop, the whole Marlovian house of cards would come tumbling down. But Shakespeare began from a different place. He was an actor himself. This was the one trump card that was unavailable to Marlowe. Richard is quintessentially Shakespearean, supremely charismatic in the theatre, because he knows that he is a role-player. He revels, and makes the audience revel, in play-acting. He is the first full embodiment of a Shakespearean obsession that culminates in Macbeth's 'poor player' and Prospero's 'These our actors'. It is Iago in *Othello* who says 'I am not what I am'. But Richard could have said it too. And, as the critic Lionel Trilling remarked in a study of *Sincerity and Authenticity* (1972), so could almost every one of Shakespeare's most memorable characters: Hamlet has no sooner heard out the Ghost than he resolves to be what he is not, a madman. Rosalind in *As You Like It* is not a boy, Portia in *The Merchant of Venice* is not a doctor of law, Romeo's beloved Juliet is not a corpse, in *Measure for Measure* the duke is not a friar and Mariana is not Isabella (nor is Helen Diana in *All's Well that Ends Well*), Edgar in *King Lear* is not Tom o' Bedlam, Hermione in *The Winter's Tale* is neither dead nor a statue.

Marlowe's characters invest everything in their aspirations. Shakespeare's are more flexible. They are not what they are. That is surely because Shakespeare was an actor and Marlowe was not. It is also one reason why Shakespeare's characters have a richer, more varied and continuous stage afterlife than Marlowe's. Only in his dreams does Richard stop acting. And when that happens, his identity collapses:

> Cold fearful drops stand on my trembling flesh.
> What? Do I fear myself? There's none else by.
> Richard loves Richard: that is, I am I.

> Is there a murderer here? No. Yes, I am.
> Then fly. What, from myself? Great reason why:
> Lest I revenge. What? Myself upon myself?
> Alack, I love myself. Wherefore? For any good
> That I myself have done unto myself?
> O no! Alas, I rather hate myself
> For hateful deeds committed by myself!

Since he has forged his identity through acting, Richard denies the possibility of an essential being that is anterior to performance. He cannot sustain a language of being –'I am', 'I am not' – because he keeps coming back to particular roles ('villain') and actions (murdering). The moment when an authentic self ought to be asserted, as in a death-bed repentance, becomes that when the self collapses. This is an actor-dramatist's way of looking at the nature of human being.

The Ghosts who appear to him in his dream the night before the last battle force him into the realization that actions have consequences: murder will bring him 'to the bar' and a verdict of 'guilty' will be pronounced. This final emphasis upon guilt is the pragmatic Shakespeare's correction of the blasphemous Marlowe towards religious and moral orthodoxy. Having been granted his earthly crown, Richard is defeated by Henry of Richmond, who has spent the night before the battle of Bosworth Field in pious prayer to the Christian God: 'O thou, whose captain I account myself, / Look on my forces with a gracious eye'. The fall of the over-reacher is thus yoked to the Tudor myth of that providential scheme of history which combined the Houses of York and Lancaster and established the dynasty that brought unity, then Reformation and ambition for imperial glory to the nation.

Further selections from critical commentaries on the play, with linking narrative, are available on the edition website, www.rscshakespeare.co.uk.

ABOUT THE TEXT

Shakespeare endures through history. He illuminates later times as well as his own. He helps us to understand the human condition. But he cannot do this without a good text of the plays. Without editions there would be no Shakespeare. That is why every twenty years or so throughout the last three centuries there has been a major new edition of his complete works. One aspect of editing is the process of keeping the texts up to date – modernizing the spelling, punctuation and typography (though not, of course, the actual words), providing explanatory notes in the light of changing educational practices (a generation ago, most of Shakespeare's classical and biblical allusions could be assumed to be generally understood, but now they can't).

But because Shakespeare did not personally oversee the publication of his plays, editors also have to make decisions about the relative authority of the early printed editions. Half of the sum of his plays only appeared posthumously, in the elaborately produced First Folio text of 1623, the original 'Complete Works' prepared for the press by Shakespeare's fellow-actors, the people who knew the plays better than anyone else. The other half had appeared in print in his lifetime, in the more compact and cheaper form of 'Quarto' editions, some of which reproduced good quality texts, others of which were to a greater or lesser degree garbled and error-strewn. In the case of *Richard III*, there are hundreds of differences between the two early editions, the Quarto of 1597 and the Folio.

Generations of editors have adopted a 'pick and mix' approach, moving between Quarto and Folio readings, making choices on either aesthetic or bibliographic grounds, and creating a composite text that Shakespeare never actually wrote. Not until the 1980s did editors follow the logic of what ought to have been obvious to anyone who works in the theatre: that the Quarto and the Folio texts represent two discrete moments in the life of *Richard III*; that plays change in the course of rehearsal, production and revival, and that the major variants between the early printed versions almost certainly reflect this process.

If you look at printers' handbooks from the age of Shakespeare, you quickly discover that one of the first rules was that, whenever possible, compositors were recommended to set their type from existing printed books rather than manuscripts. This was the age before mechanical typesetting, where each individual letter had to be picked out by hand from the compositor's case and placed on a stick (upside down and back to front) before being laid on the press. It was an age of murky rush-light and of manuscripts written in a secretary hand that had dozens of different, hard-to-decipher forms. Printers' lives were a lot easier when they were reprinting existing books rather than struggling with handwritten copy. Easily the quickest way to have created the First Folio would have been simply to reprint those eighteen plays that had already appeared in Quarto and only work from manuscript on the other eighteen.

But that is not what happened. Whenever Quartos were used, playhouse 'promptbooks' were also consulted and stage directions copied in from them. And in the case of several major plays where a reasonably well-printed Quarto was available, *Richard III* notable among them, the Folio printers were instructed to work from an alternative, playhouse-derived manuscript. This meant that the whole process of producing the first complete Shakespeare took months, even years, longer than it might have done. But for the men overseeing the project, John Hemings and Henry Condell, friends and fellow-actors who had been remembered in Shakespeare's will, the additional labour and cost were worth the effort for the sake of producing an edition that was close to the practice of the theatre. They wanted all the plays in print so that people could, as they wrote in their prefatory address to the reader, 'read him and again and again', but they also wanted 'the great variety of readers' to work from texts that were close to the theatre-life for which Shakespeare originally intended them. For this reason, the *RSC Shakespeare*, in both *Complete Works* and individual volumes, uses the Folio as base text wherever possible. Significant Quarto variants are, however, noted in the Textual Notes, and Quarto-only passages are appended after the text of *Richard III*.

The following notes highlight various aspects of the editorial process and indicate conventions used in the text of this edition:

Lists of Parts are supplied in the First Folio for only six plays, not including *Richard III*, so the list at the beginning of the play is provided by the editors, arranged by groups of character. Capitals indicate that part of the name which is used for speech headings in the script. Thus 'Lord Stanley, Earl of **DERBY**' indicates that lines spoken by this character are always headed '**DERBY**', even though he is sometimes addressed as 'Stanley'.

Locations are provided by the Folio for only two plays. Eighteenth-century editors, working in an age of elaborately realistic stage sets, were the first to provide detailed locations. Given that Shakespeare wrote for a bare stage and often an imprecise sense of place, we have relegated locations to the explanatory notes at the foot of the page, where they are given at the beginning of each scene where the imaginary location is different from the one before. We have emphasized broad geographical settings rather than specifics of the kind that suggest anachronistically realistic staging. We have therefore avoided such niceties as 'another room in the palace'.

Act and Scene Divisions were provided in the Folio in a much more thoroughgoing way than in the Quartos. Sometimes, however, they were erroneous or omitted; corrections and additions supplied by editorial tradition are indicated by square brackets. Five-act division is based on a classical model, and act breaks provided the opportunity to replace the candles in the indoor Blackfriars playhouse which the King's Men used after 1608, but Shakespeare did not necessarily think in terms of a five-part structure of dramatic composition. The Folio convention is that a scene ends when the stage is empty. Nowadays, partly under the influence of film, we tend to consider a scene to be a dramatic unit that ends with either a change of imaginary location or a significant passage of time within the narrative. Shakespeare's fluidity of composition accords well with this convention, so in addition to act and scene numbers we provide a *running scene* count in the right margin at the beginning of each new scene, in the typeface used for editorial directions. Where there is a scene break caused by a momentary bare stage, but the location does not change and extra time does not pass, we use the convention *running scene continues*. There is inevitably a degree of editorial judgment in making such calls, but the system is very valuable in suggesting the pace of the plays.

Speakers' Names are often inconsistent in Folio. We have regularized speech headings, but retained an element of deliberate inconsistency in entry directions, in order to give the flavour of Folio. For the sake of clarity, RICHARD is always so-called in his speech headings, though in the first half of the play he is sometimes addressed as 'Gloucester' and in the Folio text of the second half some of his speeches are headed '*King*'.

Verse is indicated by lines that do not run to the right margin and by capitalization of each line. The Folio printers sometimes set verse as prose, and vice versa (either out of misunderstanding or for reasons of space). We have silently corrected in such cases, although in some instances there is ambiguity, in which case we have leaned towards the preservation of Folio layout. Folio sometimes uses contraction ('turnd' rather than 'turned') to indicate whether or not the final '-ed' of a past participle is sounded, an area where there is variation for the sake of the five-beat iambic pentameter rhythm. We use the convention of a grave accent to indicate sounding (thus 'turnèd' would be two syllables), but would urge actors not to overstress. In cases where one speaker ends with a verse half-line and the next begins with the other half of the pentameter, editors since the late eighteenth century have indented the second line. We have abandoned this convention, since the Folio does not use it, and nor did actors' cues in the Shakespearean theatre. An exception is made when the second speaker actively interrupts or completes the first speaker's sentence.

Spelling is modernized, but older forms are occasionally maintained where necessary for rhythm or aural effect.

Punctuation in Shakespeare's time was as much rhetorical as grammatical. 'Colon' was originally a term for a unit of thought in an argument. The semi-colon was a new unit of punctuation (some of the Quartos lack them altogether). We have modernized punctuation throughout, but have given more weight to Folio punctuation than many editors, since, though not Shakespearean, it reflects the usage of his period. In particular, we have used the colon far more than many editors: it is exceptionally useful as a way of indicating how many Shakespearean speeches unfold clause by clause in a developing argument that gives the illusion of enacting the process of thinking in the moment. We have also kept in mind the origin of punctuation in classical times as a way of assisting the actor and orator: the comma suggests the briefest of pauses for breath, the colon a middling one and a full stop or period a longer pause. Semi-colons, by contrast, belong to an era of punctuation that was only just coming in during Shakespeare's time and that is coming to an end now: we have accordingly only used them where they occur in our copy-texts (and not always then). Dashes are sometimes used for parenthetical interjections where the Folio has brackets. They are also used for interruptions and changes in train of thought. Where a change of addressee occurs within a speech, we have used a dash preceded by a full stop (or occasionally another form of punctuation). Often the identity of the respective addressees is obvious from the context. When it is not, this has been indicated in a marginal stage direction.

Entrances and Exits are fairly thorough in Folio, which has accordingly been followed as faithfully as possible. Where characters are omitted or corrections are necessary, this is indicated by square brackets (e.g. '[*and Attendants*]'). *Exit* is sometimes silently normalized to *Exeunt* and *Manet* anglicized to 'remains'. We trust Folio positioning of entrances and exits to a greater degree than most editors.

Editorial Stage Directions such as stage business, asides, indications of addressee and of characters' position on the gallery stage are only used sparingly in Folio. Other editions mingle directions of this kind with original Folio and Quarto directions, sometimes marking them by means of square brackets. We have sought to distinguish what could be described as *directorial* interventions of this kind from Folio-style directions (either original or supplied) by placing them in the right margin in a different typeface. There is a degree of subjectivity about which directions are of which kind, but the procedure is intended as a reminder to the reader and the actor that Shakespearean stage directions are often dependent upon editorial inference alone and are not set in stone. We also depart from editorial tradition in sometimes admitting uncertainty and thus printing permissive stage directions, such as an *Aside?* (often a line may be equally effective as an aside or a direct address – it is for each production or reading to make its own decision) or a *'may exit'* or a piece of business placed between arrows to indicate that it may occur at various different moments within a scene.

Line Numbers in the left margin are editorial, for reference and to key the explanatory and textual notes.

Explanatory Notes at the foot of each page explain allusions and gloss obsolete and difficult words, confusing phraseology, occasional major textual cruces, and so on. Particular attention is given to non-standard usage, bawdy innuendo and technical terms (e.g. legal and military language). Where more than one sense is given, commas indicate shades of related meaning, slashes alternative or double meanings.

Textual Notes at the end of the play indicate major departures from the Folio. They take the following form: the reading of our text is given in bold and its source given after an equals sign, with 'Q' indicating that it derives from the First Quarto and 'Ed' that it derives from the editorial tradition. The rejected Folio ('F') reading is then given. Thus, for example, at 2.1.108 'at = Q. F = and' means that the Folio compositor erroneously printed 'and', which does not make sense in context, so we have adopted Quarto 'at'.

KEY FACTS

MAJOR PARTS: (*with percentage of lines/number of speeches/scenes on stage*) Richard III/Duke of Gloucester (32%/301/14), Duke of Buckingham (10%/91/11), Queen Elizabeth (7%/98/6), Queen Margaret (6%/33/2), George, Duke of Clarence (5%/33/3), Lady Anne (5%/51/3), Lord Hastings (4%/47/8), Duchess of York (4%/43/4), Henry, Earl of Richmond (4%/14/3), Lord Stanley, Earl of Derby (3%/32/9), King Edward IV (2%/11/1), Sir William Catesby (2%/31/9), Earl Rivers (2%/24/5), Edward, Prince of Wales (1%/19/2), Richard, Duke of York (1%/21/2).

LINGUISTIC MEDIUM: 98% verse, 2% prose.

DATE: 1592? 1594? Must follow the *Henry VI* plays, so perhaps written shortly before the theatres were closed due to plague in June 1592. Alteration of the chronicle sources to flatter Lord Stanley, Earl of Derby, has led some scholars to suppose that the play was written for the acting company of Lord Strange's Men, active at this time, whose patron was Stanley's descendant. Alternatively, Shakespeare might have been writing for Pembroke's Men in 1592: the text also includes brief praise of the Pembroke family name. Some scholars, by contrast, suppose the play to be Shakespeare's first work for the Lord Chamberlain's Men, the company formed after the post-plague reopening of the theatres in summer 1594. Support for this view might come from the way in which the play was clearly written as a showcase for Richard Burbage, the Chamberlain's leading man.

SOURCES: The main source for the representation of Richard as a hunchbacked villain is Sir Thomas More's *History of King Richard III* (c.1513). Since More was writing at the court of King Henry VIII, son of Henry VII, who defeated Richard at Bosworth Field, he had a vested interest in portraying Richard as unfavourably as possible. He got much of his information from Bishop Morton of Ely, a bitter enemy of Richard. More's account was incorporated in the major Tudor chronicles; Shakespeare probably read it via Edward Hall's *Union of the Noble and Illustre Famelies of Lancastre and York* (1548). He may also have consulted Holinshed and one or more other chronicles. The historical poem sequence known as *The Mirror for Magistrates* (1559, expanded 1563) seems to have shaped Shakespeare's treatment of the Clarence plot. The relationship to an anonymous drama *The True Tragedie of Richard the Third* (registered for publication June 1594, poorly printed) is unclear: it seems to have been older play, belonging to the Queen's Men, that was perhaps published to cash in on the success of Shakespeare's version.

TEXT: Quarto edition, 1597, with title advertising the content of the play: *The Tragedy of King Richard the third. Containing, His treacherous Plots against his brother Clarence: the pittiefull murther of his innocent nephewes: his tyrannicall vsurpation: with the whole course of his detested life, and most deserued death. As it hath beene lately Acted by the Right honourable the Lord Chamberlaine his seruants.* Reprinted 1598, with Shakespeare's name on the title page (one of the first printed plays to be so attributed), and again in 1602, 1605, 1612, 1622, 1629, 1634, indicating the play's popularity. Each Quarto was reprinted from the last, with some errors and occasional editorial correction. The 1623 Folio text derives from an independent manuscript that differed substantially from the Quarto tradition, though the Sixth Quarto and to a lesser extent the Third Quarto were consulted in its preparation. There has been much scholarly debate over the sources and relationship of the two texts: their relationship and relative authority has been justifiably described as the most difficult textual problem in all Shakespeare. It appears that the Folio, though printed much later, reflects an earlier version of the play. The Folio text is about 200 lines longer than the Quarto, a difference more probably due to Quarto cutting and streamlining than Folio expansion. The Quarto has just under 40 lines that are not in Folio. There are hundreds of variants of wording. The Folio text is generally more coherent; some of the difficulties of the Quarto have been attributed to 'memorial reconstruction' by actors, but current scholarship questions this view. Though Folio has many deficiencies, some imported from the Quarto tradition and others introduced by the compositors, it requires less editorial intervention to render it comprehensible and theatrically workable. It has been the copy text for most, though not all, scholarly editions, as it is for ours, in accordance with our Folio-based policy.

THE TRAGEDY OF RICHARD THE THIRD:
with the Landing of Earl Richmond and the Battle at Bosworth Field

RICHARD, Duke of Gloucester, later King RICHARD III

Duke of CLARENCE, his brother

Duke of BUCKINGHAM

Lord HASTINGS, the Lord Chamberlain

Sir William CATESBY

Sir Richard RATCLIFFE

Lord LOVELL

BRACKENBURY, Lord Lieutenant of the Tower

Lord Stanley, Earl of DERBY (sometimes addressed as Derby and sometimes as Stanley, here given speech prefix Derby)

KING EDWARD IV, Gloucester's older brother

QUEEN ELIZABETH, his wife

PRINCE EDWARD, their older son

Duke of YORK, their younger son

Lord RIVERS, Elizabeth's brother

Lord GREY, Elizabeth's son by her first husband

Marquis of DORSET, his brother

Sir Thomas VAUGHAN

Lady ANNE, widow of Edward, Prince of Wales, later Duchess of Gloucester

QUEEN MARGARET, widow of Henry VI

DUCHESS OF YORK, mother to Gloucester, Clarence, Edward IV

BOY ⎫
DAUGHTER ⎭ Clarence's children

Earl of RICHMOND, later King Henry VII

Earl of OXFORD

Sir JAMES BLUNT

Sir WALTER HERBERT

Sir WILLIAM BRANDON

Duke of NORFOLK

Earl of SURREY

CARDINAL, Archbishop of Canterbury

ARCHBISHOP OF YORK

BISHOP OF ELY

SIR CHRISTOPHER, a priest

Sir John, a PRIEST

Lord MAYOR of London

List of parts GREY…DORSET in the early scenes, these two may be treated as one figure **widow** historically she was betrothed, not married, to Prince Edward (son of King Henry VI), but in the play (following Hall's chronicle) she is described as his wife/widow

Three CITIZENS

JAMES TYRRELL

Two MURDERERS

MESSENGERS

KEEPER

PURSUIVANT

PAGE

Ghost of KING HENRY VI

Ghost of EDWARD, his son

Two Bishops, Soldiers, Halberdiers, Gentlemen, Lords, Citizens, Attendants

Act 1 Scene 1   *running scene 1*

Enter Richard, Duke of Gloucester, solus

RICHARD Now is the winter of our discontent
Made glorious summer by this son of York:
And all the clouds that loured upon our house
In the deep bosom of the ocean buried.
5   Now are our brows bound with victorious wreaths,
Our bruisèd arms hung up for monuments,
Our stern alarums changed to merry meetings,
Our dreadful marches to delightful measures.
Grim-visaged war hath smoothed his wrinkled front,
10   And now, instead of mounting barbèd steeds
To fright the souls of fearful adversaries,
He capers nimbly in a lady's chamber
To the lascivious pleasing of a lute.
But I, that am not shaped for sportive tricks,
15   Nor made to court an amorous looking-glass:
I, that am rudely stamped, and want love's majesty
To strut before a wanton ambling nymph:
I, that am curtailed of this fair proportion,
Cheated of feature by dissembling nature,
20   Deformed, unfinished, sent before my time
Into this breathing world, scarce half made up,
And that so lamely and unfashionable
That dogs bark at me as I halt by them —
Why, I, in this weak piping time of peace,
25   Have no delight to pass away the time,
Unless to see my shadow in the sun

1.1 *Location: near the Tower of London* **solus** alone   **2 son of York** i.e. Edward IV, whose father was
Richard Duke of York (puns on 'sun', the emblem of the House of York)   **3 loured** frowned threateningly
house family (of York)   **6 arms** armour, weapons   **for** as   **7 alarums** calls to arms/sudden attacks
8 dreadful fearsome, inspiring dread   **measures** stately dances   **9 front** forehead   **10 barbèd** armoured
11 fearful frightened (or possibly 'frightening')   **12 capers** dances with leaping movements/has sex
chamber plays on the sense of 'vagina'   **13 pleasing** attraction, delight   **14 sportive** pleasurable/
amorous/sexual   **tricks** behaviour, skills/sexual acts   **15 court . . . looking-glass** i.e. gaze lovingly at
myself in a mirror, flirt with my own reflection   **16 rudely stamped** crudely formed, roughly printed with
an image   **want** lack   **17 wanton** flirtatious, lascivious   **ambling** sauntering, walking with a sexy rolling
gait   **18 curtailed** deprived, cut short (literally refers to the docking of a dog's tail)   **19 feature** a pleasing
shape   **dissembling** cheating, deceitful   **20 sent . . . time** i.e. born prematurely   **21 made up** fully formed
22 unfashionable odd-looking, inelegant/poorly shaped   **23 halt** limp   **24 piping** characterized by
pastoral pipes, rather than warlike instruments/shrill, weak, contemptible

And descant on mine own deformity.
And therefore, since I cannot prove a lover,
To entertain these fair well-spoken days,
30   I am determinèd to prove a villain
And hate the idle pleasures of these days.
Plots have I laid, inductions dangerous,
By drunken prophecies, libels and dreams,
To set my brother Clarence and the king
35   In deadly hate the one against the other.
And if King Edward be as true and just
As I am subtle, false and treacherous,
This day should Clarence closely be mewed up,
About a prophecy, which says that 'G'
40   Of Edward's heirs the murderer shall be.
Dive, thoughts, down to my soul: here Clarence
          comes.—

Enter Clarence, guarded, and Brackenbury

Brother, good day. What means this armèd guard
That waits upon your grace?

CLARENCE His majesty,
45   Tend'ring my person's safety, hath appointed
This conduct to convey me to th'Tower.

RICHARD Upon what cause?

CLARENCE Because my name is George.

RICHARD Alack, my lord, that fault is none of yours.
50   He should, for that, commit your godfathers.
O, belike his majesty hath some intent
That you should be new-christened in the Tower.
But what's the matter, Clarence, may I know?

CLARENCE Yea, Richard, when I know, but I protest
55   As yet I do not. But, as I can learn,
He hearkens after prophecies and dreams,
And from the cross-row plucks the letter G,
And says a wizard told him that by 'G'
His issue disinherited should be:

---

27 **descant** improvise variations on (musical term), i.e. ponder, comment   29 **entertain** pass enjoyably
well-spoken courteous, harmonious   30 **determinèd** resolved/destined   32 **inductions** initial steps,
preparations   37 **subtle** cunning, sly   **false** dishonest, disloyal   38 **mewed up** imprisoned, cooped up
(like a caged bird of prey)   39 **About** as a result of   **'G'** Clarence's first name is George; Richard, however, is
the Duke of Gloucester   43 **waits upon** attends   45 **Tend'ring** holding dear, being concerned for (ironic)
46 **conduct** escort   **th'Tower** the Tower of London   50 **commit** imprison   **godfathers** sometimes
responsible for the naming of the child at baptism   51 **belike** probably/perhaps   52 **new-christened** a
grim anticipation of Clarence's death by drowning   53 **matter** reason   54 **protest** declare   56 **hearkens
after** listens to   57 **cross-row** alphabet (prefixed by a cross in children's primers)   59 **issue** children

60   And, for my name of George begins with G,
         It follows in his thought that I am he.
         These, as I learn, and such like toys as these,
         Hath moved his highness to commit me now.
      RICHARD Why, this is when men are ruled by women:
65   'Tis not the king that sends you to the Tower,
         My lady Grey his wife, Clarence, 'tis she
         That tempts him to this harsh extremity.
         Was it not she and that good man of worship,
         Anthony Woodville, her brother there,
70   That made him send Lord Hastings to the Tower,
         From whence this present day he is delivered?
         We are not safe, Clarence, we are not safe.
      CLARENCE By heaven, I think there is no man secure
         But the queen's kindred and night-walking heralds
75   That trudge betwixt the king and Mistress Shore.
         Heard you not what an humble suppliant
         Lord Hastings was to her, for his delivery?
      RICHARD Humbly complaining to her deity
         Got my Lord Chamberlain his liberty.
80   I'll tell you what: I think it is our way,
         If we will keep in favour with the king,
         To be her men and wear her livery.
         The jealous o'erworn widow and herself,
         Since that our brother dubbed them gentlewomen,
85   Are mighty gossips in our monarchy.
      BRACKENBURY I beseech your graces both to pardon me:
         His majesty hath straitly given in charge
         That no man shall have private conference,
         Of what degree soever, with your brother.
90   **RICHARD** Even so, an please your worship, Brackenbury,
         You may partake of anything we say.
         We speak no treason, man: we say the king
         Is wise and virtuous, and his noble queen

---

60 for because   **62 toys** whims, trifles   **66 lady Grey** Elizabeth's title before her marriage to Edward; Richard is being contemptuous   **68 worship** repute, honour   **69 Anthony Woodville** i.e. Earl Rivers **71 delivered** released   **74 night-walking heralds** secret, night-time messengers (a night-walker also meant a thief or a prostitute)   **75 trudge betwixt** go to and fro between   **Mistress Shore** Jane Shore, wife of a London goldsmith and Edward IV's lover; she later became Hastings' mistress   **Mistress** usual title for a woman; perhaps here with suggestive play on the sense of 'lover' or even 'female master'   **76 suppliant** petitioner   **77 delivery** release from prison   **78 complaining** appealing, lamenting, pleading   **her deity** a mocking title for Mistress Shore   **79 Lord Chamberlain** i.e. Hastings   **82 men** servants (perhaps with sexual connotations)   **livery** uniform indicating whom one served (**wear her livery** may play on a sense of 'have sex with her')   **83 o'erworn** worn out (like old clothing/sexually)   **widow** i.e. Queen Elizabeth **84 dubbed them** conferred on them the rank of   **85 gossips** chatterers/godparents   **87 straitly . . . charge** strictly ordered   **89 Of . . . soever** regardless of social rank   **90 an** if it

Well struck in years, fair and not jealous.
95   We say that Shore's wife hath a pretty foot,
A cherry lip, a bonny eye, a passing pleasing tongue,
And that the queen's kindred are made gentlefolks.
How say you sir? Can you deny all this?

BRACKENBURY With this, my lord, myself have nought
to do.

100   **RICHARD** Naught to do with Mistress Shore? I tell thee,
fellow,
He that doth naught with her, excepting one,
Were best to do it secretly, alone.

BRACKENBURY What one, my lord?

RICHARD Her husband, knave. Wouldst thou betray me?

105   **BRACKENBURY** I do beseech your grace to pardon me,
and withal
Forbear your conference with the noble duke.

CLARENCE We know thy charge, Brackenbury, and will
obey.

RICHARD We are the queen's abjects, and must obey.—
Brother, farewell. I will unto the king,
110   And whatsoe'er you will employ me in,
Were it to call King Edward's widow sister,
I will perform it to enfranchise you.
Meantime, this deep disgrace in brotherhood
Touches me deeper than you can imagine.   *Embraces him*

115   **CLARENCE** I know it pleaseth neither of us well.

RICHARD Well, your imprisonment shall not be long.
I will deliver you or else lie for you.
Meantime, have patience.

CLARENCE I must perforce. Farewell.

Exit Clarence [led by Brackenbury and Guards]

120   **RICHARD** Go, tread the path that thou shalt ne'er return.
Simple, plain Clarence, I do love thee so
That I will shortly send thy soul to heaven,
If heaven will take the present at our hands.
But who comes here? The new-delivered Hastings?

Enter Lord Hastings

125   **HASTINGS** Good time of day unto my gracious lord.

---

94 **Well . . . years** well advanced in age (Richard seems to pretend to mean 'mature, wise' or 'well-preserved')
fair attractive/just   96 **passing** surpassingly, exceptionally   101 **doth naught** Richard shifts the sense to
'sexually penetrates her vagina'   104 **betray me** i.e. by making me name the king as Shore's lover
105 **withal** moreover   106 **Forbear** restrain, cease   107 **charge** duty, instructions   108 **abjects** varies
'subjects' to incorporate sense of 'contemptible outcasts'   112 **enfranchise** free   114 **Touches** affects
117 **lie for you** take your place in prison (playing on the sense of 'lie about you')   119 **perforce** of necessity
('patience perforce' was proverbial)   123 **present** gift   124 **new-delivered** recently released

RICHARD As much unto my good Lord Chamberlain.
Well are you welcome to this open air.
How hath your lordship brooked imprisonment?
HASTINGS With patience, noble lord, as prisoners must.
130 But I shall live, my lord, to give them thanks
That were the cause of my imprisonment.
RICHARD No doubt, no doubt. And so shall Clarence too,
For they that were your enemies are his,
And have prevailed as much on him as you.
135 **HASTINGS** More pity that the eagles should be mewed,
Whiles kites and buzzards play at liberty.
RICHARD What news abroad?
HASTINGS No news so bad abroad as this at home:
The king is sickly, weak and melancholy,
140 And his physicians fear him mightily.
RICHARD Now, by Saint John, that news is bad indeed.
O, he hath kept an evil diet long,
And overmuch consumed his royal person.
'Tis very grievous to be thought upon.
145 Where is he, in his bed?
HASTINGS He is.
RICHARD Go you before, and I will follow you.

Exit Hastings

He cannot live, I hope, and must not die
Till George be packed with post-horse up to heaven.
150 I'll in to urge his hatred more to Clarence,
With lies well steeled with weighty arguments.
And, if I fail not in my deep intent,
Clarence hath not another day to live:
Which done, God take King Edward to his mercy,
155 And leave the world for me to bustle in.
For then I'll marry Warwick's youngest daughter.
What though I killed her husband and her father?
The readiest way to make the wench amends
Is to become her husband and her father:
160 The which will I, not all so much for love
As for another secret close intent,

128 brooked tolerated   **130 give them thanks** i.e. pay them back, have revenge   **135 mewed** caged
136 kites and buzzards inferior birds of prey   **137 abroad** in the world   **140 him** for him   **142 diet**
lifestyle   **149 packed** packed off, dispatched   **post-horse** all possible speed   **151 steeled** strengthened
with steel, reinforced   **152 deep** cunning/secret   **155 bustle** busy myself, be active   **156 Warwick's
youngest daughter** i.e. Lady Anne Neville; having changed sides, the Earl of Warwick died fighting against
the House of York   **157 her husband** Anne Neville was not in fact married to Prince Edward (Henry VI's
son) although she had been betrothed to him before his death   **father** father-in-law, i.e. Henry VI
161 close concealed

By marrying her which I must reach unto.
But yet I run before my horse to market:
Clarence still breathes, Edward still lives and reigns.
165　　When they are gone, then must I count my gains.

Exit

Act 1 Scene 2
running scene 1 continues

Enter the corpse of Henry the Sixth with [Gentlemen bearing]
halberds to guard it, Lady Anne being the mourner

ANNE Set down, set down your honourable load —
If honour may be shrouded in a hearse —
Whilst I awhile obsequiously lament
Th'untimely fall of virtuous Lancaster.　　*They set down the coffin*
5　　Poor key-cold figure of a holy king,
Pale ashes of the House of Lancaster,
Thou bloodless remnant of that royal blood,
Be it lawful that I invocate thy ghost,
To hear the lamentations of poor Anne,
10　　Wife to thy Edward, to thy slaughtered son,
Stabbed by the selfsame hand that made these
　　　wounds.
Lo, in these windows that let forth thy life,
I pour the helpless balm of my poor eyes.
O, cursèd be the hand that made these holes:
15　　Cursed the heart that had the heart to do it:
Cursed the blood that let this blood from hence!
More direful hap betide that hated wretch
That makes us wretched by the death of thee
Than I can wish to wolves, to spiders, toads,
20　　Or any creeping venomed thing that lives.
If ever he have child, abortive be it,
Prodigious, and untimely brought to light,
Whose ugly and unnatural aspect
May fright the hopeful mother at the view,

162 reach unto strive to carry out　**163 run . . . market** i.e. get ahead of myself (proverbial)
1.2　*Location: a London street*　**halberds** long-handled weapons with axe-like heads　**2 shrouded**
concealed/wrapped in a shroud　**hearse** probably here an open coffin, or litter beneath a frame supporting a
funereal cloth　**3 obsequiously** in a manner proper to the dead　**4 Lancaster** i.e. Henry VI, former head of
the House of Lancaster　**5 key-cold** cold as a metal key (proverbial)　**6 ashes** i.e. remains, lifeless body
8 Be it let it be　**invocate** invoke, call upon　**12 Lo** look　**windows** vents, i.e. wounds　**13 balm** healing
ointment/substance with which the dead are anointed (i.e. tears)　**17 direful hap** dreadful fortune　**betide**
befall, happen to　**19 spiders, toads** thought to be poisonous　**21 abortive** monstrous, deformed
22 Prodigious unnatural/ill-omened　**23 aspect** appearance

25 And that be heir to his unhappiness.
    If ever he have wife, let her be made
    More miserable by the death of him
    Than I am made by my young lord and thee.—
    Come, now towards Chertsey with your holy load,
30 Taken from Paul's to be interrèd there.   *They lift the coffin*
    And still as you are weary of this weight,
    Rest you, whiles I lament King Henry's corpse.
    Enter Richard, Duke of Gloucester
    RICHARD Stay, you that bear the corpse, and set it down.
    ANNE What black magician conjures up this fiend,
35 To stop devoted charitable deeds?
    RICHARD Villains, set down the corpse, or, by Saint Paul,
    I'll make a corpse of him that disobeys.
    GENTLEMAN My lord, stand back, and let the coffin pass.
    RICHARD Unmannered dog, stand'st thou when I
          command.
40 Advance thy halberd higher than my breast,
    Or, by Saint Paul, I'll strike thee to my foot,
    And spurn upon thee, beggar, for thy boldness.   *They set down*
    ANNE What, do you tremble? Are you all afraid?   *the coffin*
    Alas, I blame you not, for you are mortal,
45 And mortal eyes cannot endure the devil.—
    Avaunt, thou dreadful minister of hell!
    Thou hadst but power over his mortal body,
    His soul thou canst not have: therefore be gone.
    RICHARD Sweet saint, for charity, be not so curst.
50 **ANNE** Foul devil, for God's sake, hence, and trouble us
          not,
    For thou hast made the happy earth thy hell,
    Filled it with cursing cries and deep exclaims.
    If thou delight to view thy heinous deeds,
    Behold this pattern of thy butcheries.—   *Uncovers the body*
55 O, gentlemen, see, see dead Henry's wounds
    Open their congealed mouths and bleed afresh.—
    Blush, blush, thou lump of foul deformity,
    For 'tis thy presence that exhales this blood
    From cold and empty veins, where no blood dwells.

---

25 that may that (child)   **unhappiness** ill fortune/misery   **29 Chertsey** on the River Thames, in Surrey;
site of a famous monastery   **30 Paul's** St Paul's Cathedral in London   **31 still as** whenever   **35 devoted**
holy, devout   **40 Advance** raise   **42 spurn upon** kick   **46 Avaunt** be gone   **49 curst** ill-tempered/
cursed, damnable   **50 hence** get hence, go away   **52 exclaims** outcries, exclamations   **54 pattern**
example, model   **58 thy . . . blood** it was popularly believed that the wounds of a murder victim would bleed
in the presence of the murderer   **exhales** draws forth

60   Thy deeds, inhuman and unnatural,
         Provokes this deluge most unnatural.—
         O God, which this blood mad'st, revenge his death!
         O earth, which this blood drink'st, revenge his death!
         Either heav'n with lightning strike the murd'rer
             dead,
65   Or earth gape open wide and eat him quick,
         As thou dost swallow up this good king's blood
         Which his hell-governed arm hath butcherèd!
     RICHARD Lady, you know no rules of charity,
         Which renders good for bad, blessings for curses.
70   ANNE Villain, thou know'st nor law of God nor man:
         No beast so fierce but knows some touch of pity.
     RICHARD But I know none, and therefore am no beast.
     ANNE O, wonderful, when devils tell the truth!
     RICHARD More wonderful, when angels are so angry.
75   Vouchsafe, divine perfection of a woman,
         Of these supposèd crimes to give me leave,
         By circumstance but to acquit myself.
     ANNE Vouchsafe, defused infection of man,
         Of these known evils, but to give me leave,
80   By circumstance to curse thy cursèd self.
     RICHARD Fairer than tongue can name thee, let me have
         Some patient leisure to excuse myself.
     ANNE Fouler than heart can think thee, thou canst make
         No excuse current, but to hang thyself.
85   RICHARD By such despair, I should accuse myself.
     ANNE And by despairing shalt thou stand excused
         For doing worthy vengeance on thyself,
         That didst unworthy slaughter upon others.
     RICHARD Say that I slew them not.
90   ANNE Then say they were not slain.
         But dead they are, and devilish slave, by thee.
     RICHARD I did not kill your husband.
     ANNE Why, then he is alive.
     RICHARD Nay, he is dead, and slain by Edward's hands.
95   ANNE In thy foul throat thou liest: Queen Margaret saw
         Thy murd'rous falchion smoking in his blood,

71 so is so   73 wonderful extraordinary, astonishing   devils...truth Anne interprets Richard's am no
beast to mean that, as neither man nor beast, he must be a devil   75 Vouchsafe permit, consent   76 leave
permission   77 circumstance detailed explanation   78 defused dispersed, spreading   82 leisure time,
opportunity   84 current genuine, valid   85 despair spiritual hopelessness (thought to precede suicide)
87 worthy...thyself i.e. committing suicide (a highly sinful act)   88 unworthy dishonourable,
contemptible/causeless, unjustified   91 slave villain, wretch   95 In...liest i.e. you lie outrageously
96 falchion curved sword

The which thou once didst bend against her breast,
But that thy brothers beat aside the point.

RICHARD I was provokèd by her sland'rous tongue,
100   That laid their guilt upon my guiltless shoulders.

ANNE Thou wast provokèd by thy bloody mind,
That never dream'st on aught but butcheries.
Didst thou not kill this king?

RICHARD I grant ye.

105 ANNE Dost grant me, hedgehog? Then, God grant me too
Thou mayst be damnèd for that wicked deed.
O, he was gentle, mild and virtuous!

RICHARD The better for the king of heaven that hath
      him.

ANNE He is in heaven, where thou shalt never come.

110 RICHARD Let him thank me, that holp to send him
      thither,
For he was fitter for that place than earth.

ANNE And thou unfit for any place but hell.

RICHARD Yes, one place else, if you will hear me name it.

ANNE Some dungeon.

115 RICHARD Your bedchamber.

ANNE Ill rest betide the chamber where thou liest.

RICHARD So will it, madam, till I lie with you.

ANNE I hope so.

RICHARD I know so. But, gentle Lady Anne,
120   To leave this keen encounter of our wits,
And fall something into a slower method:
Is not the causer of the timeless deaths
Of these Plantagenets, Henry and Edward,
As blameful as the executioner?

125 ANNE Thou wast the cause and most accursed effect.

RICHARD Your beauty was the cause of that effect.
Your beauty, that did haunt me in my sleep
To undertake the death of all the world,
So I might live one hour in your sweet bosom.

130 ANNE If I thought that, I tell thee, homicide,
These nails should rend that beauty from my cheeks.

---

97 once at once   102 aught anything   105 hedgehog a contemptuous reference to Richard's crest,
which featured a wild boar   110 holp helped   115 bedchamber like hell, 'chamber' could also be
euphemistic for the vagina   118 I hope so i.e. I certainly hope it will, as I shall never lie with you (in an
ironic anticipation of future events, however, the phrase may also be construed as 'I hope to lie with you')
120 keen sharp/eager   encounter . . . wits plays on the sense of 'sexual encounter of our genitals'
122 timeless untimely, premature   125 effect agent, perpetrator (Richard then shifts the sense to
'outcome')   130 homicide murderer

RICHARD These eyes could never endure that beauty's
    wreck.
    You should not blemish it, if I stood by:
    As all the world is cheerèd by the sun,
135   So I by that: it is my day, my life.
ANNE Black night o'ershade thy day, and death thy life.
RICHARD Curse not thyself, fair creature: thou art both.
ANNE I would I were, to be revenged on thee.
RICHARD It is a quarrel most unnatural
140   To be revenged on him that loveth thee.
ANNE It is a quarrel just and reasonable
    To be revenged on him that killed my husband.
RICHARD He that bereft thee, lady, of thy husband,
    Did it to help thee to a better husband.
145 **ANNE** His better doth not breathe upon the earth.
RICHARD He lives that loves thee better than he could.
ANNE Name him.
RICHARD Plantagenet.
ANNE Why, that was he.
150 **RICHARD** The selfsame name, but one of better nature.
ANNE Where is he?
RICHARD   Here.   *Spits at him*
                    Why dost thou spit at me?
ANNE Would it were mortal poison, for thy sake.
RICHARD Never came poison from so sweet a place.
ANNE Never hung poison on a fouler toad.
155   Out of my sight, thou dost infect mine eyes.
RICHARD Thine eyes, sweet lady, have infected mine.
ANNE Would they were basilisks, to strike thee dead.
RICHARD I would they were, that I might die at once,
    For now they kill me with a living death.
160   Those eyes of thine from mine have drawn salt tears,
    Shamed their aspects with store of childish drops:
    These eyes, which never shed remorseful tear —
    No, when my father York and Edward wept,
    To hear the piteous moan that Rutland made
165   When black-faced Clifford shook his sword at him,
    Nor when thy warlike father, like a child,

---

137 thou art both i.e. day and life   **138 would** wish   **146 He lives** i.e. there is a man   **148 Plantagenet** the name was used by Richard Duke of York, Richard's father   **156 infected mine** both disease and love were thought to enter through the eyes   **157 basilisks** mythical reptiles whose gaze could kill   **158 die** plays on the sense of 'achieve sexual orgasm'   **161 aspects** appearance/looks, gazes   **163 No, when** not even when   **164 Rutland** Richard's younger brother; his death is depicted in *3 Henry VI*, Act 1 scene 3   **165 black-faced** evil, threatening, devilish   **166 father** i.e. the Earl of Warwick (originally a Yorkist, although he later changed sides)

Told the sad story of my father's death,
And twenty times made pause to sob and weep,
That all the standers-by had wet their cheeks
170   Like trees bedashed with rain: in that sad time,
My manly eyes did scorn an humble tear.
And what these sorrows could not thence exhale,
Thy beauty hath, and made them blind with
   weeping.
I never sued to friend nor enemy:
175   My tongue could never learn sweet smoothing word.
But now thy beauty is proposed my fee,
My proud heart sues, and prompts my tongue to speak.
                           She looks scornfully at him
Teach not thy lip such scorn, for it was made
For kissing, lady, not for such contempt.
180   If thy revengeful heart cannot forgive,
Lo, here I lend thee this sharp-pointed sword,   *Gives her his sword*
Which if thou please to hide in this true breast.   *↓Kneels↓*
And let the soul forth that adoreth thee,
I lay it naked to the deadly stroke
185   And humbly beg the death upon my knee.
   He lays his breast open: she offers at [it] with his sword
Nay, do not pause, for I did kill King Henry —
But 'twas thy beauty that provokèd me.
Nay, now dispatch: 'twas I that stabbed young
   Edward —
But 'twas thy heavenly face that set me on.
                             She falls the sword
190   Take up the sword again, or take up me.
ANNE Arise, dissembler. Though I wish thy death,
   I will not be thy executioner.
RICHARD Then bid me kill myself, and I will do it.   *Takes his sword back*
ANNE I have already.
195   RICHARD That was in thy rage:
   Speak it again, and even with the word,
   This hand, which for thy love did kill thy love,
   Shall for thy love kill a far truer love.
   To both their deaths shalt thou be accessory.

---

169 That so that   **170 bedashed** splattered   **171 humble** lowly   **172 exhale** draw out   **174 sued**
entreated, begged (for favour)   **175 smoothing** flattering   **176 fee** payment, reward   *lays ... open* bears
his chest   *offers* aims, makes to thrust   **189 set me on** this probably has connotations of sexual arousal
like **provokèd**   *falls* lets fall   **190 take up me** accept me (perhaps with connotations of 'possess me sexually/
make my penis erect'; Anne interprets 'raise me from my kneeling position')   **191 dissembler**
deceiver   **198 truer love** i.e. Richard himself (supposedly a truer lover than the murdered Edward)

200 ANNE I would I knew thy heart.
RICHARD 'Tis figured in my tongue.
ANNE I fear me both are false.
RICHARD Then never man was true.
ANNE Well, well, put up your sword.
205 RICHARD Say, then, my peace is made.
ANNE That shalt thou know hereafter.
RICHARD But shall I live in hope?
ANNE All men, I hope, live so.
RICHARD Vouchsafe to wear this ring.   *Puts a ring on her*
210   Look how my ring encompasseth thy finger.
        Even so thy breast encloseth my poor heart:
        Wear both of them, for both of them are thine.
        And if thy poor devoted servant may
        But beg one favour at thy gracious hand,
215   Thou dost confirm his happiness forever.
ANNE What is it?
RICHARD That it may please you leave these sad designs
        To him that hath most cause to be a mourner,
        And presently repair to Crosby House,
220   Where after I have solemnly interred
        At Chertsey monast'ry this noble king,
        And wet his grave with my repentant tears —
        I will with all expedient duty see you.
        For divers unknown reasons, I beseech you,
225   Grant me this boon.
ANNE With all my heart, and much it joys me too,
        To see you are become so penitent.—
        Tressell and Berkeley, go along with me.
RICHARD Bid me farewell.
230 ANNE 'Tis more than you deserve,
        But since you teach me how to flatter you,
        Imagine I have said farewell already.
                    Exeunt two [Tressell and Berkeley] with Anne
GENTLEMEN Towards Chertsey, noble lord?
RICHARD No, to Whitefriars. There attend my coming.
                    Exit corpse [borne by the other gentlemen]
235   Was ever woman in this humour wooed?
        Was ever woman in this humour won?

---

201 **figured in** represented by   211 **Even so** in just such a way   219 **presently** immediately   **Crosby House** Richard's London house, in Bishopsgate Street; later referred to as Crosby Place   223 **expedient duty** dutiful haste   224 **divers** various, several   **unknown** private, that cannot be divulged   225 **boon** request, favour   228 **Tressell and Berkeley** minor characters, not mentioned again in the play   234 **Whitefriars** a priory in London   235 **humour** manner, style, way

I'll have her, but I will not keep her long.
What? I, that killed her husband and his father,
To take her in her heart's extremest hate,
240   With curses in her mouth, tears in her eyes,
The bleeding witness of my hatred by,
Having God, her conscience, and these bars against
    me,
And I no friends to back my suit withal,
But the plain devil and dissembling looks?
245   And yet to win her, all the world to nothing?
Ha!
Hath she forgot already that brave prince,
Edward, her lord, whom I, some three months since,
Stabbed in my angry mood at Tewkesbury?
250   A sweeter and a lovelier gentleman,
Framed in the prodigality of nature,
Young, valiant, wise, and, no doubt, right royal,
The spacious world cannot again afford.
And will she yet abase her eyes on me,
255   That cropped the golden prime of this sweet prince,
And made her widow to a woeful bed?
On me, whose all not equals Edward's moiety?
On me, that halts and am misshapen thus?
My dukedom to a beggarly denier!
260   I do mistake my person all this while.
Upon my life, she finds, although I cannot,
Myself to be a marv'llous proper man.
I'll be at charges for a looking-glass,
And entertain a score or two of tailors
265   To study fashions to adorn my body.
Since I am crept in favour with myself,
I will maintain it with some little cost.
But first I'll turn yon fellow in his grave,
And then return lamenting to my love.

---

241 **bleeding witness** i.e. Henry's body   **by** nearby   242 **bars** obstacles   243 **suit** courtship/formal supplication   **withal** with   245 **all ... nothing** i.e. against huge odds, with everything stacked against me   247 **brave** splendid, noble   249 **mood** fit of fury   **Tewkesbury** site of the Gloucestershire battle where the Lancastrians were defeated; Edward's murder took place after the battle and is dramatized in *3 Henry VI*, Act 5 scene 5   251 **Framed ... nature** created when nature was most generous, lavish   252 **royal** majestic, noble   255 **prime** youthful manhood/springtime   257 **whose ... moiety** the entirety of whom is not worth half of Edward   258 **halt** limps   **misshapen** deformed   259 **denier** small coin worth one tenth of a penny   262 **proper** handsome, fine   263 **be ... for** buy, spend money on   264 **entertain** employ   **score ... of** twenty or forty   268 **in** into

270   Shine out, fair sun, till I have bought a glass,
       That I may see my shadow as I pass.   *Exit*

Act 1 Scene 3   *running scene 2*

Enter [Elizabeth] the Queen Mother, Lord Rivers and Lord Grey

RIVERS Have patience, madam. There's no doubt his majesty
       Will soon recover his accustomed health.
GREY In that you brook it ill, it makes him worse: *To Queen Elizabeth*
       Therefore, for God's sake, entertain good comfort,
5   And cheer his grace with quick and merry eyes.
QUEEN ELIZABETH If he were dead, what would betide on me?
GREY No other harm but loss of such a lord.
QUEEN ELIZABETH The loss of such a lord includes all harms.
GREY The heavens have blessed you with a goodly son
10   To be your comforter when he is gone.
QUEEN ELIZABETH Ah, he is young, and his minority
       Is put unto the trust of Richard Gloucester,
       A man that loves not me, nor none of you.
RIVERS Is it concluded he shall be Protector?
15   QUEEN ELIZABETH It is determined, not concluded yet:
       But so it must be, if the king miscarry.
Enter Buckingham and [Stanley, Earl of] Derby
GREY Here come the lords of Buckingham and Derby.
BUCKINGHAM Good time of day unto your royal grace.
DERBY God make your majesty joyful as you have been.
20   QUEEN ELIZABETH The Countess Richmond, good my lord of Derby,
       To your good prayer will scarcely say amen.
       Yet, Derby, notwithstanding she's your wife,
       And loves not me, be you, good lord, assured
       I hate not you for her proud arrogance.

270 **glass** mirror, looking-glass   271 **shadow** also means 'reflection'; the shadow cast by the sun will substitute for the mirror's image   1.3   *Location: the royal court, London*   3 **brook it ill** endure it with difficulty, take it badly   4 **entertain good comfort** take comfort, be cheerful   6 **betide on** happen to, befall   8 **includes** incorporates, is the sum of   9 **goodly** splendid, fine   14 **concluded** legally finalized   **Protector** guardian, who ruled on behalf of a king who was too young to do so   16 **miscarry** die   20 **Countess Richmond** Margaret Beaufort, Derby's wife; by her first husband, Edmund Tudor, she was mother to Henry, Earl of Richmond (later Henry VII)   **good my** my good

25 **DERBY** I do beseech you either not believe
The envious slanders of her false accusers,
Or, if she be accused on true report,
Bear with her weakness, which I think proceeds
From wayward sickness and no grounded malice.
30 **QUEEN ELIZABETH** Saw you the king today, my lord of
Derby?
DERBY But now the Duke of Buckingham and I
Are come from visiting his majesty.
QUEEN ELIZABETH What likelihood of his amendment,
lords?
BUCKINGHAM Madam, good hope: his grace speaks
cheerfully.
35 **QUEEN ELIZABETH** God grant him health. Did you confer
with him?
BUCKINGHAM Ay, madam. He desires to make
atonement
Between the Duke of Gloucester and your brothers,
And between them and my Lord Chamberlain,
And sent to warn them to his royal presence.
40 **QUEEN ELIZABETH** Would all were well! But that will
never be.
I fear our happiness is at the height.
Enter Richard [with Hastings and Dorset]
RICHARD They do me wrong, and I will not endure it.
Who is it that complains unto the king
That I, forsooth, am stern and love them not?
45 By holy Paul, they love his grace but lightly
That fill his ears with such dissentious rumours.
Because I cannot flatter and look fair,
Smile in men's faces, smooth, deceive and cog,
Duck with French nods and apish courtesy,
50 I must be held a rancorous enemy.
Cannot a plain man live and think no harm,
But thus his simple truth must be abused
By silken, sly, insinuating jacks?

---

26 envious malicious   **29 wayward** obstinate, wilful   **36 atonement** reconciliation   **37 brothers** only
one brother, Anthony Woodville (Earl Rivers), appears in the play, but Shakespeare may have thought of him
as two characters: Rivers and Woodville are listed separately in the opening stage directions at Act 2 scene 1,
and are addressed separately later in that scene   **39 warn** summon   **41 happiness** good fortune
44 forsooth indeed, in truth   **stern** harsh, unfriendly   **45 lightly** little   **46 dissentious** inflammatory,
quarrelsome   **47 fair** pleasing, charming   **48 smooth** flatter   **cog** fawn, flatter, deceive   **49 Duck ...
nods** i.e. bow in an affected, courtly manner   **apish** idiotic/imitative   **51 plain** unaffected, simple,
honest   **53 silken** smooth-tongued, ingratiating/elaborately dressed   **jacks** knaves, low-born men; plays
on **Jack**, a common name

GREY To who in all this presence speaks your grace?
55   RICHARD To thee, that hast nor honesty nor grace.
When have I injured thee? When done thee wrong?
Or thee? Or thee? Or any of your faction?
A plague upon you all! His royal grace —
Whom God preserve better than you would wish —
60   Cannot be quiet scarce a breathing-while,
But you must trouble him with lewd complaints.
QUEEN ELIZABETH Brother of Gloucester, you mistake the
matter.
The king, on his own royal disposition,
And not provoked by any suitor else,
65   Aiming, belike, at your interior hatred,
That in your outward action shows itself
Against my children, brothers, and myself,
Makes him to send, that he may learn the ground.
RICHARD I cannot tell. The world is grown so bad
70   That wrens make prey where eagles dare not perch.
Since every Jack became a gentleman,
There's many a gentle person made a jack.
QUEEN ELIZABETH Come, come, we know your meaning,
brother Gloucester:
You envy my advancement and my friends'.
75   God grant we never may have need of you.
RICHARD Meantime, God grants that I have need of you.
Our brother is imprisoned by your means,
Myself disgraced, and the nobility
Held in contempt, while great promotions
80   Are daily given to ennoble those
That scarce some two days since were worth a noble.
QUEEN ELIZABETH By him that raised me to this careful
height
From that contented hap which I enjoyed,
I never did incense his majesty
85   Against the Duke of Clarence, but have been
An earnest advocate to plead for him.
My lord, you do me shameful injury,
Falsely to draw me in these vile suspects.

---

54 **presence** company/royal presence   55 **nor** neither   **grace** virtue/propriety/nobility (picking up on
grace as a form of address in the previous line)   60 **breathing-while** time to draw breath   61 **lewd** wicked/
ignorant/lowly   65 **belike** probably/perhaps   68 **to send** summon (you)   70 **wrens** small, gentle birds
(unlike large, predatory **eagles**)   74 **friends** relatives   77 **brother** i.e. George, Duke of Clarence   81 **noble**
gold coin worth about a third of a pound (puns on **ennoble**)   82 **careful** full of cares   83 **hap** fortune
88 **draw me** implicate me/represent me   **suspects** suspicions

RICHARD You may deny that you were not the mean
90   Of my lord Hastings' late imprisonment.
RIVERS She may, my lord, for—
RICHARD She may, Lord Rivers? Why, who knows not
        so?
        She may do more, sir, than denying that.
        She may help you to many fair preferments,
95   And then deny her aiding hand therein,
        And lay those honours on your high desert.
        What may she not? She may, ay, marry, may she—
RIVERS What, marry, may she?
RICHARD What, marry, may she? Marry with a king,
100   A bachelor and a handsome stripling too.
        Iwis your grandam had a worser match.
QUEEN ELIZABETH My lord of Gloucester, I have too long
        borne
        Your blunt upbraidings and your bitter scoffs.
        By heaven, I will acquaint his majesty
105   Of those gross taunts that oft I have endured.
        I had rather be a country servant-maid
        Than a great queen, with this condition,
        To be so bated, scorned and stormèd at.
        Enter old Queen Margaret [unseen by the others]
        Small joy have I in being England's queen.
110 **QUEEN MARGARET** And lessened be that small, God, I   *Speaks aside*
        beseech him!   *throughout*
        Thy honour, state and seat is due to me.
RICHARD What? Threat you me with telling of the king?   *To Queen*
        I will avouch't in presence of the king.   *Elizabeth*
        I dare adventure to be sent to th'Tower.
115   'Tis time to speak, my pains are quite forgot.
QUEEN MARGARET Out, devil! I do remember them too
        well:
        Thou kill'dst my husband Henry in the Tower,
        And Edward, my poor son, at Tewkesbury.
RICHARD Ere you were queen, ay, or your husband king,   *To Queen*
120   I was a packhorse in his great affairs,   *Elizabeth*

90 **late** recent   94 **preferments** promotions, advancements   96 **desert** deserving, merit   97 **marry** by
the Virgin Mary (Richard goes on to shift the sense to 'wed')   100 **stripling** young man   101 **Iwis** indeed,
certainly   **grandam** grandmother   105 **gross** base/wicked/excessive   *Queen Margaret* historically, the
widow of Henry VI was imprisoned after the battle of Tewkesbury, and later exiled to her native
France   111 **state** rank   **seat** throne   112 **Threat** threaten   113 **avouch't** affirm, declare it
114 **adventure** risk   115 **pains** efforts (made on behalf of the king)   116 **Out** exclamation of outrage and
impatience   119 **Ere** before   120 **packhorse** workhorse

A weeder-out of his proud adversaries,
A liberal rewarder of his friends.
To royalize his blood, I spent mine own.

QUEEN MARGARET Ay, and much better blood than his
or thine.

125 RICHARD In all which time you and your husband Grey
Were factious for the House of Lancaster.—
And, Rivers, so were you.— Was not your husband
In Margaret's battle at St Albans slain?
Let me put in your minds, if you forget,
130 What you have been ere this, and what you are:
Withal, what I have been, and what I am.

QUEEN MARGARET A murd'rous villain, and so still thou
art.

RICHARD Poor Clarence did forsake his father, Warwick,
Ay, and forswore himself — which Jesu pardon! —

135 QUEEN MARGARET Which God revenge!

RICHARD To fight on Edward's party for the crown.
And for his meed, poor lord, he is mewed up.
I would to God my heart were flint, like Edward's,
Or Edward's soft and pitiful, like mine.
140 I am too childish-foolish for this world.

QUEEN MARGARET Hie thee to hell for shame, and leave
this world,
Thou cacodemon! There thy kingdom is.

RIVERS My lord of Gloucester, in those busy days
Which here you urge to prove us enemies,
145 We followed then our lord, our sovereign king.
So should we you, if you should be our king.

RICHARD If I should be? I had rather be a pedlar.
Far be it from my heart, the thought thereof.

QUEEN ELIZABETH As little joy, my lord, as you suppose
150 You should enjoy were you this country's king,
As little joy you may suppose in me,
That I enjoy, being the queen thereof.

QUEEN MARGARET A little joy enjoys the queen thereof,
For I am she, and altogether joyless.

---

121 **proud** ambitious, arrogant   **126 factious for** on the side of, promoting dissent in the interests of
127 **husband...slain** historically, Elizabeth's first husband, Sir John Grey, was killed fighting for the
Lancastrians, although in *3 Henry VI* (Act 3 scene 2) he is depicted as having fought for the Yorkists
128 battle army   **130 ere this** before now   **131 Withal** moreover   **133 Clarence...Warwick** Clarence
and the Earl of Warwick deserted the Yorkists; Clarence married Warwick's daughter, but later returned to
the Yorkist cause, events that are depicted in *3 Henry VI*   **father** father-in-law   **134 forswore himself**
broke his oath (of loyalty)   **137 meed** reward   **139 pitiful** full of pity, compassionate   **140 childish-
foolish** innocent, inexperienced   **141 Hie** hurry   **142 cacodemon** evil spirit   **144 urge** bring forward,
offer as evidence

155 I can no longer hold me patient.—   *Comes forward*
Hear me, you wrangling pirates, that fall out
In sharing that which you have pilled from me.
Which of you trembles not that looks on me?
If not, that I am queen, you bow like subjects,
160 Yet that, by you deposed, you quake like rebels.
Ah, gentle villain, do not turn away.   *To Richard*

RICHARD Foul wrinkled witch, what mak'st thou in my
        sight?

QUEEN MARGARET But repetition of what thou hast
        marred,
That will I make before I let thee go.

165 RICHARD Wert thou not banishèd on pain of death?

QUEEN MARGARET I was, but I do find more pain in
        banishment
Than death can yield me here by my abode.
A husband and a son thou ow'st to me,
And thou a kingdom; all of you allegiance.
170 The sorrow that I have, by right is yours,
And all the pleasures you usurp are mine.

RICHARD The curse my noble father laid on thee,
When thou didst crown his warlike brows with paper
And with thy scorns drew'st rivers from his eyes,
175 And then, to dry them, gav'st the duke a clout
Steeped in the faultless blood of pretty Rutland —
His curses then, from bitterness of soul
Denounced against thee, are all fall'n upon thee,
And God, not we, hath plagued thy bloody deed.

180 QUEEN ELIZABETH So just is God, to right the innocent.

HASTINGS O, 'twas the foulest deed to slay that babe,
And the most merciless that e'er was heard of!

RIVERS Tyrants themselves wept when it was reported.

DORSET No man but prophesied revenge for it.

185 BUCKINGHAM Northumberland, then present, wept to
        see it.

QUEEN MARGARET What? Were you snarling all before I
        came,

---

157 **pilled** pillaged, robbed   159 **If . . . rebels** Even if you do not bow to me as your queen, then you tremble like the rebels who deposed me   161 **gentle** noble, high-born/kind   **villain** low-born, rustic/scoundrel; the phrase is oxymoronic   162 **mak'st thou** are you doing   163 **But repetition of** merely recounting **marred** destroyed   164 **make** do   167 **abode** remaining   169 **thou** i.e. Elizabeth   172 **curse . . . paper** before his death, Richard Duke of York curses Margaret after she mockingly places a paper crown on his head (see *3 Henry VI*, Act 1 scene 4)   175 **clout** cloth   176 **pretty** youthful, fine-looking   **Rutland** York's young son; the episode with the cloth also appears in *3 Henry VI*, Act 1 scene 4   179 **plagued** punished ceaselessly   181 **that babe** i.e. Rutland   184 **No . . . prophesied** there was no man who did not prophesy

Ready to catch each other by the throat,
And turn you all your hatred now on me?
Did York's dread curse prevail so much with heaven?
190 That Henry's death, my lovely Edward's death,
Their kingdom's loss, my woeful banishment,
Should all but answer for that peevish brat?
Can curses pierce the clouds and enter heaven?
Why then give way, dull clouds, to my quick curses.
195 Though not by war, by surfeit die your king,
As ours by murder, to make him a king.—
Edward thy son, that now is Prince of Wales,   *To Elizabeth*
For Edward our son, that was Prince of Wales,
Die in his youth by like untimely violence!
200 Thyself a queen, for me that was a queen,
Outlive thy glory, like my wretched self!
Long mayst thou live to wail thy children's death,
And see another, as I see thee now,
Decked in thy rights, as thou art stalled in mine.
205 Long die thy happy days before thy death,
And, after many lengthened hours of grief,
Die neither mother, wife, nor England's queen.—
Rivers and Dorset, you were standers-by,
And so wast thou, Lord Hastings, when my son
210 Was stabbed with bloody daggers: God, I pray him,
That none of you may live his natural age,
But by some unlooked accident cut off.

RICHARD Have done thy charm, thou hateful withered
hag.

QUEEN MARGARET And leave out thee? Stay, dog, for
thou shalt hear me.
215 If heaven have any grievous plague in store
Exceeding those that I can wish upon thee,
O, let them keep it till thy sins be ripe,
And then hurl down their indignation
On thee, the troubler of the poor world's peace.
220 The worm of conscience still begnaw thy soul.
Thy friends suspect for traitors while thou liv'st,
And take deep traitors for thy dearest friends.

---

187 **catch** seize   192 **but answer for** merely equal   **peevish** foolish, childish/obstinate   194 **dull** thick,
dark, sluggish   **quick** vigorous, lively, sharp   195 **surfeit** sickness resulting from over-indulgence
199 **like** the same   204 **Decked** adorned, dressed   **stalled** installed   208 **standers-by** bystanders,
lookers-on   212 **unlooked** unforeseen, unexpected   213 **charm** magic spell, curse   **hag** witch
217 **them** i.e. the heavens   220 **still** constantly   **begnaw** eat away at, gnaw   221 **for** to be

No sleep close up that deadly eye of thine,
Unless it be while some tormenting dream
225 Affrights thee with a hell of ugly devils.
Thou elvish-marked, abortive, rooting hog,
Thou that wast sealed in thy nativity
The slave of nature and the son of hell.
Thou slander of thy heavy mother's womb,
230 Thou loathèd issue of thy father's loins,
Thou rag of honour, thou detested—

RICHARD Margaret.

QUEEN MARGARET Richard.

RICHARD Ha?

235 **QUEEN MARGARET** I call thee not.

RICHARD I cry thee mercy then, for I did think
    That thou hadst called me all these bitter names.

QUEEN MARGARET Why, so I did, but looked for no reply.
    O, let me make the period to my curse.

240 **RICHARD** 'Tis done by me, and ends in 'Margaret'.

QUEEN ELIZABETH Thus have you breathed your curse
    against yourself.

QUEEN MARGARET Poor painted queen, vain flourish of
    my fortune.
    Why strew'st thou sugar on that bottled spider,
    Whose deadly web ensnareth thee about?
245 Fool, fool, thou whet'st a knife to kill thyself.
    The day will come that thou shalt wish for me
    To help thee curse this poisonous bunch-backed toad.

HASTINGS False-boding woman, end thy frantic curse,
    Lest to thy harm thou move our patience.

250 **QUEEN MARGARET** Foul shame upon you! You have all
    moved mine.

RIVERS Were you well served, you would be taught your
    duty.

QUEEN MARGARET To serve me well, you all should do
    me duty,

---

223 deadly murderous   **226 elvish-marked** physically marked by evil elves at birth   **abortive** monstrous, deformed   **rooting hog** i.e. hunched and greedy; alludes to the boar on Richard's crest   **227 sealed . . . nativity** branded at birth   **228 slave of nature** slave to bestial natural impulses/one irredeemably marked out by nature   **229 slander** disgrace, shame   **heavy** pregnant, weighty/sorrowful   **230 issue** offspring   **231 rag** discarded scrap   **232 Margaret** Richard makes Margaret the subject of her insults to him   **236 cry thee mercy** beg your pardon   **238 looked for** expected   **239 period** end   **242 painted** artificial/made-up with cosmetics   **vain flourish** meaningless, frivolous adornment   **fortune** (rightful) position   **243 bottled** swollen (with venom), rounded, bottle-shaped   **245 thou whet'st** you are sharpening   **247 bunch-backed** hunchbacked   **248 False-boding** falsely prophesying   **frantic** deranged, mad   **251 well served** treated as befits you (Margaret maintains the sense of 'treated' and adds the sense of 'obeyed, paid respect to')   **252 duty** respect, deference

Teach me to be your queen, and you my subjects.
O, serve me well, and teach yourselves that duty.

255 **DORSET** Dispute not with her, she is lunatic.

QUEEN MARGARET Peace, Master Marquis, you are
    malapert:
Your fire-new stamp of honour is scarce current.
O, that your young nobility could judge
What 'twere to lose it, and be miserable.

260 They that stand high have many blasts to shake
    them,
And if they fall, they dash themselves to pieces.

RICHARD Good counsel, marry. Learn it, learn it,
    marquis.

DORSET It touches you, my lord, as much as me.

RICHARD Ay, and much more. But I was born so high,

265 Our eyrie buildeth in the cedar's top,
And dallies with the wind and scorns the sun.

QUEEN MARGARET And turns the sun to shade. Alas,
    alas!
Witness my son, now in the shade of death,
Whose bright out-shining beams thy cloudy wrath

270 Hath in eternal darkness folded up.
Your eyrie buildeth in our eyrie's nest.
O God, that see'st it, do not suffer it.
As it is won with blood, lost be it so!

BUCKINGHAM Peace, peace, for shame, if not for charity.

275 **QUEEN MARGARET** Urge neither charity nor shame to
    me:
Uncharitably with me have you dealt,
And shamefully my hopes by you are butchered.
My charity is outrage, life my shame,
And in that shame still live my sorrow's rage.

280 **BUCKINGHAM** Have done, have done.

QUEEN MARGARET O princely Buckingham, I'll kiss thy
    hand
In sign of league and amity with thee.
Now fair befall thee and thy noble house.

---

256 **Master Marquis** Margaret contemptuously prefaces the aristocratic 'marquis' with the form of address
for an untitled man   **malapert** impertinent   257 **fire-new** brand new, newly minted   **current** valid,
legitimate   258 **nobility** continues the coining imagery with a quibble on 'noble' (a gold coin)   264 **so
high** this high (i.e. noble)   265 **eyrie** nest/brood of young birds of prey (especially eagles, king of birds)/noble
stock of children   266 **dallies with** teases, plays with   **scorns the sun** eagles were thought to be able to
gaze unblinkingly into the sun   267 **sun** puns on **son**   272 **suffer** endure, permit   278 **My charity** the
charity I feel/the charity I am shown   **outrage** violence, hostility   **life my shame** the only life I am allowed
is a dishonourable one/I am ashamed to live   279 **still** perpetually   283 **fair** good fortune

Thy garments are not spotted with our blood,
285 Nor thou within the compass of my curse.
BUCKINGHAM Nor no one here, for curses never pass
The lips of those that breathe them in the air.
QUEEN MARGARET I will not think but they ascend the
sky,
And there awake God's gentle-sleeping peace.
290 O Buckingham, take heed of yonder dog:
Look when he fawns, he bites; and when he bites,
His venom tooth will rankle to the death.
Have not to do with him, beware of him.
Sin, death and hell have set their marks on him,
295 And all their ministers attend on him.
RICHARD What doth she say, my lord of Buckingham?
BUCKINGHAM Nothing that I respect, my gracious lord.
QUEEN MARGARET What, dost thou scorn me for my
gentle counsel?
And soothe the devil that I warn thee from?
300 O, but remember this another day,
When he shall split thy very heart with sorrow,
And say poor Margaret was a prophetess.—
Live each of you the subjects to his hate,
And he to yours, and all of you to God's.   *Exit*
305 **BUCKINGHAM** My hair doth stand on end to hear her
curses.
RIVERS And so doth mine. I muse why she's at liberty.
RICHARD I cannot blame her. By God's holy mother,
She hath had too much wrong, and I repent
My part thereof that I have done to her.
310 **QUEEN ELIZABETH** I never did her any, to my knowledge.
RICHARD Yet you have all the vantage of her wrong.
I was too hot to do somebody good,
That is too cold in thinking of it now.
Marry, as for Clarence, he is well repaid:
315 He is franked up to fatting for his pains —
God pardon them that are the cause thereof!
RIVERS A virtuous and a Christian-like conclusion,
To pray for them that have done scathe to us.

---

285 compass bounds   **286 pass** go any further than   **288 but** anything other than that   **291 Look when** whenever   **292 venom** poisonous   **rankle** inflict a festering wound   **294 marks** blemishes/ identifying insignia/aims, sights   **297 respect** deem worthy of listening to   **299 soothe** flatter, humour   **311 vantage** advantages, benefits (i.e. being queen)   **her wrong** the wrong done to her   **312 hot** eager   **do somebody good** i.e. help Edward to the crown   **313 cold** ungrateful, indifferent   **315 franked . . . fatting** penned in to be fattened up (for slaughter)   **318 scathe** harm

RICHARD So do I ever, being well advised.—

320   For had I cursed now, I had cursed myself.   *Speaks*
                                                                    to himself

Enter Catesby

CATESBY Madam, his majesty doth call for you,
       And for your grace, and yours, my gracious lord.
QUEEN ELIZABETH Catesby, I come. Lords, will you go
       with me?
RIVERS We wait upon your grace.
                              Exeunt all but [Richard of] Gloucester

325   RICHARD I do the wrong, and first begin to brawl.
       The secret mischiefs that I set abroach
       I lay unto the grievous charge of others.
       Clarence, who I indeed have cast in darkness,
       I do beweep to many simple gulls —
330   Namely, to Derby, Hastings, Buckingham —
       And tell them 'tis the queen and her allies
       That stir the king against the duke my brother.
       Now they believe it, and withal whet me
       To be revenged on Rivers, Dorset, Grey.
335   But then I sigh, and with a piece of scripture,
       Tell them that God bids us do good for evil:
       And thus I clothe my naked villainy
       With odd old ends stol'n forth of holy writ,
       And seem a saint when most I play the devil.

Enter two Murderers

340   But, soft, here come my executioners.—
       How now, my hardy, stout-resolvèd mates,
       Are you now going to dispatch this thing?
FIRST MURDERER We are, my lord, and come to have the
       warrant
       That we may be admitted where he is.
345   RICHARD Well thought upon. I have it here about me.   **Gives the warrant**
       When you have done, repair to Crosby Place.
       But, sirs, be sudden in the execution,
       Withal obdurate, do not hear him plead;
       For Clarence is well-spoken, and perhaps
350   May move your hearts to pity if you mark him.

319 **well advised** cautious   324 **wait upon** attend   326 **mischiefs** wicked, evil deeds   **abroach** in
motion   327 **lay . . . of** impose as a serious accusation against (i.e. blame on)   328 **cast in darkness**
caused to be imprisoned (with connotations of death)   329 **beweep** cry over   **gulls** idiots, gullible people
331 **allies** supporters, relatives   332 **stir** incite, stir up   333 **whet** encourage, incite   338 **ends** scraps
341 **hardy** bold   342 **dispatch** carry out (plays on the sense of 'kill')   346 **repair** make your way
347 **sudden** swift   348 **obdurate** inflexible, determined   349 **well-spoken** articulate, persuasive
350 **mark** pay attention to, listen to

FIRST MURDERER Tut, tut! My lord, we will not stand to
      prate:
    Talkers are no good doers. Be assured
    We go to use our hands and not our tongues.
RICHARD Your eyes drop millstones when fools' eyes fall
      tears.
355   I like you, lads. About your business straight.
    Go, go, dispatch.
FIRST MURDERER We will, my noble lord.   [*Exeunt*]

Act 1 Scene 4   *running scene 3*

Enter Clarence and Keeper

KEEPER Why looks your grace so heavily today?
CLARENCE O, I have passed a miserable night,
    So full of fearful dreams, of ugly sights,
    That, as I am a Christian faithful man,
5   I would not spend another such a night,
    Though 'twere to buy a world of happy days,
    So full of dismal terror was the time.
KEEPER What was your dream, my lord? I pray you tell
      me.
CLARENCE Methoughts that I had broken from the
      Tower,
10   And was embarked to cross to Burgundy,
    And in my company my brother Gloucester,
    Who from my cabin tempted me to walk
    Upon the hatches: there we looked toward England,
    And cited up a thousand heavy times,
15   During the wars of York and Lancaster
    That had befall'n us. As we paced along
    Upon the giddy footing of the hatches,
    Methought that Gloucester stumbled, and in falling
    Struck me, that thought to stay him, overboard,
20   Into the tumbling billows of the main.
    O lord, methought, what pain it was to drown!
    What dreadful noise of water in mine ears,
    What sights of ugly death within mine eyes.
    Methoughts I saw a thousand fearful wrecks:

---

351 **prate** chat   354 **eyes drop millstones** proverbial image of hard-heartedness   **fall** let fall, drop
355 **straight** straight away   **1.4** *Location: the Tower of London*   **Keeper** guard (this role could be
conflated with Brackenbury)   1 **heavily** sadly   5 **spend** pass/expend (like money)   6 **Though 'twere**
even if it were   7 **dismal** ominous, sinister   13 **hatches** deck   14 **cited up** recalled   17 **giddy** swaying,
unstable   19 **stay** steady, restrain   20 **main** sea

25   A thousand men that fishes gnawed upon:
      Wedges of gold, great anchors, heaps of pearl,
      Inestimable stones, unvalued jewels,
      All scattered in the bottom of the sea.
      Some lay in dead men's skulls, and in the holes
30   Where eyes did once inhabit, there were crept,
      As 'twere in scorn of eyes, reflecting gems,
      That wooed the slimy bottom of the deep,
      And mocked the dead bones that lay scattered by.
KEEPER Had you such leisure in the time of death
35   To gaze upon these secrets of the deep?
CLARENCE Methought I had, and often did I strive
      To yield the ghost. But still the envious flood
      Stopped in my soul, and would not let it forth
      To find the empty, vast and wand'ring air,
40   But smothered it within my panting bulk,
      Which almost burst to belch it in the sea.
KEEPER Awaked you not in this sore agony?
CLARENCE No, no, my dream was lengthened after life.
      O, then began the tempest to my soul,
45   I passed, methought, the melancholy flood,
      With that sour ferryman which poets write of,
      Unto the kingdom of perpetual night.
      The first that there did greet my stranger soul,
      Was my great father-in-law, renownèd Warwick,
50   Who spake aloud, 'What scourge for perjury
      Can this dark monarchy afford false Clarence?'
      And so he vanished. Then came wand'ring by
      A shadow like an angel, with bright hair
      Dabbled in blood, and he shrieked out aloud,
55   'Clarence is come: false, fleeting, perjured Clarence,
      That stabbed me in the field by Tewkesbury.
      Seize on him, Furies, take him unto torment!'
      With that, methought, a legion of foul fiends
      Environed me, and howlèd in mine ears

---

27 **Inestimable** impossible to count or value   **unvalued** priceless   37 **yield the ghost** die   **envious flood** malicious sea   38 **Stopped in** shut up, blocked in   39 **vast** boundless/empty   40 **bulk** body   42 **sore** serious, extreme   45 **melancholy flood** the River Styx, which had to be crossed to get to Hades, the classical underworld   46 **sour ferryman** Charon, who ferried souls to Hades   47 **kingdom . . . night** Hades, the underworld   48 **stranger** foreign, newly arrived   50 **perjury** oath-breaking; Clarence broke his oath of allegiance to Warwick by returning to fight for the Yorkists after he and Warwick had changed sides to support the Lancastrians   51 **monarchy** kingdom (the underworld)   **afford** offer, give to   53 **shadow** ghost (of Prince Edward, Henry VI's son)   54 **shrieked** ghosts were traditionally supposed to speak in shrill voices   55 **fleeting** fickle, capricious   56 **field** battlefield   57 **Furies** in classical mythology, three female spirits of vengeance   58 **legion** army   59 **Environed** surrounded

60   Such hideous cries, that with the very noise
      I trembling waked, and for a season after
      Could not believe but that I was in hell,
      Such terrible impression made the dream.
   KEEPER No marvel, lord, though it affrighted you,
65   I am afraid, methinks, to hear you tell it.
   CLARENCE Ah, keeper, keeper, I have done these things,
      That now give evidence against my soul,
      For Edward's sake, and see how he requites me.
      O God! If my deep prayers cannot appease thee,
70   But thou wilt be avenged on my misdeeds,
      Yet execute thy wrath in me alone,
      O, spare my guiltless wife and my poor children.
      Keeper, I prithee sit by me awhile.
      My soul is heavy, and I fain would sleep.
75   KEEPER I will, my lord. God give your grace good rest.   *Clarence sleeps*
   Enter Brackenbury, the Lieutenant
   BRACKENBURY Sorrow breaks seasons and reposing
            hours,
      Makes the night morning, and the noontide night.
      Princes have but their titles for their glories,
      An outward honour for an inward toil,
80   And, for unfelt imaginations,
      They often feel a world of restless cares:
      So that between their titles and low name,
      There's nothing differs but the outward fame.
   Enter [the] two Murderers
   FIRST MURDERER Ho, who's here?
85   BRACKENBURY What wouldst thou, fellow? And how
            cam'st thou hither?
   SECOND MURDERER I would speak with Clarence, and I
            came hither on my legs.
   BRACKENBURY What, so brief?
90   FIRST MURDERER 'Tis better, sir, than to be tedious. Let   *Gives*
            him see our commission, and talk no more.   *Brackenbury a paper*
   BRACKENBURY I am in this commanded to deliver   *Reads*
      The noble Duke of Clarence to your hands.
      I will not reason what is meant hereby,

61 **season** while, time   64 **though** if   68 **requites** rewards, repays   73 **prithee** beg you (literally 'I pray thee')   74 **heavy** oppressed, burdened, sorrowful   76 **breaks** cracks, disrupts   **seasons** natural rhythms of time   **reposing hours** time for rest   77 **noontide** midday   78 **for** as   79 **for** at the cost of, as the result of   80 **for** in exchange for   **unfelt imaginations** abstract concepts that cannot actually be experienced, illusory glories   81 **cares** anxieties   82 **low name** those of ordinary humble status   83 **fame** reputation, name   94 **reason** deduce, work out

95   Because I will be guiltless from the meaning.
There lies the duke asleep, and there the keys.
I'll to the king and signify to him
That thus I have resigned to you my charge.   *Exit*
FIRST MURDERER You may, sir, 'tis a point of wisdom.
100   Fare you well.
SECOND MURDERER What, shall we stab him as he
sleeps?
FIRST MURDERER No: he'll say 'twas done cowardly, when
he wakes.
105   **SECOND MURDERER** Why he shall never wake until the
great judgement day.
FIRST MURDERER Why, then he'll say we stabbed him
sleeping.
SECOND MURDERER The urging of that word 'judgement'
110   hath bred a kind of remorse in me.
FIRST MURDERER What? Art thou afraid?
SECOND MURDERER Not to kill him, having a warrant,
but to be damned for killing him, from the which
no warrant can defend me.
115   **FIRST MURDERER** I thought thou hadst been resolute.
SECOND MURDERER So I am, to let him live.
FIRST MURDERER I'll back to the Duke of Gloucester and
tell him so.
SECOND MURDERER Nay, I prithee stay a little. I hope
120   this passionate humour of mine will change. It was   *They pause or*
wont to hold me but while one tells twenty.   *count to twenty*
FIRST MURDERER How dost thou feel thyself now?
SECOND MURDERER Some certain dregs of conscience
are yet within me.
125   **FIRST MURDERER** Remember our reward, when the deed's
done.
SECOND MURDERER Come, he dies. I had forgot the
reward.
FIRST MURDERER Where's thy conscience now?
130   **SECOND MURDERER** O, in the Duke of Gloucester's purse.
FIRST MURDERER When he opens his purse to give us
our reward, thy conscience flies out.
SECOND MURDERER 'Tis no matter, let it go. There's few
or none will entertain it.

---

95 **will** want to   97 **signify to** inform   109 **urging of** bringing forth/emphasis on   119 **stay** wait
120 **passionate humour** emotional mood   **It . . . me** it usually lasts   121 **tells twenty** counts to twenty
134 **entertain** receive, be hospitable to

135　FIRST MURDERER What if it come to thee again?

SECOND MURDERER I'll not meddle with it: it makes a
man a coward. A man cannot steal, but it accuseth
him: a man cannot swear, but it checks him: a man
cannot lie with his neighbour's wife, but it detects

140　him. 'Tis a blushing shamefaced spirit that mutinies
in a man's bosom: it fills a man full of obstacles:
it made me once restore a purse of gold that, by
chance, I found: it beggars any man that keeps it: it is
turned out of towns and cities for a dangerous thing:

145　and every man that means to live well endeavours to
trust to himself and live without it.

FIRST MURDERER 'Tis even now at my elbow, persuading
me not to kill the duke.

SECOND MURDERER Take the devil in thy mind, and

150　believe him not: he would insinuate with thee but to
make thee sigh.

FIRST MURDERER I am strong-framed, he cannot prevail
with me.

SECOND MURDERER Spoke like a tall man that respects

155　thy reputation. Come, shall we fall to work?

FIRST MURDERER Take him on the costard with the hilts
of thy sword, and then throw him into the malmsey-
butt in the next room.

SECOND MURDERER O, excellent device; and make a sop

160　of him.

FIRST MURDERER Soft, he wakes.

SECOND MURDERER Strike!

FIRST MURDERER No, we'll reason with him.

CLARENCE Where art thou, keeper? Give me a cup of
wine.

165　SECOND MURDERER You shall have wine enough, my
lord, anon.

CLARENCE In God's name, what art thou?

FIRST MURDERER A man, as you are.

CLARENCE But not, as I am, royal.

FIRST MURDERER Nor you, as we are, loyal.

---

138 checks rebukes   139 lie have sex   142 restore return   143 keeps retains/maintains, supports
144 for as   145 well prosperously/virtuously   150 him i.e. conscience   insinuate ingratiate himself
154 tall brave   156 Take strike   costard head (literally, a type of large apple)   157 malmsey-butt barrel
of strong, sweet wine from Greece   159 device plan   sop piece of bread soaked in wine   163 reason
converse, talk   165 anon soon

170 CLARENCE Thy voice is thunder, but thy looks are
     humble.
     FIRST MURDERER My voice is now the king's, my looks
     mine own.
     CLARENCE How darkly and how deadly dost thou speak!
     Your eyes do menace me: why look you pale?
     Who sent you hither? Wherefore do you come?
175 SECOND MURDERER To, to, to—
     CLARENCE To murder me?
     BOTH Ay, ay.
     CLARENCE You scarcely have the hearts to tell me so,
     And therefore cannot have the hearts to do it.
180 Wherein, my friends, have I offended you?
     FIRST MURDERER Offended us you have not, but the
     king.
     CLARENCE I shall be reconciled to him again.
     SECOND MURDERER Never, my lord: therefore prepare to
     die.
     CLARENCE Are you drawn forth among a world of men
185 To slay the innocent? What is my offence?
     Where is the evidence that doth accuse me?
     What lawful quest have given their verdict up
     Unto the frowning judge? Or who pronounced
     The bitter sentence of poor Clarence' death,
190 Before I be convict by course of law?
     To threaten me with death is most unlawful.
     I charge you, as you hope for any goodness
     That you depart and lay no hands on me.
     The deed you undertake is damnable.
195 FIRST MURDERER What we will do, we do upon
     command.
     SECOND MURDERER And he that hath commanded is our
     king.
     CLARENCE Erroneous vassals, the great king of kings
     Hath in the table of his law commanded
     That thou shalt do no murder. Will you then
200 Spurn at his edict and fulfil a man's?
     Take heed, for he holds vengeance in his hand,
     To hurl upon their heads that break his law.

---

174 Wherefore why   184 drawn forth selected   187 quest inquest, those holding a judicial inquiry
190 convict convicted   192 charge command   197 Erroneous misguided, erring   vassals servants,
slaves   king of kings i.e. God   198 table...law i.e. the Ten Commandments   199 do no murder the
Sixth Commandment (Exodus 20:13)   200 Spurn at reject, scorn

SECOND MURDERER And that same vengeance doth he
     hurl on thee,
    For false forswearing and for murder, too.
205   Thou didst receive the sacrament to fight
    In quarrel of the House of Lancaster.
FIRST MURDERER And, like a traitor to the name of God,
    Didst break that vow, and with thy treacherous blade
    Unripp'dst the bowels of thy sovereign's son.
210 **SECOND MURDERER** Whom thou wast sworn to cherish
    and defend.
FIRST MURDERER How canst thou urge God's dreadful
    law to us,
    When thou hast broke it in such dear degree?
CLARENCE Alas, for whose sake did I that ill deed?
    For Edward, for my brother, for his sake.
215   He sends you not to murder me for this,
    For in that sin he is as deep as I.
    If God will be avengèd for the deed,
    O, know you yet he doth it publicly.
    Take not the quarrel from his powerful arm:
220   He needs no indirect or lawless course
    To cut off those that have offended him.
FIRST MURDERER Who made thee, then, a bloody
    minister,
    When gallant-springing brave Plantagenet,
    That princely novice, was struck dead by thee?
225 **CLARENCE** My brother's love, the devil and my rage.
FIRST MURDERER Thy brother's love, our duty and thy
    faults,
    Provoke us hither now to slaughter thee.
CLARENCE If you do love my brother, hate not me.
    I am his brother and I love him well.
230   If you are hired for meed, go back again,
    And I will send you to my brother Gloucester,
    Who shall reward you better for my life
    Than Edward will for tidings of my death.
SECOND MURDERER You are deceived, your brother
    Gloucester hates you.

---

204 false forswearing breaking your oath (forbidden by the Ninth Commandment) **205 receive the sacrament** take Communion as a means of affirming your oath **206 In quarrel of** in the cause of **209 Unripp'dst** tore open **bowels** intestines, entrails **sovereign's son** i.e. Prince Edward, son of Henry VI **211 dreadful** inspiring dread and awe **212 dear** extreme, grievous (a) **219 quarrel** (settling of the) dispute **220 indirect** devious, oblique **221 cut off** kill **222 bloody** violent, bloodthirsty **223 gallant-springing** gallant and youthful, growing promisingly **224 novice** youth, beginner **225 My brother's love** love for my brother **230 meed** money, reward

235   **CLARENCE** O no, he loves me, and he holds me dear.
      Go you to him from me.
    FIRST MURDERER Ay, so we will.
    CLARENCE Tell him, when that our princely father York
      Blessed his three sons with his victorious arm,
240   He little thought of this divided friendship.
      Bid Gloucester think on this, and he will weep.
    FIRST MURDERER Ay, millstones, as he lessoned us to
      weep.
    CLARENCE O, do not slander him, for he is kind.
    FIRST MURDERER Right, as snow in harvest.
245   Come, you deceive yourself:
      'Tis he that sends us to destroy you here.
    CLARENCE It cannot be, for he bewept my fortune,
      And hugged me in his arms, and swore, with sobs
      That he would labour my delivery.
250   **FIRST MURDERER** Why, so he doth, when he delivers you
      From this earth's thraldom to the joys of heaven.
    SECOND MURDERER Make peace with God, for you must
      die, my lord.
    CLARENCE Have you that holy feeling in your souls
      To counsel me to make my peace with God,
255   And are you yet to your own souls so blind
      That you will war with God by murd'ring me?
      O, sirs, consider, they that set you on
      To do this deed will hate you for the deed.
    SECOND MURDERER What shall we do?   *To First Murderer*
260   **CLARENCE** Relent, and save your souls.
      Which of you, if you were a prince's son,
      Being pent from liberty, as I am now,
      If two such murderers as yourselves came to you,
      Would not entreat for life as you would beg,
265   Were you in my distress?
    FIRST MURDERER Relent? No: 'tis cowardly and
      womanish.
    CLARENCE Not to relent is beastly, savage, devilish.
      My friend, I spy some pity in thy looks.   *To Second Murderer*
      O, if thine eye be not a flatterer,
270   Come thou on my side, and entreat for me,
      A begging prince what beggar pities not?

---

240 friendship also kinship   **242 lessoned** taught   **243 is kind** is gentle, well-meaning/has feelings of
natural kinship   **249 labour my delivery** strive to obtain my release   **251 thraldom** servitude,
enslavement   **253 feeling** sensibility, awareness   **262 pent** shut up   **267 beastly** not human, lacking in
reason

SECOND MURDERER Look behind you, my lord.

FIRST MURDERER Take that, and that: if all this will not
do,   *Stabs him*

I'll drown you in the malmsey-butt within.
                                                    Exit [with the body]

275 **SECOND MURDERER** A bloody deed, and desperately
dispatched.

How fain, like Pilate, would I wash my hands

Of this most grievous murder!

Enter First Murderer

FIRST MURDERER How now? What mean'st thou, that
thou help'st me not?

By heaven, the duke shall know how slack you have
been!

280 **SECOND MURDERER** I would he knew that I had saved
his brother.

Take thou the fee, and tell him what I say,

For I repent me that the duke is slain.   *Exit*

FIRST MURDERER So do not I. Go, coward as thou art.

Well, I'll go hide the body in some hole

285 Till that the duke give order for his burial.

And when I have my meed, I will away,

For this will out, and then I must not stay.   *Exit*

Act 2 Scene 1   *running scene 4*

*Flourish. Enter the King, sick, the Queen, Lord Marquis
Dorset, Rivers, Hastings, Catesby, Buckingham, Woodville
[and others]*

KING EDWARD IV Why, so. Now have I done a good day's
work.

You peers, continue this united league.

I every day expect an embassage

From my redeemer to redeem me hence,

5   And more to peace my soul shall part to heaven,

Since I have made my friends at peace on earth.—

Dorset and Rivers, take each other's hand:

Dissemble not your hatred, swear your love.

275 **desperately dispatched** carried out in desperation, executed recklessly (**desperately** has connotations
of spiritual hopelessness)   276 **fain** willingly   **Pilate . . . murder** Pontius Pilate, the Roman governor of
Judaea involved in the crucifixion of Christ, washed his hands before the discontented crowd as a means of
exonerating himself from blame   287 **out** get out, be known ('murder will out' was proverbial)
2.1 *Location: the royal court, London*   **Flourish** trumpet fanfare signalling the arrival of a person in
authority   3 **embassage** message   8 **Dissemble not** (in shaking hands) do not conceal, disguise

RIVERS By heaven, my soul is purged from grudging
          hate,

10   And with my hand I seal my true heart's love.   *Gives his hand to*
HASTINGS So thrive I, as I truly swear the like!   *Hastings*
KING EDWARD IV Take heed you dally not before your
          king,
      Lest he that is the supreme king of kings
      Confound your hidden falsehood, and award
15   Either of you to be the other's end.
HASTINGS So prosper I, as I swear perfect love.
RIVERS And I, as I love Hastings with my heart.
KING EDWARD IV Madam, yourself is not exempt from
          this,
      Nor you, son Dorset, Buckingham, nor you;
20   You have been factious one against the other.
      Wife, love Lord Hastings: let him kiss your hand,
      And what you do, do it unfeignedly.
QUEEN ELIZABETH There, Hastings, I will never more
          remember
      Our former hatred, so thrive I and mine.
25   **KING EDWARD IV** Dorset, embrace him.— Hastings, love
          Lord Marquis.
DORSET This interchange of love, I here protest,
      Upon my part shall be inviolable.
HASTINGS And so swear I.   *They embrace*
KING EDWARD IV Now, princely Buckingham, seal thou
          this league
30   With thy embracements to my wife's allies,
      And make me happy in your unity.
BUCKINGHAM Whenever Buckingham doth turn his hate   *To the Queen*
      Upon your grace, but with all duteous love
      Doth cherish you and yours, God punish me
35   With hate in those where I expect most love.
      When I have most need to employ a friend,
      And most assurèd that he is a friend,
      Deep, hollow, treacherous, and full of guile
      Be he unto me. This do I beg of heaven,
40   When I am cold in love to you or yours.   *Embrace*

---

9 from of   **10 true** honest, faithful   **11 thrive I** may I thrive   **12 dally** trifle, feign, mock   **13 king of
kings** i.e. God   **14 Confound** overthrow, catch out   **award** sentence, appoint   **15 end** (cause of) death
19 son i.e. stepson   **20 factious** divisive, generators of factions   **22 unfeignedly** sincerely, without
deception   **26 protest** declare   **30 allies** relatives   **33 but . . . Doth** i.e. and does not, with all duteous love
38 Deep cunning   **hollow** insincere   **guile** cunning, deceit

KING EDWARD IV A pleasing cordial, princely
　　　Buckingham,
　　Is this thy vow unto my sickly heart.
　　There wanteth now our brother Gloucester here,
　　To make the blessèd period of this peace.
45 **BUCKINGHAM** And, in good time,
　　Here comes Sir Richard Ratcliffe and the duke.
Enter Ratcliffe and [Richard, Duke of] Gloucester
RICHARD Good morrow to my sovereign king and queen.
　　And, princely peers, a happy time of day!
KING EDWARD IV Happy, indeed, as we have spent the
　　　day.
50 　　Gloucester, we have done deeds of charity,
　　Made peace of enmity, fair love of hate,
　　Between these swelling wrong-incensèd peers.
RICHARD A blessèd labour, my most sovereign lord.
　　Among this princely heap, if any here,
55 　　By false intelligence, or wrong surmise,
　　Hold me a foe, if I unwillingly, or in my rage,
　　Have aught committed that is hardly borne
　　To any in this presence, I desire
　　To reconcile me to his friendly peace.
60 　　'Tis death to me to be at enmity:
　　I hate it, and desire all good men's love.—
　　First, madam, I entreat true peace of you,
　　Which I will purchase with my duteous service.—
　　Of you, my noble cousin Buckingham,
65 　　If ever any grudge were lodged between us.—
　　Of you and you, Lord Rivers, and of Dorset,
　　That all without desert have frowned on me.—
　　Of you, Lord Woodville, and, Lord Scales, of you:
　　Dukes, earls, lords, gentlemen, indeed, of all.
70 　　I do not know that Englishman alive
　　With whom my soul is any jot at odds
　　More than the infant that is born tonight.
　　I thank my God for my humility.
QUEEN ELIZABETH A holy day shall this be kept hereafter.
75 　　I would to God all strifes were well compounded.—

---

41 cordial heart-restoring medicine   **43 wanteth** only lacks   **44 period** end, completion   **45 in good
time** right on time, at the perfect moment   **47 morrow** morning   **52 swelling** proud, arrogant/incensed,
angry   **wrong-incensèd** full of wrongly directed anger/enraged by perceived wrongs   **54 heap** gathering,
group (casual and demeaning term in this context)   **55 intelligence** information   **surmise** assumption,
conjecture   **57 is hardly borne** has caused offence, is resented   **67 desert** deserving, justification
68 Lord Scales actually another title of Lord Rivers; Shakespeare erroneously supposes another character;
some editors omit the line   **72 the … tonight** a newborn baby   **75 well compounded** settled as effectively

My sovereign lord, I do beseech your highness
To take our brother Clarence to your grace.
RICHARD Why, madam, have I offered love for this
To be so flouted in this royal presence?
80   Who knows not that the gentle duke is dead?

They all start

You do him injury to scorn his corpse.
KING EDWARD IV Who knows not he is dead? Who knows
   he is?
QUEEN ELIZABETH All-seeing heaven, what a world is
   this?
BUCKINGHAM Look I so pale, Lord Dorset, as the rest?
85 DORSET Ay, my good lord, and no man in the presence
   But his red colour hath forsook his cheeks.
KING EDWARD IV Is Clarence dead? The order was
   reversed.
RICHARD But he, poor man, by your first order died,
   And that a wingèd Mercury did bear:
90   Some tardy cripple bare the countermand,
   That came too lag to see him burièd.
   God grant that some, less noble and less loyal,
   Nearer in bloody thoughts, and not in blood,
   Deserve not worse than wretched Clarence did,
95   And yet go current from suspicion.

Enter [Lord Stanley,] Earl of Derby

DERBY A boon, my sovereign, for my service done.   *Kneels*
KING EDWARD IV I prithee peace. My soul is full of sorrow.
DERBY I will not rise, unless your highness hear me.
KING EDWARD IV Then say at once what is it thou
   requests.
100 DERBY The forfeit, sovereign, of my servant's life,   *Rises*
   Who slew today a riotous gentleman
   Lately attendant on the Duke of Norfolk.
KING EDWARD IV Have I a tongue to doom my brother's
   death,
   And shall that tongue give pardon to a slave?
105   My brother killed no man: his fault was thought,

77 to your grace into your favour   79 flouted mocked   80 gentle kind, mild/noble   86 forsook
abandoned   89 that i.e. that first order   Mercury swift messenger of the Roman gods, usually depicted with
wings on his cap and sandals   90 tardy slow   bare the countermand brought the order revoking the
first   91 lag late, slowly   92 God . . . suspicion I pray God there are none, less noble and loyal than
Clarence, more involved in treachery yet less closely related to the king, who deserve worse than Clarence's
fate yet go free from suspicion (a pointed remark aimed at Elizabeth and her relatives)   95 go current pass
as legitimate coin   96 boon request for a favour   100 forfeit . . . life revocation of the death penalty that his
servant has incurred   103 doom . . . death sentence (doom) my brother to death

And yet his punishment was bitter death.
Who sued to me for him? Who, in my wrath,
Kneeled at my feet, and bid me be advised?
Who spoke of brotherhood? Who spoke of love?
110 Who told me how the poor soul did forsake
The mighty Warwick and did fight for me?
Who told me, in the field at Tewkesbury
When Oxford had me down, he rescued me,
And said, 'Dear brother, live, and be a king'?
115 Who told me, when we both lay in the field,
Frozen almost to death, how he did lap me
Even in his garments, and did give himself,
All thin and naked, to the numb cold night?
All this from my remembrance brutish wrath
120 Sinfully plucked, and not a man of you
Had so much grace to put it in my mind.
But when your carters or your waiting vassals
Have done a drunken slaughter, and defaced
The precious image of our dear Redeemer,
125 You straight are on your knees for pardon, pardon,
And I, unjustly too, must grant it you.
But for my brother not a man would speak,
Nor I, ungracious, speak unto myself
For him, poor soul. The proudest of you all
130 Have been beholding to him in his life,
Yet none of you would once beg for his life.
O God, I fear thy justice will take hold
On me, and you, and mine, and yours for this!—
Come, Hastings, help me to my closet.
135 Ah, poor Clarence.

Exeunt some with King and Queen

RICHARD This is the fruits of rashness. Marked you not
How that the guilty kindred of the queen
Looked pale when they did hear of Clarence' death?
O, they did urge it still unto the king!
140 God will revenge it. Come, lords, will you go
To comfort Edward with our company.

BUCKINGHAM We wait upon your grace.   *Exeunt*

---

107 sued pleaded   **108 be advised** to reconsider, reflect/to be cautious   **110 forsake** abandon, renounce   **112 field** battlefield   **113 down** on the ground, unhorsed/at his mercy   **116 lap** enfold, swathe   **118 thin** thinly dressed   **numb** numbing   **119 remembrance** memory   **122 carters** cart drivers   **waiting vassals** attendant servants   **123 defaced … Redeemer** i.e. committed murder (since man is made in God's image)   **125 straight** straight away   **127 But** yet   **128 ungracious** wickedly, lacking divine grace   **129 proudest** most splendid, eminent/most self-esteeming   **130 beholding** beholden, indebted   **133 On of you** i.e. the assembled company   **134 closet** private room/bedchamber   **136 Marked** observed, noticed   **139 still** constantly

Act 2 Scene 2

*Enter the old Duchess of York with the two children of
Clarence*

BOY Good grandam, tell us, is our father dead?
DUCHESS OF YORK No, boy.
DAUGHTER Why do you weep so oft, and beat your
  breast,
  And cry 'O Clarence, my unhappy son'?
5 **BOY** Why do you look on us, and shake your head,
  And call us orphans, wretches, castaways,
  If that our noble father were alive?
 DUCHESS OF YORK My pretty cousins, you mistake me
  both:
  I do lament the sickness of the king,
10 As loath to lose him, not your father's death.
  It were lost sorrow to wail one that's lost.
 BOY Then you conclude, my grandam, he is dead.
  The king mine uncle is to blame for it.
  God will revenge it, whom I will importune
15 With earnest prayers all to that effect.
 DAUGHTER And so will I.
 DUCHESS OF YORK Peace, children, peace. The king doth
  love you well.
  Incapable and shallow innocents,
  You cannot guess who caused your father's death.
20 **BOY** Grandam, we can, for my good uncle Gloucester
  Told me the king, provoked to it by the queen,
  Devised impeachments to imprison him;
  And when my uncle told me so, he wept,
  And pitied me, and kindly kissed my cheek,
25 Bade me rely on him as on my father,
  And he would love me dearly as a child.
 DUCHESS OF YORK Ah, that deceit should steal such
  gentle shape,
  And with a virtuous visor hide deep vice!

2.2   **1 grandam** grandmother   **6 wretches** exiles/miserable people   **castaways** rejected ones
8 cousins a general term for relatives   **10 As** being   **11 lost** wasted, pointless (sense then shifts to 'gone')
14 importune urge, entreat persistently   **18 Incapable** inexperienced, unknowing   **shallow** naive
22 impeachments accusations, charges   **24 kindly** gently, benevolently/as a family member   **27 gentle
shape** an appearance of nobility, a benevolent guise   **28 visor** mask

He is my son — ay, and therein my shame.
30   Yet from my dugs he drew not this deceit.
BOY Think you my uncle did dissemble, grandam?
DUCHESS OF YORK Ay, boy.
BOY I cannot think it. Hark, what noise is this?   *Wailing within*
Enter the Queen with her hair about her ears, Rivers and
Dorset after her
QUEEN ELIZABETH Ah, who shall hinder me to wail and
            weep,
35   To chide my fortune, and torment myself?
        I'll join with black despair against my soul,
        And to myself become an enemy.
DUCHESS OF YORK What means this scene of rude
            impatience?
QUEEN ELIZABETH To make an act of tragic violence.
40   Edward, my lord, thy son, our king, is dead.
        Why grow the branches when the root is gone?
        Why wither not the leaves that want their sap?
        If you will live, lament: if die, be brief,
        That our swift-wingèd souls may catch the king's,
45   Or, like obedient subjects, follow him
        To his new kingdom of ne'er-changing night.
DUCHESS OF YORK Ah, so much interest have I in thy
            sorrow
        As I had title in thy noble husband.
        I have bewept a worthy husband's death,
50   And lived with looking on his images:
        But now two mirrors of his princely semblance
        Are cracked in pieces by malignant death,
        And I for comfort have but one false glass,
        That grieves me when I see my shame in him.
55   Thou art a widow, yet thou art a mother,
        And hast the comfort of thy children left.
        But death hath snatched my husband from mine
            arms,
        And plucked two crutches from my feeble hands,
        Clarence and Edward. O, what cause have I,

---

30 dugs breasts (breast milk was popularly thought to convey some of the qualities of the mother)   *hair* ...
ears dishevelled and loose hair was a theatrical convention signifying distress   **35 chide** berate, chastise
36 black profound, dark, hellish   **37 to ... enemy** i.e. commit suicide   **38 rude impatience** uncontrolled
outburst, violent want of endurance   **39 act** deed/division of a play (continuing the theatrical image begun
with **scene**)   **42 want** lack   **43 brief** quick   **44 catch** catch up with   **47 interest** right, entitlement
48 title in claim on (as Edward's mother)   **50 his images** i.e. his sons   **51 mirrors** i.e. images, reflections
semblance likeness   **53 false glass** i.e. Richard, a distorted, false image of his father

60   Thine being but a moiety of my moan,
     To overgo thy woes and drown thy cries.
BOY Ah, aunt, you wept not for our father's death: *To the Queen*
     How can we aid you with our kindred tears?
DAUGHTER Our fatherless distress was left unmoaned.
65   Your widow-dolour likewise be unwept.   *To the Queen*
QUEEN ELIZABETH Give me no help in lamentation,
     I am not barren to bring forth complaints.
     All springs reduce their currents to mine eyes,
     That I, being governed by the watery moon,
70   May send forth plenteous tears to drown the world.
     Ah, for my husband, for my dear lord Edward!
CHILDREN Ah, for our father, for our dear lord Clarence!
DUCHESS OF YORK Alas for both, both mine, Edward and
     Clarence!
QUEEN ELIZABETH What stay had I but Edward? And
     he's gone.
75   **CHILDREN** What stay had we but Clarence? And he's
     gone.
DUCHESS OF YORK What stays had I but they? And they
     are gone.
QUEEN ELIZABETH Was never widow had so dear a loss.
CHILDREN Were never orphans had so dear a loss!
DUCHESS OF YORK Was never mother had so dear a loss.
80   Alas, I am the mother of these griefs!
     Their woes are parcelled, mine is general.
     She for an Edward weeps, and so do I:
     I for a Clarence weep, so doth not she:
     These babes for Clarence weep, and so do I:
85   I for an Edward weep, so do not they.
     Alas, you three, on me, threefold distressed,
     Pour all your tears! I am your sorrow's nurse,
     And I will pamper it with lamentation.
DORSET Comfort, dear mother. God is much displeased   *To the Queen*
90   That you take with unthankfulness, his doing.
     In common worldly things, 'tis called ungrateful,
     With dull unwillingness to repay a debt
     Which with a bounteous hand was kindly lent,

---

60 **moiety** small portion   61 **overgo** exceed   63 **kindred** similar, belonging to relatives   64 **unmoaned** unlamented, not grieved for   65 **widow-dolour** widow's grief   **be** shall be   67 **barren to** so infertile that I cannot   **complaints** grief, lamentations   68 **reduce** return, bring together   69 **watery moon** i.e. the moon, which controls the tides   74 **stay** support   77 **Was never widow** there was never a widow who **dear** grievous/costly   81 **parcelled** in specific parts, divided between them   **general** all-encompassing 87 **nurse** nourisher, feeder   88 **pamper** cram, feed luxuriously   92 **dull** sluggish, reluctant

Much more to be thus opposite with heaven,
95   For it requires the royal debt it lent you.
RIVERS   Madam, bethink you, like a careful mother
       Of the young prince your son: send straight for him
       Let him be crowned. In him your comfort lives.
       Drown desperate sorrow in dead Edward's grave
100   And plant your joys in living Edward's throne.
Enter Richard, Buckingham, [Stanley, Earl of] Derby,
Hastings and Ratcliffe
RICHARD   Sister, have comfort. All of us have cause   *To the Queen*
       To wail the dimming of our shining star,
       But none can help our harms by wailing them.—
       Madam, my mother, I do cry you mercy: *Kneels*
105   I did not see your grace. Humbly on my knee
       I crave your blessing.
DUCHESS OF YORK   God bless thee, and put meekness in
           thy breast,
       Love, charity, obedience and true duty.   *↓Richard rises↓*
RICHARD   Amen.— And make me die a good old man.   *Aside*
110   That is the butt-end of a mother's blessing;
       I marvel that her grace did leave it out.
BUCKINGHAM   You cloudy princes and heart-sorrowing
           peers,
       That bear this heavy mutual load of moan,
       Now cheer each other in each other's love.
115   Though we have spent our harvest of this king,
       We are to reap the harvest of his son.
       The broken rancour of your high-swoll'n hates,
       But lately splintered, knit, and joined together,
       Must gently be preserved, cherished, and kept.
120   Meseemeth good, that, with some little train,
       Forthwith from Ludlow the young prince be fet
       Hither to London, to be crowned our king.
RIVERS   Why with some little train, my lord of
           Buckingham?

---

94 **opposite** antagonistic, adversarial   95 **For it requires** because it reclaims   96 **careful** caring
104 **cry you mercy** beg your pardon   107 **meekness** humility   110 **butt-end** concluding part
111 **grace** quibbling on the duchess' title and on the sense of 'religious virtue'   112 **cloudy** gloomy
113 **moan** sorrow, grief   117 **broken rancour** divisive animosity (**broken** begins an image of an injured
limb)   **high-swoll'n** very inflamed/proud   118 **But lately splintered** only recently splinted, reset (though
at the same time continuing the imagery of fragmentation)   119 **kept** looked after   120 **Meseemeth** it
seems to me   **little train** small retinue of attendants and accompanying nobles   121 **Forthwith**
immediately   **Ludlow** Ludlow Castle, in Shropshire, near the Welsh border   **fet** fetched

BUCKINGHAM Marry, my lord, lest by a multitude,
125   The new-healed wound of malice should break out,
    Which would be so much the more dangerous
    By how much the estate is green and yet
      ungoverned.
    Where every horse bears his commanding rein,
    And may direct his course as please himself,
130   As well the fear of harm, as harm apparent,
    In my opinion, ought to be prevented.
RICHARD I hope the king made peace with all of us,
    And the compact is firm and true in me.
RIVERS And so in me, and so, I think, in all.
135   Yet since it is but green, it should be put
    To no apparent likelihood of breach,
    Which haply by much company might be urged:
    Therefore I say with noble Buckingham,
    That it is meet so few should fetch the prince.
140 HASTINGS And so say I.
RICHARD Then be it so, and go we to determine
    Who they shall be that straight shall post to Ludlow.
    Madam, and you my sister, will you go
    To give your censures in this business?
Exeunt. Buckingham and Richard remain
145 BUCKINGHAM My lord, whoever journeys to the prince,
    For God's sake, let not us two stay at home.
    For by the way I'll sort occasion,
    As index to the story we late talked of,
    To part the queen's proud kindred from the prince.
150 RICHARD My other self, my counsel's consistory,
    My oracle, my prophet, my dear cousin,
    I, as a child, will go by thy direction.
    Towards Ludlow then, for we'll not stay behind.
Exeunt

---

124 **multitude** large group   127 **estate** state, kingdom   **green** new, vulnerable (with suggestions of the prince's youth)   128 **Where … himself** when each horse is in control of his own reins and may go where he pleases (i.e. in the absence of a strong rider to govern)   130 **As … apparent** both the fear of possible harm as well as actual harm   132 **with** between   133 **compact** agreement, contract   135 **green** new, not tested   136 **apparent** evident, real   **breach** breakage, rupture   137 **haply** perhaps/probably   **urged** encouraged   139 **meet** appropriate, suitable   142 **post** hasten   144 **censures** opinions   147 **by** on **sort occasion** arrange an opportunity   148 **index** preface   **story** plan, business   **late** recently 150 **counsel's** innermost thoughts' (puns on advisory 'council')   **consistory** council chamber, meeting place   152 **direction** instruction, guidance

Act 2 Scene 3

Enter one Citizen at one door, and another at the other

FIRST CITIZEN Good morrow, neighbour. Whither away
    so fast?

SECOND CITIZEN I promise you, I scarcely know myself.
    Hear you the news abroad?

FIRST CITIZEN Yes, that the king is dead.

5 **SECOND CITIZEN** Ill news, by'r lady, seldom comes the
    better:

    I fear, I fear 'twill prove a giddy world.

Enter another Citizen

THIRD CITIZEN Neighbours, God speed.

FIRST CITIZEN Give you good morrow, sir.

THIRD CITIZEN Doth the news hold of good King
    Edward's death?

10 **SECOND CITIZEN** Ay, sir, it is too true, God help the
    while.

THIRD CITIZEN Then, masters, look to see a troublous
    world.

FIRST CITIZEN No, no. By God's good grace his son shall
    reign.

THIRD CITIZEN Woe to that land that's governed by a
    child.

SECOND CITIZEN In him there is a hope of government,
15   Which in his nonage, council under him,
    And in his full and ripened years, himself,
    No doubt shall then, and till then govern well.

FIRST CITIZEN So stood the state when Henry the Sixth
    Was crowned in Paris but at nine months old.

20 **THIRD CITIZEN** Stood the state so? No, no, good friends,
    God wot,
    For then this land was famously enriched
    With politic grave counsel; then the king
    Had virtuous uncles to protect his grace.

FIRST CITIZEN Why, so hath this, both by his father and
    mother.

2.3 *Location: a London street* **3 abroad** at large, in the outside world **5 by'r lady** by Our Lady (the Virgin Mary) **seldom . . . better** is rarely followed by better things **6 giddy** inconstant, unstable **7 God speed** God be with you; a standard greeting **8 Give . . . morrow** God give you good day; a standard greeting **9 Doth . . . hold** is the news true **10 God . . . while** i.e. God help us **while** age, times **11 masters** sirs **look** expect **15 nonage** minority, youth **council under him** the Privy Council, a group of the king's ministers, governing for him **20 so** in the same condition **wot** knows **22 politic grave counsel** wise and reverend guidance **23 protect** act as formal guardians for

25	**THIRD CITIZEN** Better it were they all came by his father,
	Or by his father there were none at all.
	For emulation, who shall now be nearest,
	Will touch us all too near, if God prevent not.
	O, full of danger is the Duke of Gloucester,
30	And the queen's sons and brothers haught and
	proud:
	And were they to be ruled, and not to rule,
	This sickly land might solace as before.
	FIRST CITIZEN Come, come, we fear the worst. All will be
	well.
	THIRD CITIZEN When clouds are seen, wise men put on
	their cloaks;
35	When great leaves fall, then winter is at hand;
	When the sun sets, who doth not look for night?
	Untimely storms makes men expect a dearth.
	All may be well; but, if God sort it so,
	'Tis more than we deserve or I expect.
40	**SECOND CITIZEN** Truly, the hearts of men are full of fear.
	You cannot reason almost with a man
	That looks not heavily and full of dread.
	THIRD CITIZEN Before the days of change, still is it so.
	By a divine instinct men's minds mistrust
45	Pursuing danger. As by proof, we see
	The water swell before a boist'rous storm.
	But leave it all to God. Whither away?
	SECOND CITIZEN Marry, we were sent for to the justices.
	THIRD CITIZEN And so was I. I'll bear you company.

Exeunt

Act 2 Scene 4   *running scene 6*

*Enter [the] Archbishop, young York, the Queen and the
Duchess*

ARCHBISHOP OF YORK Last night, I heard, they lay at
Stony Stratford

---

27 **emulation** rivalry   **nearest** most closely related to the king/most influential over the king   28 **touch** . . .
near affect us all too closely   30 **haught** haughty, aspiring   32 **solace** take comfort, be happy   36 **look for**
expect   37 **dearth** famine, shortage   38 **sort** ordain, arrange   41 **cannot reason almost** can scarcely
reason   42 **heavily** gravely, anxiously   43 **still** always   44 **mistrust** suspect   45 **proof** experience
46 **boist'rous** violent   47 **Whither away?** Where are you going?   48 **justices** Justices of the Peace; the
reason for this is never stated   **2.4**   *Location: the royal court, London*   1 **lay** spent the night   **Stony
Stratford** small town in Buckinghamshire

And at Northampton they do rest tonight.
Tomorrow, or next day, they will be here.
DUCHESS OF YORK I long with all my heart to see the
    prince.
5   I hope he is much grown since last I saw him.
QUEEN ELIZABETH But I hear, no. They say my son of
    York
Has almost overta'en him in his growth.
YORK Ay, mother, but I would not have it so.
DUCHESS OF YORK Why, my good cousin, it is good to
    grow.
10   YORK Grandam, one night as we did sit at supper,
My uncle Rivers talked how I did grow
More than my brother. 'Ay', quoth my uncle
    Gloucester,
'Small herbs have grace, great weeds do grow apace.'
And since, methinks, I would not grow so fast,
15   Because sweet flowers are slow and weeds make
    haste.
DUCHESS OF YORK Good faith, good faith, the saying did
    not hold
In him that did object the same to thee.
He was the wretched'st thing when he was young,
So long a-growing and so leisurely,
20   That, if his rule were true, he should be gracious.
ARCHBISHOP OF YORK And so no doubt he is, my
    gracious madam.
DUCHESS OF YORK I hope he is, but yet let mothers
    doubt.
YORK Now, by my troth, if I had been remembered,
I could have given my uncle's grace a flout,
25   To touch his growth nearer than he touched mine.
DUCHESS OF YORK How, my young York? I prithee let
    me hear it.
YORK Marry, they say my uncle grew so fast
That he could gnaw a crust at two hours old.

---

2 Northampton Northamptonshire town twelve miles further from London than Stony Stratford, an apparent confusion explained by Shakespeare's sources: Richard and Buckingham met the Prince at Stony Stratford, then (Rivers, Vaughan and Grey having been arrested) took him back to Northampton before resuming the journey to London **9 cousin** general term for a relative **13 grace** virtuous qualities; possibly Richard quibbles on 'herb of grace' or rue, a herb with medicinal qualities whose name means 'sorrow' **apace** quickly **16 hold** apply, prove true **17 object the same** suggest it, apply it **23 troth** faith **been remembered** remembered **24 flout** taunt, mocking insult **25 touch...mine** mock his growth more pointedly than he mocked mine **28 gnaw...old** various historical accounts claim that Richard was born with teeth, something considered abnormal and ominous

'Twas full two years ere I could get a tooth.
30   Grandam, this would have been a biting jest.
DUCHESS OF YORK I prithee, pretty York, who told thee
        this?
YORK Grandam, his nurse.
DUCHESS OF YORK His nurse? Why, she was dead ere
        thou wast born.
YORK If 'twere not she, I cannot tell who told me.
35   QUEEN ELIZABETH A parlous boy. Go to, you are too
        shrewd.
DUCHESS OF YORK Good madam, be not angry with the
        child.
QUEEN ELIZABETH Pitchers have ears.

Enter a Messenger

ARCHBISHOP OF YORK Here comes a messenger. What
        news?
MESSENGER Such news, my lord, as grieves me to report.
40   QUEEN ELIZABETH How doth the prince?
MESSENGER Well, madam, and in health.
DUCHESS OF YORK What is thy news?
MESSENGER Lord Rivers and Lord Grey are sent to
        Pomfret,
        And with them Sir Thomas Vaughan, prisoners.
45   DUCHESS OF YORK Who hath committed them?
MESSENGER The mighty dukes, Gloucester and
        Buckingham.
ARCHBISHOP OF YORK For what offence?
MESSENGER The sum of all I can, I have disclosed.
        Why or for what the nobles were committed
50   Is all unknown to me, my gracious lord.
QUEEN ELIZABETH Ay me, I see the ruin of my house.
        The tiger now hath seized the gentle hind,
        Insulting tyranny begins to jut
        Upon the innocent and aweless throne.
55   Welcome, destruction, blood and massacre.
        I see, as in a map, the end of all.
DUCHESS OF YORK Accursèd and unquiet wrangling
        days,

---

30 biting sharp/to do with teeth   **35 parlous** mischievous, wily   **Go to** expression of dismissive impatience
shrewd sharp-tongued, cheeky   **37 Pitchers have ears** proverbial; pitchers were jugs with large handles
('ears') – Elizabeth means that the boy has been eavesdropping on adult conversation   **43 Pomfret**
Pontefract castle, in Yorkshire   **48 can** know, can say   **51 house** family   **52 hind** female deer
53 Insulting threatening, harmful/exulting scornfully   **jut** thrust, shove/project, encroach   **54 aweless**
inspiring no awe or dread   **throne** i.e. Prince Edward   **56 map** chart of the world/diagram/summary,
epitome

How many of you have mine eyes beheld?
My husband lost his life to get the crown,
60   And often up and down my sons were tossed,
For me to joy and weep their gain and loss.
And being seated, and domestic broils
Clean overblown, themselves the conquerors,
Make war upon themselves, brother to brother,
65   Blood to blood, self against self. O, preposterous
And frantic outrage, end thy damnèd spleen,
Or let me die, to look on earth no more!
QUEEN ELIZABETH Come, come, my boy, we will to   *To young York*
          sanctuary.—
Madam, farewell.   *To the Duchess*
70 DUCHESS OF YORK Stay, I will go with you.
QUEEN ELIZABETH You have no cause.
ARCHBISHOP OF YORK My gracious lady, go,
And thither bear your treasure and your goods.
For my part, I'll resign unto your grace
75   The seal I keep: and so betide to me
As well I tender you and all of yours!
Go, I'll conduct you to the sanctuary.   *Exeunt*

Act 3 Scene 1   *running scene 7*

*The trumpets sound. Enter young Prince [Edward], the Dukes
of Gloucester [Richard] and Buckingham, Lord Cardinal with
others*

BUCKINGHAM Welcome, sweet prince, to London, to
          your chamber.
RICHARD Welcome, dear cousin, my thoughts'
          sovereign.
     The weary way hath made you melancholy.
PRINCE EDWARD No, uncle, but our crosses on the way
5   Have made it tedious, wearisome, and heavy.
     I want more uncles here to welcome me.

---

62 **seated** in power, having gained the throne   **broils** turmoil   63 **overblown** blown over
65 **preposterous** unnatural (literally, in reverse order)   66 **frantic outrage** insane violence   **spleen** fury
(the spleen was thought to be the seat of extreme emotion)   68 **sanctuary** churches and their precincts
provided sanctuary from arrest; Elizabeth went to Westminster Abbey   75 **seal** great seal of England, used
by the king to authenticate documents; the Archbishop was its official keeper   **so . . . you** may my fortunes
depend on the care I show you   **3.1**   *Location: London; exact location unspecified, possibly a street*
1 **chamber** London was known as the *camera regis*, Latin for the 'king's chamber'   **2 my thoughts'**
sovereign my chief concern/head of my thoughts   **4 crosses** troubles (i.e. the arrests of Rivers, Vaughan
and Grey)   **5 heavy** laborious, burdensome, sorrowful   **6 want** lack/desire

RICHARD Sweet prince, the untainted virtue of your
　　　years
　　Hath not yet dived into the world's deceit.
　　No more can you distinguish of a man
10　　Than of his outward show, which — God he knows —
　　Seldom or never jumpeth with the heart.
　　Those uncles which you want were dangerous:
　　Your grace attended to their sugared words,
　　But looked not on the poison of their hearts.
15　　God keep you from them, and from such false friends.
PRINCE EDWARD God keep me from false friends, but they
　　　were none.
RICHARD My lord, the Mayor of London comes to greet
　　　you.

Enter Lord Mayor

LORD MAYOR　God bless your grace with health and
　　happy days.
PRINCE EDWARD I thank you, good my lord, and thank
　　　you all.—
20　　I thought my mother, and my brother York,
　　Would long ere this have met us on the way.
　　Fie, what a slug is Hastings, that he comes not
　　To tell us whether they will come or no.

Enter Lord Hastings

BUCKINGHAM And, in good time, here comes the
　　sweating lord.
25　　**PRINCE EDWARD** Welcome, my lord. What, will our
　　mother come?
HASTINGS On what occasion, God he knows, not I,
　　The queen your mother, and your brother York,
　　Have taken sanctuary. The tender prince
　　Would fain have come with me to meet your grace,
30　　But by his mother was perforce withheld.
BUCKINGHAM Fie, what an indirect and peevish course
　　Is this of hers?— Lord Cardinal, will your grace
　　Persuade the queen to send the Duke of York
　　Unto his princely brother presently?—

---

11 **jumpeth** accords, agrees　13 **attended** paid attention, listened　21 **ere** before　22 **slug** sluggard, lazy
fellow　26 **On what occasion** for what reason　28 **tender** young　**prince** i.e. Edward's younger brother,
Richard　29 **fain** willingly　30 **perforce** forcibly　31 **indirect** devious/oblique, lengthy/erroneous
peevish obstinate/perverse　34 **presently** immediately

35   If she deny, Lord Hastings, go with him,
      And from her jealous arms pluck him perforce.
CARDINAL My lord of Buckingham, if my weak oratory
      Can from his mother win the Duke of York,
      Anon expect him here. But if she be obdurate
40   To mild entreaties, God forbid
      We should infringe the holy privilege
      Of blessèd sanctuary. Not for all this land
      Would I be guilty of so great a sin.
BUCKINGHAM You are too senseless obstinate, my lord,
45   Too ceremonious and traditional.
      Weigh it but with the grossness of this age,
      You break not sanctuary in seizing him.
      The benefit thereof is always granted
      To those whose dealings have deserved the place,
50   And those who have the wit to claim the place:
      This prince hath neither claimed it nor deserved it,
      And therefore, in mine opinion, cannot have it.
      Then, taking him from thence that is not there,
      You break no privilege nor charter there.
55   Oft have I heard of sanctuary men,
      But sanctuary children ne'er till now.
CARDINAL My lord, you shall o'er-rule my mind for
         once.—
      Come on, Lord Hastings, will you go with me?
HASTINGS I go, my lord.   *Exeunt Cardinal and Hastings*
60 PRINCE EDWARD Good lords, make all the speedy haste
         you may.—
      Say, uncle Gloucester, if our brother come,
      Where shall we sojourn till our coronation?
RICHARD Where it think'st best unto your royal self.
      If I may counsel you, some day or two
65   Your highness shall repose you at the Tower:
      Then where you please, and shall be thought most fit
      For your best health and recreation.
PRINCE EDWARD I do not like the Tower, of any place.—
      Did Julius Caesar build that place, my lord?   *To Buckingham*

---

36 jealous suspicious, mistrustful, over-protective   **37 oratory** rhetorical skill   **39 Anon** shortly
obdurate inflexible, determined   **44 senseless** unreasonably, foolishly   **46 Weigh...with** if you only
judge it by   **grossness** low standards, coarseness   **48 benefit** protection   **49 dealings** actions, conduct
50 wit intelligence, mature judgement   **53 thence...there** a place that cannot really be considered as
sanctuary in his case   **54 charter** privilege, legal right   **62 sojourn** stay, reside   **65 repose you** settle
yourself, rest   **Tower** a royal residence as well as a much-feared prison   **68 any place** all places

70 **BUCKINGHAM** He did, my gracious lord, begin that place,
     Which, since, succeeding ages have re-edified.
   PRINCE EDWARD Is it upon record? Or else reported
     Successively from age to age, he built it?
   BUCKINGHAM Upon record, my gracious lord.
75 **PRINCE EDWARD** But say, my lord, it were not registered,
     Methinks the truth should live from age to age,
     As 'twere retailed to all posterity,
     Even to the general ending day.
   RICHARD So wise so young, they say, do never live long.   *Aside*
80 **PRINCE EDWARD** What say you, uncle?
   RICHARD I say, without characters, fame lives long.—
     Thus, like the formal Vice, Iniquity,   *Aside*
     I moralize two meanings in one word.
   PRINCE EDWARD That Julius Caesar was a famous man.
85   With what his valour did enrich his wit,
     His wit set down to make his valour live.
     Death makes no conquest of his conqueror,
     For now he lives in fame, though not in life.
     I'll tell you what, my cousin Buckingham—
90 **BUCKINGHAM** What, my gracious lord?
   PRINCE EDWARD An if I live until I be a man,
     I'll win our ancient right in France again,
     Or die a soldier, as I lived a king.
   RICHARD Short summers lightly have a forward spring.   *Aside*
   Enter young York, Hastings and Cardinal
95 **BUCKINGHAM** Now, in good time, here comes the Duke of
       York.
   PRINCE EDWARD Richard of York, how fares our noble
       brother?
   YORK Well, my dear lord, so must I call you now.
   PRINCE EDWARD Ay, brother, to our grief, as it is yours:
     Too late he died that might have kept that title,
100   Which by his death hath lost much majesty.
   RICHARD How fares our cousin, noble lord of York?

---

71 re-edified rebuilt, developed   **72 upon record** written down   **75 registered** recorded   **77 retailed**
recounted, retold   **78 general ending day** universal doomsday, the end of the world   **79 So…long**
proverbial: 'too soon wise to live long'   **81 characters** written records   **82 formal Vice** conventional Vice
figure of morality plays, an allegorical character named after a particular sin and known for wordplay and
grim humour   **Iniquity** sinfulness; a stock name for a Vice figure   **83 moralize** interpret (perhaps playing
on the idea of expounding God's word for the purpose of moral teaching)   **85 With…live** i.e. he used his
intellect to write down the courageous military exploits that had enriched it, in order to ensure that his
reputation lived on   **87 his conqueror** the one who conquers death   **91 An if** if   **94 lightly** usually
forward early   **98 grief** Edward refers to the death of his father   **99 late** recently

YORK I thank you, gentle uncle. O, my lord,
　　You said that idle weeds are fast in growth:
　　The prince my brother hath outgrown me far.

105　**RICHARD** He hath, my lord.

YORK And therefore is he idle?

RICHARD O, my fair cousin, I must not say so.

YORK Then he is more beholding to you than I.

RICHARD He may command me as my sovereign,

110　But you have power in me as in a kinsman.

YORK I pray you, uncle, give me this dagger.

RICHARD My dagger, little cousin? With all my heart.

PRINCE EDWARD A beggar, brother?

YORK Of my kind uncle, that I know will give,

115　And being but a toy, which is no grief to give.

RICHARD A greater gift than that I'll give my cousin.

YORK A greater gift? O, that's the sword to it.

RICHARD Ay, gentle cousin, were it light enough.

YORK O, then, I see, you will part but with light gifts.

120　In weightier things you'll say a beggar nay.

RICHARD It is too weighty for your grace to wear.

YORK I weigh it lightly, were it heavier.

RICHARD What, would you have my weapon, little lord?

YORK I would, that I might thank you as you call me.

125　**RICHARD** How?

YORK Little.

PRINCE EDWARD My lord of York will still be cross in talk.
　　Uncle, your grace knows how to bear with him.

YORK You mean to bear me, not to bear with me.—

130　Uncle, my brother mocks both you and me,
　　Because that I am little, like an ape,
　　He thinks that you should bear me on your
　　　　shoulders.

BUCKINGHAM With what a sharp-provided wit he
　　reasons!　　　　　　　　　　　　　　　　　　　　*Aside*
　　To mitigate the scorn he gives his uncle,

---

103 **idle** useless   108 **beholding** beholden, indebted   110 **as in** in that I am   111 **dagger** perhaps maintaining the link between Richard and the medieval Vice figure, who traditionally carried a dagger   112 **With . . . heart** very willingly (but also implying that he would gladly stab York with it)   115 **toy** trifle   **grief** hardship   117 **to it** that goes with it   118 **light** not heavy (York shifts the sense to 'trifling, cheap')   120 **a beggar nay** no to a beggar   122 **weigh it lightly** consider it a trifle/do not think it weighs very much   **were it** even if it were   123 **have** continues the grim play on 'receive as a gift/receive in death'   127 **still** always   **cross** contrary, perverse   131 **like . . . shoulders** professional fools or tame bears carried apes on their backs at fairs; attention is drawn here to Richard's hunched back   140 **bear** puns on the name of the animal   133 **sharp-provided** quick and ready   134 **mitigate** moderate, lessen

135   He prettily and aptly taunts himself.
            So cunning and so young is wonderful.
        RICHARD My lord, will't please you pass along?
            Myself and my good cousin Buckingham
            Will to your mother, to entreat of her
140   To meet you at the Tower and welcome you.
        YORK What, will you go unto the Tower, my lord?
        PRINCE EDWARD My Lord Protector will have it so.
        YORK I shall not sleep in quiet at the Tower.
        RICHARD Why, what should you fear?
145   **YORK** Marry, my uncle Clarence' angry ghost.
            My grandam told me he was murdered there.
        PRINCE EDWARD I fear no uncles dead.
        RICHARD Nor none that live, I hope.
        PRINCE EDWARD An if they live, I hope I need not fear.
150   But come, my lord and with a heavy heart,
            Thinking on them, go I unto the Tower.
        A sennet.

                        Exeunt Prince, York, Hastings and Dorset.
                        Richard, Buckingham and Catesby remain
        BUCKINGHAM Think you, my lord, this little prating York
            Was not incensèd by his subtle mother
            To taunt and scorn you thus opprobriously?
155   **RICHARD** No doubt, no doubt. O, 'tis a perilous boy:
            Bold, quick, ingenious, forward, capable.
            He is all the mother's, from the top to toe.
        BUCKINGHAM Well, let them rest.— Come hither,
                Catesby.
            Thou art sworn as deeply to effect what we intend
160   As closely to conceal what we impart.
            Thou know'st our reasons urged upon the way,
            What think'st thou? Is it not an easy matter
            To make William Lord Hastings of our mind,
            For the instalment of this noble duke
165   In the seat royal of this famous isle?
        CATESBY He for his father's sake so loves the prince,
            That he will not be won to aught against him.

135 prettily cleverly, charmingly   **136 cunning** crafty, clever   *sennet* trumpet call signalling the
continuation of a procession   **152 prating** chattering, prattling   **153 incensèd** urged on, incited   **subtle**
cunning   **154 opprobriously** scornfully, insultingly   **155 perilous** wily, dangerous, mischievous
156 forward spirited, ready   **capable** responsive, receptive   **157 all the mother's** exactly like his mother
158 let them rest enough of them, leave them for the moment; or perhaps literally 'let them take their
rest'   **159 deeply** profoundly, solemnly   **160 closely** secretly   **161 urged** proposed, discussed   **way** i.e.
the journey from Ludlow to London   **163 of . . . For** share our opinion and intention regarding   **166 He . . .
father's** Hastings for Edward IV's   **167 won to aught** persuaded to do anything

BUCKINGHAM What think'st thou, then, of Stanley? Will
    not he?

CATESBY He will do all in all as Hastings doth.

170 **BUCKINGHAM** Well, then, no more but this: go, gentle
    Catesby,

And, as it were far off sound thou Lord Hastings,

How he doth stand affected to our purpose,

And summon him tomorrow to the Tower,

To sit about the coronation.

175   If thou dost find him tractable to us,

Encourage him, and tell him all our reasons.

If he be leaden, icy-cold, unwilling,

Be thou so too, and so break off the talk,

And give us notice of his inclination,

180 For we tomorrow hold divided councils,

Wherein thyself shalt highly be employed.

RICHARD Commend me to Lord William. Tell him,
    Catesby,

His ancient knot of dangerous adversaries

Tomorrow are let blood at Pomfret Castle,

185 And bid my lord, for joy of this good news,

Give Mistress Shore one gentle kiss the more.

BUCKINGHAM Good Catesby, go effect this business
    soundly.

CATESBY My good lords both, with all the heed I can.

RICHARD Shall we hear from you, Catesby, ere we sleep?

190 **CATESBY** You shall, my lord.

RICHARD At Crosby House, there shall you find us both.

Exit Catesby

BUCKINGHAM Now my lord, what shall we do if we
    perceive

Lord Hastings will not yield to our complots?

RICHARD Chop off his head: something we will
    determine:

195 And look when I am king, claim thou of me

The earldom of Hereford, and all the movables

Whereof the king my brother was possessed.

---

171 **as . . . off** in a roundabout way, indirectly   **sound** sound out, probe   172 **affected to** disposed towards
174 **sit** confer, sit in council   180 **divided councils** two separate meetings   181 **highly** crucially
182 **Lord William** i.e. Hastings   183 **ancient knot** long-standing group (**knot** may play on the sense of
'tumour')   184 **are let blood** i.e. will be executed; literally, refers to surgical bloodletting   186 **Mistress
Shore** Hastings' mistress Jane Shore (formerly mistress of Edward IV)   188 **heed** care   193 **complots**
conspiracies, schemes   196 **movables** portable property

BUCKINGHAM I'll claim that promise at your grace's
    hand.
RICHARD And look to have it yielded with all kindness.
200   Come, let us sup betimes, that afterwards
    We may digest our complots in some form.   *Exeunt*

Act 3 Scene 2

Enter a Messenger to the door of Hastings

MESSENGER My lord, my lord!
HASTINGS Who knocks?   *Within*
MESSENGER One from the lord Stanley.
HASTINGS What is't o'clock?   *Within*
5   **MESSENGER** Upon the stroke of four.
Enter Lord Hastings
HASTINGS Cannot my lord Stanley sleep these tedious
    nights?
MESSENGER So it appears by that I have to say.
    First, he commends him to your noble self.
HASTINGS What then?
10   **MESSENGER** Then certifies your lordship that this night
    He dreamt the boar had razèd off his helm.
    Besides, he says there are two councils kept,
    And that may be determined at the one
    Which may make you and him to rue at th'other:
15   Therefore he sends to know your lordship's pleasure,
    If you will presently take horse with him,
    And with all speed post with him toward the north,
    To shun the danger that his soul divines.
HASTINGS Go, fellow, go, return unto thy lord,
20   Bid him not fear the separated council:
    His honour and myself are at the one,
    And at the other is my good friend Catesby,
    Where nothing can proceed that toucheth us
    Whereof I shall not have intelligence.
25   Tell him his fears are shallow, without instance.
    And for his dreams, I wonder he's so simple
    To trust the mock'ry of unquiet slumbers.

---

200 sup betimes have supper early   **201 digest** arrange (plays on the sense of literal digestion)   **form** good order   **3.2** *Location: outside Hastings' house*   **6 tedious** weary, long   **11 boar** Richard's heraldic emblem   **razèd** pulled, torn   **helm** helmet   **13 that … determined** decisions may be taken **14 to rue** grieve   **15 pleasure** will, inclination   **16 presently** immediately   **17 post** ride swiftly   **21 His honour** Lord Stanley   **23 toucheth** affects, relates to   **24 have intelligence** be informed   **25 without instance** lacking evidence   **27 mock'ry** foolish delusions, false images

To fly the boar before the boar pursues,
Were to incense the boar to follow us

30   And make pursuit where he did mean no chase.
Go, bid thy master rise and come to me
And we will both together to the Tower,
Where he shall see the boar will use us kindly.

MESSENGER I'll go, my lord, and tell him what you say.

Exit

Enter Catesby

35   CATESBY Many good morrows to my noble lord.

HASTINGS Good morrow, Catesby. You are early stirring.
What news, what news, in this our tott'ring state?

CATESBY It is a reeling world, indeed, my lord,
And I believe will never stand upright

40   Till Richard wear the garland of the realm.

HASTINGS How? Wear the garland? Dost thou mean the
crown?

CATESBY Ay, my good lord.

HASTINGS I'll have this crown of mine cut from my
shoulders
Before I'll see the crown so foul misplaced.

45   But canst thou guess that he doth aim at it?

CATESBY Ay, on my life, and hopes to find you forward
Upon his party for the gain thereof:
And thereupon he sends you this good news,
That this same very day your enemies,

50   The kindred of the queen, must die at Pomfret.

HASTINGS Indeed, I am no mourner for that news,
Because they have been still my adversaries.
But that I'll give my voice on Richard's side
To bar my master's heirs in true descent,

55   God knows I will not do it, to the death.

CATESBY God keep your lordship in that gracious mind.

HASTINGS But I shall laugh at this a twelvemonth hence,
That they which brought me in my master's hate,
I live to look upon their tragedy.

60   Well, Catesby, ere a fortnight make me older,
I'll send some packing that yet think not on't.

---

28 **fly** flee   29 **Were** would be   30 **mean** (originally) intend   33 **use** treat   **kindly** gently, courteously
(plays on the sense of 'according to his (boar-like) nature')   40 **garland** i.e. crown (with connotations of a
victor's garland)   43 **crown** head   44 **foul** wickedly, wrongfully/in an ugly manner (perhaps recalling
Richard's appearance)   46 **forward . . . party** ready to support him, eagerly on his side   54 **master's** i.e.
Edward IV's   58 **they** i.e. the queen's relatives   **in** into

CATESBY 'Tis a vile thing to die, my gracious lord,
When men are unprepared and look not for it.
HASTINGS O, monstrous, monstrous! And so falls it out
65 With Rivers, Vaughan, Grey: and so 'twill do
With some men else, that think themselves as safe
As thou and I — who, as thou know'st, are dear
To princely Richard and to Buckingham.
CATESBY The princes both make high account of you.—
70 For they account his head upon the bridge.   *Aside*
HASTINGS I know they do, and I have well deserved it.
Enter Lord Stanley [Earl of Derby]
Come on, come on, where is your boar-spear, man?   *To Derby*
Fear you the boar, and go so unprovided?
DERBY My lord, good morrow.— Good morrow, Catesby.
75 You may jest on, but, by the holy rood,
I do not like these several councils, I.
HASTINGS My lord, I hold my life as dear as yours,
And never in my days, I do protest,
Was it so precious to me as 'tis now.
80 Think you, but that I know our state secure,
I would be so triumphant as I am?
DERBY The lords at Pomfret, when they rode from
London,
Were jocund and supposed their states were sure,
And they indeed had no cause to mistrust:
85 But yet you see how soon the day o'ercast.
This sudden stab of rancour I misdoubt:
Pray God, I say, I prove a needless coward.
What, shall we toward the Tower? The day is spent.
HASTINGS Come, come, have with you. Wot you what,
my lord?
90 Today the lords you talk of are beheaded.
LORD DERBY They, for their truth, might better wear
their heads
Than some that have accused them wear their hats.
But come, my lord, let's away.

---

64 **monstrous** unnatural **falls it out** it has happened   69 **make high account** hold you in high
estimation (in the context of the following line, **high** plays on the sense of 'high up, aloft')   70 **account**
consider, expect   **the bridge** London Bridge, on which traitors' heads were displayed on poles
73 **unprovided** unprepared, ill-equipped   75 **rood** (Christ's) cross   76 **several** separate   78 **protest**
declare   81 **triumphant** cheerful/exultant (over my enemies' deaths)   83 **jocund** merry, cheerful   **states
were sure** positions were secure   84 **mistrust** doubt, suspect   86 **This ... misdoubt** i.e. this sudden
hostile attack has made me fearful, mistrustful   88 **spent** coming to an end (although the scene begins at
4 a.m.; perhaps Stanley refers figuratively to his own 'time', i.e. life)   89 **have with you** literally 'I'll join you'
or as a reprimand 'come along now'   **Wot** know   91 **truth** loyalty, honesty   92 **hats** i.e. official positions
(Stanley has Richard's role as royal Protector in mind)

Enter a Pursuivant

HASTINGS Go on before: I'll talk with this good fellow.—

Exeunt Derby and Catesby

95   How now, sirrah? How goes the world with thee?

PURSUIVANT The better that your lordship please to ask.

HASTINGS I tell thee, man, 'tis better with me now
    Than when thou met'st me last where now we meet:
    Then was I going prisoner to the Tower,

100   By the suggestion of the queen's allies.
    But now, I tell thee — keep it to thyself —
    This day those enemies are put to death,
    And I in better state than e'er I was.

PURSUIVANT God hold it to your honour's good content.

105 HASTINGS Gramercy, fellow. There, drink that for me.

Throws him his purse

PURSUIVANT I thank your honour.   *Exit*

Enter a Priest

PRIEST Well met, my lord. I am glad to see your honour.

HASTINGS I thank thee, good Sir John, with all my heart.
    I am in your debt for your last exercise:

110   Come the next Sabbath, and I will content you.   *Whispers in his ear*

PRIEST I'll wait upon your lordship.

Enter Buckingham

BUCKINGHAM What, talking with a priest, Lord
    Chamberlain?
    Your friends at Pomfret, they do need the priest:
    Your honour hath no shriving work in hand.

115 HASTINGS Good faith, and when I met this holy man,
    The men you talk of came into my mind.
    What, go you toward the Tower?

BUCKINGHAM I do, my lord, but long I cannot stay there.
    I shall return before your lordship thence.

120 HASTINGS Nay, like enough, for I stay dinner there.

BUCKINGHAM And supper too, although thou know'st it   *Aside*
    not.—
    Come, will you go?

HASTINGS I'll wait upon your lordship.   *Exeunt*

Pursuivant state messenger with the power to execute warrants   **94 before** ahead   **95 sirrah** sir (used to inferiors)   **100 suggestion** instigation, prompting   **103 state** prosperity, position, circumstances **104 hold** keep, maintain   **105 Gramercy** great thanks   **108 Sir** conventional title for a clergyman **109 I . . . exercise** Hastings apologizes for not attending the last church service (during which he was in prison)   **exercise** religious service   **110 content** recompense   **114 shriving work** business of saying confession and receiving absolution   **119 thence** from there   **120 stay** stay for

Act 3 Scene 3   *running scene 9*

Enter Sir Richard Ratcliffe with Halberds, carrying the nobles
[Rivers, Grey and Vaughan] to death at Pomfret

RIVERS Sir Richard Ratcliffe, let me tell thee this:
    Today shalt thou behold a subject die
    For truth, for duty, and for loyalty.
GREY God bless the prince from all the pack of you.
5   A knot you are of damnèd blood-suckers!
VAUGHAN You live that shall cry woe for this hereafter.
RATCLIFFE Dispatch. The limit of your lives is out.
RIVERS O Pomfret, Pomfret! O thou bloody prison!
    Fatal and ominous to noble peers!
10   Within the guilty closure of thy walls
    Richard the Second here was hacked to death.
    And, for more slander to thy dismal seat,
    We give to thee our guiltless blood to drink.
GREY Now Margaret's curse is fall'n upon our heads,
15   When she exclaimed on Hastings, you and I,
    For standing by when Richard stabbed her son.
RIVERS Then cursed she Richard, then cursed she
      Buckingham,
    Then cursed she Hastings. O, remember, God,
    To hear her prayer for them, as now for us:
20   And for my sister and her princely sons,
    Be satisfied, dear God, with our true blood,
    Which, as thou know'st, unjustly must be spilt.
RATCLIFFE Make haste: the hour of death is expiate.
RIVERS Come, Grey, come, Vaughan, let us here
      embrace.
25   Farewell, until we meet again in heaven.   *Exeunt*

Act 3 Scene 4   *running scene 10*

Enter Buckingham, Derby, Hastings, Bishop of Ely, Norfolk,
Ratcliffe, Lovell, with others. [They take their seats] at a table

HASTINGS Now, noble peers, the cause why we are met
    Is to determine of the coronation.
    In God's name speak: when is the royal day?

3.3 *Location: Pomfret (Pontefract) castle, Yorkshire*   5 **knot** tight group   7 **Dispatch** get on with
it   10 **closure** enclosure   12 **for . . . seat** to add to the disgrace associated with this place   **dismal seat**
ominous position   15 **exclaimed on** cried out against, condemned   **Hastings . . . I** in fact, Margaret does
not mention Grey (see Act 1 scene 3)   20 **for** instead of   23 **expiate** reached, fully come   3.4 *Location:*
council chamber, the Tower of London   2 **of** about

BUCKINGHAM Is all things ready for the royal time?

5   **DERBY** It is, and wants but nomination.

BISHOP OF ELY Tomorrow, then, I judge a happy day.

BUCKINGHAM Who knows the Lord Protector's mind
     herein?
    Who is most inward with the noble duke?

BISHOP OF ELY Your grace, we think, should soonest
    know his mind.

10 **BUCKINGHAM** We know each other's faces: for our
    hearts,
    He knows no more of mine, than I of yours,
    Or I of his, my lord, than you of mine.—
    Lord Hastings, you and he are near in love.

HASTINGS I thank his grace, I know he loves me well.

15   But, for his purpose in the coronation,
    I have not sounded him, nor he delivered
    His gracious pleasure any way therein:
    But you, my honourable lords, may name the time,
    And in the duke's behalf I'll give my voice,

20   Which I presume he'll take in gentle part.

Enter [Richard of] Gloucester

BISHOP OF ELY In happy time, here comes the duke
    himself.

RICHARD My noble lords and cousins all, good morrow.
    I have been long a sleeper: but I trust
    My absence doth neglect no great design

25   Which by my presence might have been concluded.

BUCKINGHAM Had you not come upon your cue, my
    lord,
    William Lord Hastings had pronounced your part —
    I mean your voice — for crowning of the king.

RICHARD Than my lord Hastings no man might be
    bolder:

30   His lordship knows me well, and loves me well.—
    My lord of Ely, when I was last in Holborn,
    I saw good strawberries in your garden there:
    I do beseech you send for some of them.

---

5 **wants but nomination** requires only the appointing of the date   6 **happy** auspicious, favourable
8 **inward** intimate   9 **mind** temperament/opinion on the coronation/intentions in general   10 **for** as for
13 **near in love** close, intimate   16 **sounded** questioned, sounded out   19 **in** on   **voice** vote
20 **take...part** accept in a gracious manner   22 **cousins** term of address between nobles   24 **neglect**
cause the neglect of   27 **part** role (continues the theatrical language begun with **cue**)   29 **bolder** more
confident

BISHOP OF ELY Marry, and will, my lord, with all my
    heart.   *Exit Bishop*

35   **RICHARD** Cousin of Buckingham, a word with you.
    Catesby hath sounded Hastings in our business,   *They speak aside*
    And finds the testy gentleman so hot
    That he will lose his head ere give consent
    His master's child, as worshipfully he terms it,
40   Shall lose the royalty of England's throne.
    BUCKINGHAM Withdraw yourself a while. I'll go with
    you.   *Exeunt [Richard and Buckingham]*
    DERBY We have not yet set down this day of triumph.
    Tomorrow, in my judgement, is too sudden,
    For I myself am not so well provided
45   As else I would be, were the day prolonged.
    Enter the Bishop of Ely
    BISHOP OF ELY Where is my lord, the Duke of
    Gloucester?
    I have sent for these strawberries.
    HASTINGS His grace looks cheerfully and smooth this
    morning:
    There's some conceit or other likes him well,
50   When that he bids good morrow with such spirit.
    I think there's never a man in Christendom
    Can lesser hide his love or hate than he,
    For by his face straight shall you know his heart.
    DERBY What of his heart perceive you in his face
55   By any livelihood he showed today?
    HASTINGS Marry, that with no man here he is offended:
    For, were he, he had shown it in his looks.
    Enter Richard and Buckingham
    RICHARD I pray you all, tell me what they deserve
    That do conspire my death with devilish plots
60   Of damnèd witchcraft, and that have prevailed
    Upon my body with their hellish charms.
    HASTINGS The tender love I bear your grace, my lord,
    Makes me most forward in this princely presence
    To doom th'offenders, whosoe'er they be:
65   I say, my lord, they have deservèd death.

---

37 **testy** headstrong, short-tempered **hot** angry/impetuous 38 **head** plays on the etymology of **testy**, i.e.
teste, Old French for 'head' 39 **worshipfully** respectfully 42 **set down** confirmed 44 **provided**
prepared 45 **prolonged** postponed, delayed 48 **smooth** seemingly amiable or friendly 49 **conceit** idea,
fancy **likes** pleases 53 **straight** instantly 55 **livelihood** liveliness 61 **charms** magic spells 64 **doom**
sentence

RICHARD Then be your eyes the witness of their evil.
Look how I am bewitched: behold, mine arm   *Points to his arm*
Is like a blasted sapling, withered up:
And this is Edward's wife, that monstrous witch,
70   Consorted with that harlot, strumpet Shore,
That by their witchcraft thus have markèd me.
HASTINGS If they have done this deed, my noble lord—
RICHARD If? Thou protector of this damnèd strumpet—
Talk'st thou to me of 'ifs'? Thou art a traitor.
75   Off with his head! Now, by Saint Paul I swear,
I will not dine until I see the same. —
Lovell and Ratcliffe, look that it be done.
The rest that love me, rise and follow me.

Exeunt. Lovell and Ratcliffe with
the Lord Hastings remain

HASTINGS Woe, woe for England! Not a whit for me,
80   For I, too fond, might have prevented this.
Stanley did dream the boar did rouse our helms;
And I did scorn it and disdain to fly.
Three times today my foot-cloth horse did stumble,
And started, when he looked upon the Tower,
85   As loath to bear me to the slaughter-house.
O, now I need the priest that spake to me:
I now repent I told the pursuivant,
As too triumphing how mine enemies
Today at Pomfret bloodily were butchered,
90   And I myself secure in grace and favour.
O Margaret, Margaret, now thy heavy curse
Is lighted on poor Hastings' wretched head!
RATCLIFFE Come, come, dispatch. The duke would be at
   dinner.
Make a short shrift: he longs to see your head.
95   HASTINGS O, momentary grace of mortal men,
Which we more hunt for than the grace of God!
Who builds his hope in air of your good looks,
Lives like a drunken sailor on a mast,
Ready with every nod to tumble down
100   Into the fatal bowels of the deep.

---

68 blasted shrivelled, blighted by supernatural means   **69 is** i.e. is the doing of   **monstrous** unnatural
70 Consorted associated, in conjunction   **Shore** Jane Shore, Hastings' mistress and formerly Edward
IV's   **76 the same** i.e. Hastings' beheading accomplished   **80 fond** foolish   **81 rouse** move violently, pull
from our heads   **83 foot-cloth horse** horse with a long ornate cloth draped over its back   **84 started**
shied, moved suddenly   **85 As** as if   **loath** reluctant, unwilling   **88 triumphing** exulting victoriously
94 shrift) confession (to a priest)   **95 grace** fortune, favour (in the next line, the sense shifts to 'divine grace,
mercy')   **97 Who** he who   **in air** on the insubstantial foundation, in the emptiness   **good** favouring,
approving

LOVELL Come, come, dispatch: 'tis bootless to exclaim.
HASTINGS O bloody Richard! Miserable England!
I prophesy the fearful'st time to thee
That ever wretched age hath looked upon.
105   Come, lead me to the block: bear him my head.
They smile at me who shortly shall be dead. *Exeunt*

[Act 3 Scene 5]   *running scene 11*

Enter Richard and Buckingham, in rotten armour,
marvellous ill-favoured

RICHARD Come, cousin, canst thou quake and change
   thy colour,
Murder thy breath in middle of a word,
And then again begin, and stop again,
As if thou were distraught and mad with terror?
5   **BUCKINGHAM** Tut, I can counterfeit the deep tragedian,
Speak and look back, and pry on every side,
Tremble and start at wagging of a straw:
Intending deep suspicion, ghastly looks
Are at my service, like enforcèd smiles,
10   And both are ready in their offices
At any time to grace my stratagems.
But what, is Catesby gone?
RICHARD He is, and see, he brings the mayor along.
Enter the Mayor and Catesby
BUCKINGHAM Lord Mayor—
15   **RICHARD** Look to the drawbridge there!
BUCKINGHAM Hark, a drum!
RICHARD Catesby, o'erlook the walls.
BUCKINGHAM Lord Mayor, the reason we have sent—
RICHARD Look back, defend thee, here are enemies.
20   **BUCKINGHAM** God and our innocency defend and guard
   us!
Enter Lovell and Ratcliffe, with Hastings' head

---

101 bootless useless   **exclaim** protest, cry out   **3.5** *Location: within the walls of the Tower of London*   **rotten** rusty/old, decaying   ***marvellous ill-favoured*** (looking) extremely unsightly   **1 change thy colour** i.e. make yourself look pale with fear   **2 Murder** i.e. cut off, catch   **5 counterfeit** imitate   **deep** artful, cunning   **tragedian** tragic actor   **6 back** behind me, over my shoulder (presumably in alarm or distrust)   **pry** peer (nervously or suspiciously)   **7 at wagging** at the mere stirring, shaking   **8 Intending** expressing, pretending   **ghastly** full of fear   **9 service** command   **enforcèd** false, deliberate   **10 offices** roles, tasks   **17 o'erlook** look over (seems to suggest that the scene takes place on the battlements)

RICHARD Be patient, they are friends: Ratcliffe and
        Lovell.
LOVELL Here is the head of that ignoble traitor,
        The dangerous and unsuspected Hastings.
RICHARD So dear I loved the man that I must weep.
25   I took him for the plainest harmless creature
        That breathed upon the earth a Christian,
        Made him my book, wherein my soul recorded
        The history of all her secret thoughts.
        So smooth he daubed his vice with show of virtue
30   That, his apparent open guilt omitted —
        I mean, his conversation with Shore's wife —
        He lived from all attainder of suspects.
BUCKINGHAM Well, well, he was the covert'st sheltered
        traitor
        That ever lived.
35   Would you imagine, or almost believe,
        Were't not that, by great preservation
        We live to tell it, that the subtle traitor
        This day had plotted, in the council house,
        To murder me and my good lord of Gloucester?
40 **MAYOR** Had he done so?
RICHARD What? Think you we are Turks or infidels?
        Or that we would, against the form of law,
        Proceed thus rashly in the villain's death,
        But that the extreme peril of the case,
45   The peace of England and our person's safety,
        Enforced us to this execution?
MAYOR Now fair befall you! He deserved his death,
        And your good graces, both have well proceeded
        To warn false traitors from the like attempts.
50 **BUCKINGHAM** I never looked for better at his hands,
        After he once fell in with Mistress Shore.
        Yet had we not determined he should die
        Until your lordship came to see his end,
        Which now the loving haste of these our friends,
55   Something against our meanings, have prevented;
        Because, my lord, I would have had you heard

21 **patient** calm   25 **plainest** most honest   27 **book** i.e. diary, personal notebook   28 **history** narrative, record   29 **smooth** plausibly   30 **his … omitted** apart from his manifest guilt   31 **conversation** sexual relationship   32 **from** free from   **attainder of suspects** stain of suspicion   33 **covert'st sheltered** most secretly concealed   35 **almost** even   37 **subtle** cunning   41 **Turks** i.e. barbarians, non-Christians   42 **form** order, code   43 **rashly** hastily   47 **fair** good fortune   48 **proceeded** acted (perhaps with connotations of 'taken legal proceedings')   50 **looked for** expected   51 **fell in** plays on the sense of 'penetrated sexually'   52 **had … die** we had determined that he should not die   53 **see** attend to, manage

The traitor speak, and timorously confess
The manner and the purpose of his treasons,
That you might well have signified the same
60   Unto the citizens, who haply may
Misconster us in him and wail his death.
MAYOR But, my good lord, your grace's words shall serve
As well as I had seen and heard him speak:
And do not doubt, right noble princes both,
65   But I'll acquaint our duteous citizens
With all your just proceedings in this case.
RICHARD And to that end we wished your lordship here,
T'avoid the censures of the carping world.
BUCKINGHAM Which since you come too late of our
intent,
70   Yet witness what you hear we did intend.
And so, my good Lord Mayor, we bid farewell.

Exit Mayor

RICHARD Go, after, after, cousin Buckingham.
The mayor towards Guildhall hies him in all post:
There, at your meetest vantage of the time,
75   Infer the bastardy of Edward's children:
Tell them how Edward put to death a citizen
Only for saying he would make his son
Heir to the crown, meaning indeed his house,
Which, by the sign thereof was termèd so.
80   Moreover, urge his hateful luxury
And bestial appetite in change of lust,
Which stretched unto their servants, daughters,
wives,
Even where his raging eye or savage heart,
Without control, lusted to make a prey.
85   Nay, for a need, thus far come near my person:
Tell them, when that my mother went with child
Of that insatiate Edward, noble York
My princely father then had wars in France,
And by true computation of the time,
90   Found that the issue was not his begot —

---

57 timorously with fear, tremblingly   **60 haply** perhaps   **61 Misconster** misconstrue   **us in him** our role in or motives for his death   **63 as** as if   **68 carping** fault-finding, dissatisfied   **69 of** regarding **70 witness** testify to   **73 Guildhall** central building in which civic affairs were conducted   **hies . . . post** hurries as quickly as possible   **74 meetest vantage** best opportunity   **75 Infer** allege   **78 house** both home and either shop or inn   **79 sign** i.e. sign bearing the name (The Crown) of the shop or inn   **80 luxury** lechery, lust   **81 change of lust** constantly requiring new sexual partners   **83 Even where** wherever **85 for a need** if necessary   **come . . . person** i.e. tell a tale that will affect me too   **86 went . . . Of** was pregnant with   **89 true** exact, accurate   **90 his begot** conceived by him

Which well appearèd in his lineaments,
Being nothing like the noble duke my father.
Yet touch this sparingly, as 'twere far off,
Because, my lord, you know my mother lives.
95 BUCKINGHAM Doubt not, my lord, I'll play the orator
As if the golden fee for which I plead
Were for myself. And so, my lord, adieu.
RICHARD If you thrive well, bring them to Baynard's
Castle,
Where you shall find me well accompanied
100 With reverend fathers and well-learnèd bishops.
BUCKINGHAM I go: and towards three or four o'clock
Look for the news that the Guildhall affords.

Exit Buckingham

RICHARD Go, Lovell, with all speed to Doctor Shaw.—
Go thou to Friar Penker: bid them both   *To Catesby or Ratcliffe*
105 Meet me within this hour at Baynard's Castle.

Exeunt [all but Richard]

Now will I go to take some privy order
To draw the brats of Clarence out of sight,
And to give order that no manner person
Have any time recourse unto the princes.   *Exit*

[Act 3 Scene 6]   *running scene 12*

Enter a Scrivener

SCRIVENER Here is the indictment of the good Lord
Hastings,   *Shows a paper*
Which in a set hand fairly is engrossed,
That it may be today read o'er in Paul's.
And mark how well the sequel hangs together:
5 Eleven hours I have spent to write it over,
For yesternight by Catesby was it sent me,

---

91 well... lineaments was obvious in Edward's features, appearance   **93 sparingly** carefully, discreetly, with restraint   **96 golden fee** i.e. the crown (**fee** perhaps plays on the legal sense of 'inherited estate'; the sense of 'payment' anticipates the reward Buckingham expects for his services)   **98 thrive well** are successful   **Baynard's Castle** London residence owned by the Duchess of York, situated by the River Thames near Blackfriars   **103 Shaw... Penker** both clergymen who supported Richard   **106 take... order** make some secret arrangements   **108 manner** manner of   **109 recourse** means of access
3.6 *Location: London   Scrivener* professional scribe, particularly of legal documents   **1 indictment** formal statement of charges   **2 a set hand** formal handwriting   **fairly** elegantly   **engrossed** written in large characters appropriate for legal documents ('gross' in its sense of 'wicked, reprehensible' may pick up on its moral opposite, 'fair')   **3 Paul's** St Paul's Cathedral (where public proclamations were often made)   **4 the sequel** the following/the sequence of events/subsequent scribal copy he produced

The precedent was full as long a-doing.
And yet within these five hours Hastings lived,
Untainted, unexamined, free, at liberty.
10   Here's a good world the while! Who is so gross
That cannot see this palpable device?
Yet who so bold, but says he sees it not?
Bad is the world, and all will come to nought
When such ill dealing must be seen in thought.

Exit

[Act 3 Scene 7]   *running scene 13*

Enter Richard and Buckingham, at several doors

RICHARD How now, how now? What say the citizens?
BUCKINGHAM Now, by the holy mother of our lord,
    The citizens are mum, say not a word.
RICHARD Touched you the bastardy of Edward's
    children?
5   BUCKINGHAM I did: with his contract with Lady Lucy,
    And his contract by deputy in France,
    Th'unsatiate greediness of his desire,
    And his enforcement of the city wives,
    His tyranny for trifles, his own bastardy,
10   As being got, your father then in France,
    And his resemblance, being not like the duke.
    Withal I did infer your lineaments,
    Being the right idea of your father,
    Both in your form and nobleness of mind:
15   Laid open all your victories in Scotland,
    Your discipline in war, wisdom in peace,
    Your bounty, virtue, fair humility:
    Indeed, left nothing fitting for your purpose
    Untouched, or slightly handled, in discourse.
20   And when my oratory drew toward end,

7 **precedent** preceding document, first draft (from which the final copy has been made)   9 **Untainted** unstained by accusation   **unexamined** not questioned, interrogated   **free** at liberty/innocent/untroubled   10 **the while** these days   **gross** stupid   11 **palpable device** obvious contrivance   14 **seen in thought** i.e. not acknowledged openly   3.7 *Location: Baynard's Castle, London*   **several** separate   3 **mum** silent   4 **Touched you** did you mention   5 **contract** betrothal   6 **contract ... France** in *3 Henry VI* (Act 3 scene 3) the Earl of Warwick goes to France as Edward's **deputy** to secure a betrothal with the King of France's sister-in-law; he and the French king are furious and humiliated when word comes that Edward has abruptly married Elizabeth instead   8 **enforcement** coercion/rape   9 **tyranny for trifles** severe punishment of minor crimes/oppressive behaviour even with regard to trivialities   10 **got** begot, conceived   15 **Laid open** revealed/described/elaborated on   16 **discipline** strategic skill   17 **bounty** generosity   **fair** honourable   18 **fitting for** relevant to   19 **slightly** neglectfully

I bid them that did love their country's good
Cry 'God save Richard, England's royal king!'
RICHARD And did they so?
BUCKINGHAM No, so God help me, they spake not a
        word,
25   But, like dumb statues or breathing stones,
        Stared each on other and looked deadly pale:
        Which when I saw, I reprehended them,
        And asked the mayor what meant this wilful silence:
        His answer was, the people were not used
30   To be spoke to but by the recorder.
        Then he was urged to tell my tale again:
        'Thus saith the duke, thus hath the duke inferred' —
        But nothing spoke in warrant from himself.
        When he had done, some followers of mine own,
35   At lower end of the hall, hurled up their caps,
        And some ten voices cried, 'God save King Richard!'
        And thus I took the vantage of those few:
        'Thanks, gentle citizens and friends,' quoth I,
        'This general applause and cheerful shout
40   Argues your wisdom and your love to Richard.'
        And even here brake off, and came away.
RICHARD What tongueless blocks were they? Would they
        not speak?
        Will not the mayor then and his brethren come?
BUCKINGHAM The mayor is here at hand. Intend some
        fear:
45   Be not you spoke with, but by mighty suit.
        And look you get a prayer-book in your hand,
        And stand between two churchmen, good my lord,
        For on that ground I'll make a holy descant:
        And be not easily won to our requests.
50   Play the maid's part: still answer nay, and take it.
RICHARD I go. And if you plead as well for them
        As I can say nay to thee for myself,
        No doubt we bring it to a happy issue.

---

30 recorder civic official in the City of London   **32 inferred** alleged   **33 in . . . himself** on his own
authority   **35 hall** i.e. the Guildhall   **37 the vantage** advantage   **39 general** public/widespread
40 Argues demonstrates   **41 even here** at this point   **brake** broke   **42 blocks** blockheads, idiots
43 brethren members of the town corporation   **44 Intend** pretend, feign   **fear** an intimidating manner/
religious veneration/fearfulness   **45 suit** request, entreaty   **46 look** make sure   **48 ground** base melody
descant accompaniment to or improvised variation on the **ground**, or underlying melody   **49 won**
persuaded   **50 maid's** young woman's/virgin's   **still** constantly, repeatedly   **and take it** yet have sex all
the same   **52 for myself** on my own behalf/for my own advantage   **53 issue** outcome

BUCKINGHAM Go, go, up to the leads. The Lord Mayor
    knocks.   *[Exit Richard]*

Enter the Mayor and Citizens

55   Welcome, my lord. I dance attendance here:
       I think the duke will not be spoke withal.

Enter Catesby

       Now, Catesby, what says your lord to my request.

CATESBY He doth entreat your grace, my noble lord,
       To visit him tomorrow or next day:

60   He is within, with two right reverend fathers,
       Divinely bent to meditation,
       And in no worldly suits would he be moved,
       To draw him from his holy exercise.

BUCKINGHAM Return, good Catesby, to the gracious
       duke:

65   Tell him myself, the Mayor and Alderman,
       In deep designs, in matter of great moment,
       No less importing than our general good,
       Are come to have some conference with his grace.

CATESBY I'll signify so much unto him straight.   *Exit*

70 **BUCKINGHAM** Ah, ha, my lord, this prince is not an
       Edward!
       He is not lulling on a lewd love-bed,
       But on his knees at meditation:
       Not dallying with a brace of courtesans,
       But meditating with two deep divines:

75   Not sleeping, to engross his idle body,
       But praying, to enrich his watchful soul.
       Happy were England, would this virtuous prince
       Take on his grace the sovereignty thereof:
       But sure I fear we shall not win him to it.

80 **MAYOR** Marry, God defend his grace should say us nay!

BUCKINGHAM I fear he will. — Here Catesby comes
       again.

Enter Catesby

       Now, Catesby, what says his grace?

CATESBY He wonders to what end you have assembled
       Such troops of citizens to come to him,

---

54 **leads** lead-covered flat roof   55 **dance attendance** am being kept waiting, am eager to be seen
61 **bent** occupied, concerned/bent over (in prayer)   62 **suits** affairs, petitions (especially legal)
63 **exercise** prayers   66 **deep** very important, profound   **moment** significance   67 **No less importing**
concerning no less a matter   71 **lulling** lolling, reclining   73 **dallying** toying sexually, having sex   **brace**
pair   74 **deep** learned, profoundly wise   **divines** priests   75 **engross** fatten   76 **watchful** alert/awake
77 **Happy** fortunate   78 **his grace** plays on the ducal title and on the sense of 'divine grace' (suggesting a
God-given right to the crown)   80 **defend** forbid

85   His grace not being warned thereof before.
        He fears, my lord, you mean no good to him.
     BUCKINGHAM Sorry I am my noble cousin should
        Suspect me that I mean no good to him.
        By heaven, we come to him in perfect love,
90   And so once more return and tell his grace.

                                          Exit [Catesby]

        When holy and devout religious men
        Are at their beads, 'tis hard to draw them thence,
        So sweet is zealous contemplation.

     Enter Richard aloft, between two Bishops. [Catesby returns]

     MAYOR See, where his grace stands 'tween two
           clergymen.
95   BUCKINGHAM Two props of virtue for a Christian prince,
        To stay him from the fall of vanity:
        And, see, a book of prayer in his hand,
        True ornaments to know a holy man.—
        Famous Plantagenet, most gracious prince,
100   Lend favourable ear to our requests,
        And pardon us the interruption
        Of thy devotion and right Christian zeal.
     RICHARD My lord, there needs no such apology:
        I do beseech your grace to pardon me,
105   Who, earnest in the service of my God,
        Deferred the visitation of my friends.
        But, leaving this, what is your grace's pleasure?
     BUCKINGHAM Even that, I hope, which pleaseth God
           above,
        And all good men of this ungoverned isle.
110 RICHARD I do suspect I have done some offence
        That seems disgracious in the city's eye,
        And that you come to reprehend my ignorance.
     BUCKINGHAM You have, my lord: would it might please
           your grace,
        On our entreaties, to amend your fault.
115 RICHARD Else wherefore breathe I in a Christian land?
     BUCKINGHAM Know then, it is your fault that you resign
        The supreme seat, the throne majestical,

---

89 perfect complete   **92 beads** rosary beads   **93 zealous** pious, devout   *aloft* i.e. on the upper staging
level, or gallery   **95 props** supports   **96 stay** keep   **fall of** moral fall caused by   **102 right** rightful/
genuine, true/extremely   **106 visitation** visit (especially by an ecclesiastical body); Richard is deliberately
employing language with religious connotations   **111 disgracious** disliked   **112 reprehend my**
ignorance rebuke me for the fault I am unaware of   **115 Else ... land?** Why else do I live as a Christian (if
not to amend my faults)?

The sceptred office of your ancestors,
Your state of fortune and your due of birth,
120   The lineal glory of your royal house,
To the corruption of a blemished stock;
Whiles, in the mildness of your sleepy thoughts,
Which here we waken to our country's good,
The noble isle doth want his proper limbs:
125   His face defaced with scars of infamy,
His royal stock graft with ignoble plants,
And almost shouldered in the swallowing gulf
Of dark forgetfulness and deep oblivion.
Which to recure, we heartily solicit
130   Your gracious self to take on you the charge
And kingly government of this your land —
Not as Protector, steward, substitute,
Or lowly factor for another's gain;
But as successively from blood to blood,
135   Your right of birth, your empery, your own.
For this, consorted with the citizens,
Your very worshipful and loving friends,
And by their vehement instigation,
In this just cause come I to move your grace.
140   **RICHARD** I cannot tell if to depart in silence,
Or bitterly to speak in your reproof
Best fitteth my degree or your condition.
If not to answer, you might haply think
Tongue-tied ambition, not replying, yielded
145   To bear the golden yoke of sovereignty,
Which fondly you would here impose on me.
If to reprove you for this suit of yours,
So seasoned with your faithful love to me,
Then on the other side I checked my friends.
150   Therefore, to speak, and to avoid the first,
And then, in speaking, not to incur the last,
Definitively thus I answer you:

118 sceptred involving the bearing of a royal sceptre   **119 state** position, rank/kingship   **of fortune** to which fortune entitles you   **120 lineal** hereditary   **121 blemished** morally tainted (through illegitimacy)   **stock** family tree (sense subsequently shifts to 'tree trunk')   **124 want** lack   **proper** rightful, own   **125 infamy** bad reputation, disgrace   **126 graft** grafted, i.e. united (as in horticulture)   **plants** may pun on 'Plantagenet'   **127 shouldered** shoved (possibly 'immersed up to the shoulders')   **gulf** abyss/whirlpool   **129 recure** redress, cure   **133 factor** agent   **134 successively** by right of succession   **135 empery** sovereign dominions   **136 consorted** united, in league   **137 worshipful** honourable/respectful   **139 move** persuade   **142 degree** rank or perhaps 'spiritual condition'   **condition** social status   **143 not to** I do not   **haply** perhaps   **144 yielded** consented   **146 fondly** foolishly   **149 checked** (would have) rebuked

Your love deserves my thanks, but my desert
Unmeritable shuns your high request.
155 First, if all obstacles were cut away,
And that my path were even to the crown,
As the ripe revenue and due of birth,
Yet so much is my poverty of spirit,
So mighty and so many my defects,
160 That I would rather hide me from my greatness —
Being a bark to brook no mighty sea —
Than in my greatness covet to be hid,
And in the vapour of my glory smothered.
But, God be thanked, there is no need of me,
165 And much I need to help you, were there need.
The royal tree hath left us royal fruit,
Which, mellowed by the stealing hours of time,
Will well become the seat of majesty,
And make, no doubt, us happy by his reign.
170 On him I lay that you would lay on me,
The right and fortune of his happy stars,
Which God defend that I should wring from him!
BUCKINGHAM My lord, this argues conscience in your
       grace,
But the respects thereof are nice and trivial,
175 All circumstances well considerèd.
You say that Edward is your brother's son:
So say we too, but not by Edward's wife,
For first was he contract to Lady Lucy —
Your mother lives a witness to his vow —
180 And afterward by substitute betrothed
To Bona, sister to the King of France.
These both put off, a poor petitioner,
A care-crazed mother to a many sons,
A beauty-waning and distressèd widow,
185 Even in the afternoon of her best days,
Made prize and purchase of his wanton eye,

---

153 **desert**   154 **Unmeritable** unworthiness   155 **cut away** with sinister connotations of 'cut off, killed'
156 **even** direct, smooth   157 **revenue** possession/yield, income   160 **greatness** i.e. kingship   161 **bark**
ship   **brook** endure, withstand   162 **in . . . hid** desire to be enveloped by greatness   163 **vapour** mist/
spray   165 **much I need** I would need a great deal (i.e. I am inadequate)   166 **royal tree** i.e. King Edward
IV   167 **mellowed** matured   **stealing** creeping (forward)   168 **become** suit, befit   **seat** throne
170 **that** what   171 **happy** auspicious, favourable   172 **defend** forbid   **wring** wrench   173 **argues**
shows, is evidence of   174 **respects thereof** factors in your argument   **nice** unimportant, trifling
178 **contract . . . vow** the verbal contract entered into at betrothal was considered binding   180 **substitute**
deputy, delegate   181 **sister** sister-in-law   182 **petitioner** Elizabeth Grey catches Edward's eye when she
entreats him for the return of her dead husband's lands (see *3 Henry VI*, Act 3 scene 2)   183 **care-crazed**
fraught, worn out with anxiety   186 **purchase** booty, plunder   **wanton** lustful

Seduced the pitch and height of his degree
To base declension and loathed bigamy.
By her, in his unlawful bed, he got
190   This Edward, whom our manners call the prince.
More bitterly could I expostulate,
Save that, for reverence to some alive,
I give a sparing limit to my tongue.
Then, good my lord, take to your royal self
195   This proffered benefit of dignity:
If not to bless us and the land withal,
Yet to draw forth your noble ancestry
From the corruption of abusing times,
Unto a lineal true-derivèd course.
200   MAYOR Do, good my lord: your citizens entreat you.   *To Richard*
BUCKINGHAM Refuse not, mighty lord, this proffered
        love.
CATESBY O, make them joyful, grant their lawful suit!
RICHARD Alas, why would you heap this care on me?
        I am unfit for state and majesty.
205   I do beseech you, take it not amiss:
        I cannot nor I will not yield to you.
BUCKINGHAM If you refuse it — as, in love and zeal,
        Loath to depose the child, your brother's son,
        As well we know your tenderness of heart
210   And gentle, kind, effeminate remorse,
        Which we have noted in you to your kindred
        And equally indeed to all estates —
        Yet know, whe'er you accept our suit or no,
        Your brother's son shall never reign our king,
215   But we will plant some other in the throne
        To the disgrace and downfall of your house:
        And in this resolution here we leave you.—
        Come, citizens, we will entreat no more.
                        Exeunt [*Buckingham with Citizens*]
CATESBY Call him again, sweet prince. Accept their suit.
220   If you deny them all the land will rue it.
RICHARD Will you enforce me to a world of cares?
        Call them again. I am not made of stones,

---

187 **pitch** height (literally, the highest point in a falcon's flight)   188 **base declension** descent to
baseness   **bigamy** i.e. because Edward had been engaged to two other women previously   190 **our
manners** courtesy   191 **expostulate** expound on, argue about   192 **some alive** i.e. Richard and
Edward's mother, the Duchess of York   193 **sparing** considerate, forbearing   195 **benefit** benevolent
bestowal   **dignity** honour, high rank, kingship   199 **true-derivèd** legitimate, directly descended
203 **care** duty, trouble, source of anxiety   207 **as** being, because (you are)   **zeal** devotion
210 **effeminate** tender, gentle   212 **estates** social ranks

> But penetrable to your kind entreaties,
> Albeit against my conscience and my soul.

Enter Buckingham and the rest

225 Cousin of Buckingham, and sage, grave men,
> Since you will buckle fortune on my back,
> To bear her burden, whe'er I will or no,
> I must have patience to endure the load:
> But if black scandal or foul-faced reproach
230 Attend the sequel of your imposition,
> Your mere enforcement shall acquittance me
> From all the impure blots and stains thereof;
> For God doth know, and you may partly see,
> How far I am from the desire of this.

235 **MAYOR** God bless your grace! We see it and will say it.
RICHARD In saying so, you shall but say the truth.
BUCKINGHAM Then I salute you with this royal title:
> Long live King Richard, England's worthy king!
ALL Amen.
240 **BUCKINGHAM** Tomorrow may it please you to be
> crowned?
RICHARD Even when you please, for you will have it so.
BUCKINGHAM Tomorrow, then, we will attend your
> grace.
> And so most joyfully we take our leave.
RICHARD Come, let us to our holy work again.—   *To the Bishops*
245 Farewell, my cousins: farewell, gentle friends.

Exeunt

Act 4 Scene 1   *running scene 14*

*Enter the Queen, Anne Duchess of Gloucester [leading a girl],
the Duchess of York and Marquis Dorset*

DUCHESS OF YORK Who meets us here? My niece
> Plantagenet
> Led in the hand of her kind aunt of Gloucester?
> Now, for my life, she's wand'ring to the Tower,
> On pure heart's love to greet the tender prince.
5 Daughter, well met.
ANNE God give your graces both
> A happy and a joyful time of day.

226 **buckle** i.e. like armour; **my back** draws attention to Richard's hunched back   **230 sequel**
consequences   **231 Your…me** the fact that you forced me shall acquit me   **mere** absolute   **241 Even**
just, exactly   **4.1** *Location: outside the Tower of London*   **Anne…Gloucester** i.e. Lady Anne, who
has married Richard at some point since his wooing of her in Act 1 scene 2   **leading a girl** probably
Clarence's daughter   **1 niece** granddaughter   **4 tender** young

QUEEN ELIZABETH As much to you, good sister. Whither
    away?
ANNE No further than the Tower, and, as I guess,
10   Upon the like devotion as yourselves,
      To gratulate the gentle princes there.
QUEEN ELIZABETH Kind sister, thanks: we'll enter all
    together.
Enter the Lieutenant [Brackenbury]
      And, in good time, here the lieutenant comes.
      Master Lieutenant, pray you, by your leave,
15   How doth the prince, and my young son of York?
BRACKENBURY Right well, dear madam. By your
    patience,
      I may not suffer you to visit them:
      The king hath strictly charged the contrary.
QUEEN ELIZABETH The king? Who's that?
20   **BRACKENBURY** I mean the Lord Protector.
QUEEN ELIZABETH The lord protect him from that kingly
    title!
      Hath he set bounds between their love and me?
      I am their mother: who shall bar me from them?
DUCHESS OF YORK I am their father's mother: I will see
    them.
25   **ANNE** Their aunt I am in law, in love their mother:
      Then bring me to their sights. I'll bear thy blame
      And take thy office from thee, on my peril.
BRACKENBURY No, madam, no; I may not leave it so:
      I am bound by oath, and therefore pardon me. *Exit*
Enter Stanley [Earl of Derby]
30   **DERBY** Let me but meet you, ladies, one hour hence,
      And I'll salute your grace of York as mother,
      And reverend looker-on, of two fair queens.—
      Come, madam, you must straight to Westminster,   *To Anne*
      There to be crownèd Richard's royal queen.
35   **QUEEN ELIZABETH** Ah, cut my lace asunder,
      That my pent heart may have some scope to beat,
      Or else I swoon with this dead-killing news!

---

10 like devotion same devoted purpose   **11 gratulate** greet, welcome   **17 suffer** allow   **22 bounds** boundaries   **25 in law** i.e. by marriage   **27 office** responsibility, official duty   **31 mother** mother-in-law (of Elizabeth and Anne)   **32 looker-on** beholder   **two fair queens** i.e. Elizabeth and Anne (as wife of Richard, who is shortly to be crowned)   **33 straight** (go) straight away   **35 lace** cords that fastened the tightly laced bodice (often cut when a woman became faint)   **36 pent** confined, penned in

ANNE Despiteful tidings! O, unpleasing news!

DORSET Be of good cheer. Mother, how fares your grace?

40 QUEEN ELIZABETH O Dorset, speak not to me, get thee
gone!
Death and destruction dogs thee at thy heels:
Thy mother's name is ominous to children.
If thou wilt outstrip death, go cross the seas,
And live with Richmond, from the reach of hell.

45 Go, hie thee, hie thee from this slaughter-house,
Lest thou increase the number of the dead
And make me die the thrall of Margaret's curse,
Nor mother, wife, nor England's counted queen.

DERBY Full of wise care is this your counsel, madam.—

50 Take all the swift advantage of the hours.   *To Dorset*
You shall have letters from me to my son
In your behalf, to meet you on the way.
Be not ta'en tardy by unwise delay.

DUCHESS OF YORK O ill-dispersing wind of misery!

55 O my accursèd womb, the bed of death!
A cockatrice hast thou hatched to the world,
Whose unavoided eye is murderous.

DERBY Come, madam, come: I in all haste was sent.   *To Anne*

ANNE And I with all unwillingness will go.

60 O, would to God that the inclusive verge
Of golden metal that must round my brow
Were red-hot steel, to sear me to the brains!
Anointed let me be with deadly venom,
And die, ere men can say, 'God save the queen!'

65 QUEEN ELIZABETH Go, go, poor soul, I envy not thy glory:
To feed my humour wish thyself no harm.

ANNE No? Why? When he that is my husband now
Came to me, as I followed Henry's corpse,
When scarce the blood was well washed from his
hands

70 Which issued from my other angel husband

---

38 Despiteful cruel, malicious   **44 Richmond** i.e. Henry Tudor, Earl of Richmond (later Henry VII), who had sought refuge in Brittany   **from** away from   **45 hie** hurry   **47 thrall** slave   **48 Nor** neither **counted** accounted, acknowledged   **51 letters … way** i.e. the letters will be sent to Dorset while en route/ the letters will ask George Stanley to meet Dorset on the way and assist his journey/the letters will enable Dorset to be introduced to and assisted by Richmond when he reaches Brittany   **son** stepson (Richmond), or possibly Stanley's own son George   **53 ta'en tardy** caught by surprise   **54 ill-dispersing** evil-spreading **56 cockatrice** basilisk, a mythical reptile that could kill with its gaze   **57 unavoided** unavoidable **60 inclusive** enclosing   **verge** band, rim   **63 Anointed** anointing with holy oil was a key part of the coronation   **66 To … harm** do not wish yourself harm just to satisfy my mood   **70 other angel husband** my other (first) husband, who was an angel/my first husband, who was a different (i.e. good) type of angel (implying that Richard is the fallen angel Lucifer)

And that dear saint which then I weeping
    followed —
O, when I say I looked on Richard's face,
This was my wish: 'Be thou', quoth I, 'accursed
For making me, so young, so old a widow!
75   And, when thou wed'st, let sorrow haunt thy bed;
And be thy wife — if any be so mad —
More miserable by the life of thee
Than thou hast made me by my dear lord's death!'
Lo, ere I can repeat this curse again,
80   Within so small a time, my woman's heart
Grossly grew captive to his honey words
And proved the subject of mine own soul's curse,
Which hitherto hath held mine eyes from rest,
For never yet one hour in his bed
85   Did I enjoy the golden dew of sleep,
But with his timorous dreams was still awaked.
Besides, he hates me for my father Warwick,
And will, no doubt, shortly be rid of me.
QUEEN ELIZABETH Poor heart, adieu! I pity thy
    complaining.
90   **ANNE** No more than with my soul I mourn for yours.
DORSET Farewell, thou woeful welcomer of glory.
ANNE Adieu, poor soul, that tak'st thy leave of it.
DUCHESS OF YORK Go thou to Richmond, and good
    fortune guide thee.—   *To Dorset*
Go thou to Richard, and good angels tend thee.—   *To Anne*
95   Go thou to sanctuary, and good thoughts possess   *To Queen*
    thee.—   *Elizabeth*
I to my grave, where peace and rest lie with me.
Eighty odd years of sorrow have I seen,
And each hour's joy wrecked with a week of teen.   *She starts to*
QUEEN ELIZABETH Stay, yet look back with me unto the   *leave*
    Tower.
100   Pity, you ancient stones, those tender babes
Whom envy hath immured within your walls,
Rough cradle for such little pretty ones,
Rude ragged nurse, old sullen playfellow
For tender princes: use my babies well.
105   So foolish sorrows bids your stones farewell. *Exeunt*

---

74 old experienced/worn-out   **81 Grossly** stupidly/excessively/coarsely   **86 timorous** full of fear
87 Warwick with Clarence, the Earl of Warwick deserted the Yorkist cause   **89 complaining** lamentations
98 teen grief, suffering   **101 immured** imprisoned, closed in   **103 Rude** harsh, rough   **ragged** rugged,
eroded   **sullen** dismal, melancholy   **105 So** such/thus   **foolish** fond, doting

Act 4 Scene 2

running scene 15

Sound a sennet. Enter Richard in pomp, Buckingham,
Catesby, Ratcliffe, Lovell, [a Page and others. A throne is
brought forth]

RICHARD Stand all apart.— Cousin of Buckingham.
BUCKINGHAM My gracious sovereign?
RICHARD Give me thy hand.   *Sound [trumpets]*

He ascends the throne

Thus high, by thy advice and thy assistance,   *Richard and*
5   Is King Richard seated.   *Buckingham speak aside*
But shall we wear these glories for a day?
Or shall they last, and we rejoice in them?
BUCKINGHAM Still live they and forever let them last!
RICHARD Ah, Buckingham, now do I play the touch,
10   To try if thou be current gold indeed:
Young Edward lives. Think now what I would speak.
BUCKINGHAM Say on, my loving lord.
RICHARD Why, Buckingham, I say I would be king,
BUCKINGHAM Why, so you are, my thrice-renownèd
    lord.
15 **RICHARD** Ha? Am I king? 'Tis so: but Edward lives.
BUCKINGHAM True, noble prince.
RICHARD O, bitter consequence,
That Edward still should live — true noble prince.
Cousin, thou wast not wont to be so dull.
20   Shall I be plain? I wish the bastards dead,
And I would have it suddenly performed.
What say'st thou now? Speak suddenly, be brief.
BUCKINGHAM Your grace may do your pleasure.
RICHARD Tut, tut, thou art all ice: thy kindness freezes.
25   Say, have I thy consent that they shall die?
BUCKINGHAM Give me some little breath, some pause,
    dear lord,
Before I positively speak in this:
I will resolve you herein presently.   *Exit*
CATESBY The king is angry: see, he gnaws his lip.   *Aside*

4.2 *Location: the royal court, London* **pomp** ceremony, splendour, celebration   **1 apart** aside   **9 play the touch** act the touchstone (used to test the validity of gold)   **10 try** test   **current** genuine   **17 consequence** outcome   **18 true noble prince** Richard adapts Buckingham's phrase so that it applies to Edward   **19 wont . . . dull** accustomed to be so stupid   **21 suddenly** immediately   **26 breath** breathing space   **27 positively** definitively, directly   **28 resolve** answer

30 **RICHARD** I will converse with iron-witted fools
   And unrespective boys: none are for me
   That look into me with considerate eyes.
   High-reaching Buckingham grows circumspect.—
   Boy!
35 **PAGE** My lord?   *Comes forward*
   RICHARD Know'st thou not any whom corrupting gold
   Will tempt unto a close exploit of death?
   PAGE I know a discontented gentleman,
   Whose humble means match not his haughty spirit:
40 Gold were as good as twenty orators,
   And will, no doubt, tempt him to anything.
   RICHARD What is his name?
   PAGE His name, my lord, is Tyrrell.
   RICHARD I partly know the man. Go, call him hither,
        boy.   *Exit [Page]*
45 The deep-revolving witty Buckingham
   No more shall be the neighbour to my counsels.
   Hath he so long held out with me untired,
   And stops he now for breath? Well, be it so.
   Enter Stanley
   How now, Lord Stanley, what's the news?
50 **DERBY** Know, my loving lord, the marquis Dorset
   As I hear, is fled to Richmond,
   In the parts where he abides.   *Stands apart*
   RICHARD Come hither, Catesby. Rumour it abroad
   That Anne, my wife, is very grievous sick:
55 I will take order for her keeping close.
   Inquire me out some mean poor gentleman,
   Whom I will marry straight to Clarence' daughter:
   The boy is foolish, and I fear not him.
   Look, how thou dream'st! I say again, give out
60 That Anne my queen is sick and like to die:
   About it, for it stands me much upon,
   To stop all hopes whose growth may damage me.
                                    [Exit Catesby]
   I must be married to my brother's daughter,
   Or else my kingdom stands on brittle glass.

---

30 **iron-witted** dull-witted, stupid, obtuse   31 **unrespective** inattentive, disrespectful   32 **considerate**
thoughtful   33 **High-reaching** ambitious   37 **close** secret   39 **haughty** proud, aspiring   40 **orators**
persuasive speakers   45 **deep-revolving** deeply thoughtful, musing   **witty** sharp, clever   46 **counsels**
secrets, confidences   47 **held out** kept up   55 **take order** make arrangements   **close** shut away
56 **mean** humble, low-ranking   58 **The boy** i.e. Clarence's son   59 **how thou dream'st** i.e. pay attention
(perhaps Catesby is shocked)   **give out** make it known   61 **it...upon** it is very important for me
63 **brother's daughter** i.e. Edward IV's daughter Elizabeth

65   Murder her brothers, and then marry her:
         Uncertain way of gain! But I am in
         So far in blood that sin will pluck on sin:
         Tear-falling pity dwells not in this eye.

      Enter [Page, with] Tyrrell
         Is thy name Tyrrell?

70   TYRRELL James Tyrrell, and your most obedient subject.
      RICHARD Art thou, indeed?
      TYRRELL Prove me, my gracious lord.   *King Richard and Tyrrell*
      RICHARD Dar'st thou resolve to kill a friend of mine?   *speak aside*
      TYRRELL Please you:

75   But I had rather kill two enemies.
      RICHARD Why, then thou hast it: two deep enemies,
         Foes to my rest and my sweet sleep's disturbers
         Are they that I would have thee deal upon —
         Tyrrell, I mean those bastards in the Tower.

80   TYRRELL Let me have open means to come to them,
         And soon I'll rid you from the fear of them.
      RICHARD Thou sing'st sweet music. Hark, come hither,
         Tyrrell
         Go, by this token: rise, and lend thine ear.   *Gives a token*
         There is no more but so: say it is done,   *Whispers*

85   And I will love thee, and prefer thee for it.
      TYRRELL I will dispatch it straight.
                        Exit [Tyrrell, with the Page]

      Enter Buckingham
      BUCKINGHAM My lord, I have considered in my mind
         The late request that you did sound me in.
      RICHARD Well, let that rest. Dorset is fled to Richmond.

90   BUCKINGHAM I hear the news, my lord.
      RICHARD Stanley, he is your wife's son. Well, look unto
         it.
      BUCKINGHAM My lord, I claim the gift, my due by
         promise,
         For which your honour and your faith is pawned:
         Th'earldom of Hereford and the movables

95   Which you have promisèd I shall possess.
      RICHARD Stanley, look to your wife: if she convey
         Letters to Richmond, you shall answer it.

---

67 **pluck on** draw on   68 **Tear-falling pity** mercy, compassion that induces weeping   72 **Prove** test, try
73 **friend** plays on the sense of 'relative'   78 **deal upon** deal with, act against   80 **open** unrestricted
83 **token** some symbol of authority, perhaps a ring   84 **There…so** that is all there is to it   85 **prefer**
advance, promote   88 **late** recent   **sound me in** ask me about   91 **he** i.e. Richmond   93 **pawned**
pledged   94 **movables** portable property   96 **look to** beware, watch   97 **answer** be answerable for

BUCKINGHAM What says your highness to my just
     request?
RICHARD I do remember me, Henry the Sixth
100   Did prophesy that Richmond should be king,
    When Richmond was a little peevish boy.
    A king, perhaps—
BUCKINGHAM May it please you to resolve me in my suit.
RICHARD Thou troublest me: I am not in the vein. *Exit*
105 BUCKINGHAM And is it thus? Repays he my deep service
    With such contempt? Made I him king for this?
    O, let me think on Hastings, and be gone
    To Brecknock, while my fearful head is on!   *Exit*

[Act 4 Scene 3]

running scene 15 continues

Enter Tyrrell

TYRRELL The tyrannous and bloody act is done,
    The most arch deed of piteous massacre
    That ever yet this land was guilty of.
    Dighton and Forrest, who I did suborn
5   To do this piece of ruthful butchery,
    Albeit they were fleshed villains, bloody dogs,
    Melted with tenderness and mild compassion,
    Wept like to children in their deaths' sad story.
    'O, thus', quoth Dighton, 'lay the gentle babes.'
10   'Thus, thus', quoth Forrest, 'girdling one another
    Within their alabaster innocent arms.
    Their lips were four red roses on a stalk,
    And in their summer beauty kissed each other.
    A book of prayers on their pillow lay,
15   Which one', quoth Forrest, 'almost changed my
      mind.
    But O! The devil'— there the villain stopped.
    When Dighton thus told on: 'We smotherèd
    The most replenishèd sweet work of nature,
    That from the prime creation e'er she framed.'
20   Hence both are gone with conscience and remorse:

---

101 peevish foolish, childish **103 resolve** answer, satisfy **104 vein** mood **108 Brecknock** Brecon in Wales, Buckingham's family seat **4.3 2 arch** extreme, foremost **4 suborn** bribe **5 ruthful** lamentable, sad **6 fleshed** experienced (hunting term referring to feeding hounds with raw meat to excite them for the chase) **8 their . . . story** in telling the sad story of their deaths **10 girdling** hugging, encircling **11 alabaster** i.e. white (the substance was often used for human figures that formed part of funeral monuments) **15 Which one** which, which thing **18 replenishèd** complete, perfect **19 prime** first **framed** created **20 gone** overcome

They could not speak, and so I left them both,
To bear this tidings to the bloody king.

Enter Richard

And here he comes.—
All heath, my sovereign lord!

25 **RICHARD** Kind Tyrrell, am I happy in thy news?

TYRRELL If to have done the thing you gave in charge
Beget your happiness, be happy then,
For it is done.

RICHARD But didst thou see them dead?

30 **TYRRELL** I did, my lord.

RICHARD And buried, gentle Tyrrell?

TYRRELL The chaplain of the Tower hath buried them,
But where, to say the truth, I do not know.

RICHARD Come to me, Tyrrell, soon and after supper,
35 When thou shalt tell the process of their death.
Meantime, but think how I may do thee good,
And be inheritor of thy desire.
Farewell till then.

TYRRELL I humbly take my leave.   [*Exit*]

40 **RICHARD** The son of Clarence have I pent up close,
His daughter meanly have I matched in marriage,
The sons of Edward sleep in Abraham's bosom,
And Anne my wife hath bid the world good night.
Now, for I know the Breton Richmond aims
45 At young Elizabeth, my brother's daughter,
And by that knot looks proudly on the crown,
To her go I, a jolly thriving wooer.

Enter Ratcliffe

RATCLIFFE My lord!

RICHARD Good or bad news, that thou com'st in so
bluntly?

50 **RATCLIFFE** Bad news, my lord: Morton is fled to
Richmond,
And Buckingham, backed with the hardy Welshmen,
Is in the field, and still his power increaseth.

RICHARD Ely with Richmond troubles me more near
Than Buckingham and his rash-levied strength.

---

22 bloody bloodthirsty   **26 gave in charge** ordered   **34 soon and** i.e. soon   **35 process** account,
story   **37 be ... desire** you shall get what you wish   **40 close** securely, privately   **41 meanly ...
marriage** I have married to a low-ranking man   **42 Abraham's bosom** i.e. heaven   **44 for** because
Breton from Brittany (where Richmond is taking refuge)   **46 by that knot** through that marriage
49 bluntly unceremoniously, abruptly   **50 Morton** John Morton, Bishop of Ely (whom Richard asks for
strawberries in Act 3 scene 4)   **51 hardy** bold, resolute   **52 power** army   **53 near** deeply   **54 rash-
levied** rapidly mustered

55   Come, I have learned that fearful commenting
         Is leaden servitor to dull delay:
         Delay leads impotent and snail-paced beggary.
         Then fiery expedition be my wing,
         Jove's Mercury, and herald for a king!
60   Go, muster men. My counsel is my shield:
         We must be brief when traitors brave the field.

                                                Exeunt

[Act 4 Scene 4]   *running scene 16*

         Enter old Queen Margaret

         QUEEN MARGARET So, now prosperity begins to mellow
         And drop into the rotten mouth of death.
         Here in these confines slyly have I lurked,
         To watch the waning of mine enemies.
5   A dire induction am I witness to,
         And will to France, hoping the consequence
         Will prove as bitter, black, and tragical.
         Withdraw thee, wretched Margaret. Who comes
           here?
         Enter Duchess [of York] and Queen [Elizabeth]
         QUEEN ELIZABETH Ah, my poor princes! Ah, my tender
           babes!
10   My unblowed flowers, new-appearing sweets!
         If yet your gentle souls fly in the air
         And be not fixed in doom perpetual,
         Hover about me with your airy wings
         And hear your mother's lamentation!
15   QUEEN MARGARET Hover about her: say that right for   *Aside*
           right
         Hath dimmed your infant morn to agèd night.
         DUCHESS OF YORK So many miseries have crazed my
           voice,
         That my woe-wearied tongue is still and mute.
         Edward Plantagenet, why art thou dead?

55 **fearful commenting** nervous talk   56 **leaden servitor** the slow servant   57 **leads** precedes, generates
beggary ruin   58 **expedition** speed, quick action   59 **Jove's Mercury** swift messenger of Jove, king of the
Roman gods   60 **My … shield** the best advice is to arm myself/arms shall be my advisers (i.e. let us not
waste time discussing matters)   61 **brief** swift   **brave the field** challenge us on the battlefield
4.4 *Location: unspecified; probably somewhere near the royal court*   1 **mellow** ripen   3 **confines**
regions, territories (of England)   5 **induction** introduction, opening scene   6 **consequence** unfolding
events and their conclusion   10 **unblowed** young and unopened, not yet in bloom   **sweets** flowers/dear
ones   12 **in doom perpetual** eternally in the place appointed for you   15 **right for right** even-handed
justice   17 **crazed** cracked   19 **Edward Plantagenet** could refer to Edward IV or his son

20	QUEEN MARGARET Plantagenet doth quit Plantagenet:	*Aside*
	Edward for Edward pays a dying debt.	
	QUEEN ELIZABETH Wilt thou, O God, fly from such gentle	
	lambs,	
	And throw them in the entrails of the wolf?	
	When didst thou sleep when such a deed was done?	
25	QUEEN MARGARET When holy Harry died, and my sweet	*Aside*
	son.	
	DUCHESS OF YORK Dead life, blind sight, poor mortal	
	living ghost,	
	Woe's scene, world's shame, grave's due by life	
	usurped,	
	Brief abstract and record of tedious days,	
	Rest thy unrest on England's lawful earth,	*Sits down*
30	Unlawfully made drunk with innocent blood!	
	QUEEN ELIZABETH Ah, that thou wouldst as soon afford a	
	grave	
	As thou canst yield a melancholy seat!	
	Then would I hide my bones, not rest them here.	
	Ah, who hath any cause to mourn but we?	*Sits with her*
35	QUEEN MARGARET If ancient sorrow be most reverend,	*Comes forward*
	Give mine the benefit of seniory,	
	And let my griefs frown on the upper hand.	
	If sorrow can admit society,	*Sits with them*
	I had an Edward, till a Richard killed him:	
40	I had a husband, till a Richard killed him:	
	Thou hadst an Edward, till a Richard killed him:	
	Thou hadst a Richard, till a Richard killed him.	
	DUCHESS OF YORK I had a Richard too, and thou didst	
	kill him;	
	I had a Rutland too, thou holp'st to kill him.	
45	QUEEN MARGARET Thou hadst a Clarence too, and	
	Richard killed him.	
	From forth the kennel of thy womb hath crept	
	A hell-hound that doth hunt us all to death:	

---

20 **quit** requite, repay   21 **Edward for Edward** probably refers to Elizabeth's son and Margaret's (with Henry VI)   23 **entrails** insides, intestines   25 **Harry** Henry VI (Margaret's husband)   27 **grave's...usurped** i.e. one who should have died but remains living   28 **abstract** summary/epitome   29 **lawful** own proper, that is rightfully England's   31 **thou** i.e. the earth   **afford** offer   36 **seniory** seniority   37 **on...hand** from the superior position   38 **admit society** permit company   39 **Edward** Margaret's son with Henry VI (murdered by Richard, Edward IV and Clarence; see *3 Henry VI*, Act 5 scene 5)   40 **husband** Henry VI (murdered by Richard; see *3 Henry VI*, Act 5 scene 6)   41 **Edward** Elizabeth's eldest son with Edward IV   42 **Richard** Elizabeth's second son, the young Duke of York   43 **Richard** the Duke of York, the Duchess' husband (killed by Margaret and Clifford; see *3 Henry VI*, Act 1 scene 4)   44 **Rutland** the Duchess' youngest son (murdered by Clifford; see *3 Henry IV*, Act 1 scene 3)   **holp'st** helped

That dog, that had his teeth before his eyes,
To worry lambs and lap their gentle blood,
50   That foul defacer of God's handiwork,
That reigns in gallèd eyes of weeping souls,
That excellent grand tyrant of the earth,
Thy womb let loose, to chase us to our graves.
O upright, just, and true-disposing God,
55   How do I thank thee, that this carnal cur
Preys on the issue of his mother's body,
And makes her pew-fellow with others' moan!

DUCHESS OF YORK O Harry's wife, triumph not in my
         woes!
God witness with me, I have wept for thine.

60   **QUEEN MARGARET** Bear with me: I am hungry for
         revenge,
And now I cloy me with beholding it.
Thy Edward he is dead, that killed my Edward:
The other Edward dead, to quit my Edward:
Young York he is but boot, because both they
65   Matched not the high perfection of my loss.
Thy Clarence he is dead that stabbed my Edward,
And the beholders of this frantic play,
Th'adulterate Hastings, Rivers, Vaughan, Grey,
Untimely smothered in their dusky graves.
70   Richard yet lives, hell's black intelligencer,
Only reserved their factor to buy souls
And send them thither. But at hand, at hand,
Ensues his piteous and unpitied end:
Earth gapes, hell burns, fiends roar, saints pray,
75   To have him suddenly conveyed from hence.
Cancel his bond of life, dear God, I pray,
That I may live and say, 'The dog is dead!'

QUEEN ELIZABETH O, thou didst prophesy the time would
         come

---

48 **teeth ... eyes** i.e. could bite before he could see properly; Richard was born with teeth   49 **worry** seize
by the throat   50 **defacer ... handiwork** i.e. murderer (perhaps also alludes to Richard's own deformed
physique)   51 **gallèd** irritated, swollen (from weeping)   52 **excellent** supreme   54 **upright** righteous,
just   **true-disposing** arranging all justly   55 **carnal cur** flesh-eating dog   56 **issue** offspring, children
57 **pew-fellow** fellow mourner   **moan** lamentations, grief   58 **triumph** glory, exult   61 **cloy me** gorge
myself   62 **Thy Edward** Edward IV   **my Edward** Margaret's son with Henry VI   63 **other Edward**
Elizabeth's eldest son with Edward IV   64 **Young York** Elizabeth's second son, the young Duke of York
but boot merely added to make up the total   **both they** Edward IV and his eldest son   65 **perfection ...
loss** completeness, extent of the loss I experience/excellence of the people I have lost   67 **frantic** mad,
frenzied   68 **Th'adulterate** the adulterous (Hastings; refers to his affair with Jane Shore)   70 **intelligencer**
spy, secret agent   71 **Only reserved** solely kept alive (to be)/exclusively selected (as)   **factor** agent,
representative

That I should wish for thee to help me curse
80   That bottled spider, that foul bunch-backed toad!
QUEEN MARGARET I called thee then vain flourish of my
                fortune:
        I called thee then poor shadow, painted queen,
        The presentation of but what I was,
        The flattering index of a direful pageant,
85   One heaved a-high, to be hurled down below,
        A mother only mocked with two fair babes,
        A dream of what thou wast, a garish flag,
        To be the aim of every dangerous shot;
        A sign of dignity, a breath, a bubble;
90   A queen in jest, only to fill the scene.
        Where is thy husband now? Where be thy brothers?
        Where be thy two sons? Wherein dost thou joy?
        Who sues, and kneels and says, 'God save the queen'?
        Where be the bending peers that flattered thee?
95   Where be the thronging troops that followed thee?
        Decline all this, and see what now thou art:
        For happy wife, a most distressèd widow:
        For joyful mother, one that wails the name:
        For one being sued to, one that humbly sues:
100   For queen, a very caitiff crowned with care:
        For she that scorned at me, now scorned of me:
        For she being feared of all, now fearing one:
        For she commanding all, obeyed of none.
        Thus hath the course of justice whirled about,
105   And left thee but a very prey to time,
        Having no more but thought of what thou wast,
        To torture thee the more, being what thou art.
        Thou didst usurp my place, and dost thou not
        Usurp the just proportion of my sorrow?
110   Now thy proud neck bears half my burdened yoke,
        From which even here I slip my wearied head,
        And leave the burden of it all on thee.

---

80 bottled swollen (with venom), rounded, bottle-shaped   **bunch-backed** hunchbacked   **81 vain flourish** meaningless, frivolous adornment   **82 shadow** illusory, fragile image/actor   **painted** artificial/made-up with cosmetics   **83 presentation** imitation   **84 flattering index** deceptively attractive prologue   **pageant** play   **86 mocked** taunted/imitated, play-acted   **87 dream** mere image   **flag** army's identifying banner, highly visible in battle/type of flower belonging to the iris family   **89 sign** mere symbol/military banner   **dignity** monarchy   **90 in jest** for entertainment/pretend   **fill the** fulfil the requirements of/make up numbers in   **93 sues** pays court, entreats   **94 bending** bowing/yielding   **95 troops** retinues   **96 Decline** go through in order (grammatical term)   **97 For** instead of   **98 name** i.e. of **mother**   **100 caitiff** wretch   **care** troubles, grief   **101 of** by   **104 course…about** an image that recalls the popular conception of fortune as a wheel that raised humans up and cast them down as it came full circle   **105 very** absolute   **106 thought** i.e. memory

Farewell, York's wife, and queen of sad mischance:
These English woes shall make me smile in France.   *Starts to leave*

115 QUEEN ELIZABETH O thou well skilled in curses, stay
      awhile,
    And teach me how to curse mine enemies!
  QUEEN MARGARET Forbear to sleep the night, and fast
      the day:
    Compare dead happiness with living woe:
    Think that thy babes were sweeter than they were,
120   And he that slew them fouler than he is.
    Bett'ring thy loss makes the bad causer worse:
    Revolving this will teach thee how to curse.
  QUEEN ELIZABETH My words are dull. O, quicken them
      with thine!
  QUEEN MARGARET Thy woes will make them sharp, and
      pierce like mine.   *Exit Margaret*
125 DUCHESS OF YORK Why should calamity be full of
      words?
  QUEEN ELIZABETH Windy attorneys to their client's
      woes,
    Airy succeeders of intestine joys,
    Poor breathing orators of miseries!
    Let them have scope: though what they will impart
130   Help nothing else, yet do they ease the heart.
  DUCHESS OF YORK If so, then be not tongue-tied: go with
      me.
    And in the breath of bitter words let's smother
    My damnèd son, that thy two sweet sons smothered.   *Trumpet*
    The trumpet sounds: be copious in exclaims.
  Enter King Richard and his train
135 RICHARD Who intercepts me in my expedition?
  DUCHESS OF YORK O, she that might have intercepted
      thee,
    By strangling thee in her accursèd womb,
    From all the slaughters, wretch, that thou hast done!
  QUEEN ELIZABETH Hid'st thou that forehead with a
      golden crown

---

113 **mischance** misfortune   117 **Forbear** refrain, refuse   121 **Bett'ring** amplifying   **bad causer** person
responsible for the evil   122 **Revolving** considering, reflecting on   123 **dull** lifeless, sluggish/blunt
quicken enliven/sharpen   126 **Windy . . . woes** (words are) empty, wind-blown representatives of the grief
of the speakers   127 **intestine** internal (both in the sense of 'experienced within' and in the sense of
'digestive', the latter making words into farts)   129 **scope** range, room   134 **exclaims** outcries,
exclamations   135 **expedition** military enterprise/haste   136 **might** i.e. should   138 **From** i.e. to prevent

140 Where't should be branded, if that right were right,
    The slaughter of the prince that owed that crown,
    And the dire death of my poor sons and brothers?
    Tell me, thou villain slave, where are my children?
DUCHESS OF YORK Thou toad, thou toad, where is thy
        brother Clarence?
145 And little Ned Plantagenet, his son?
QUEEN ELIZABETH Where is the gentle Rivers, Vaughan,
        Grey?
DUCHESS OF YORK Where is kind Hastings?
RICHARD A flourish, trumpets! Strike alarum, drums!
    Let not the heavens hear these tell-tale women
150 Rail on the lord's anointed. Strike, I say!
                                        Flourish. Alarums
    Either be patient and entreat me fair,
    Or with the clamorous report of war
    Thus will I drown your exclamations.
DUCHESS OF YORK Art thou my son?
155 **RICHARD** Ay, I thank God, my father, and yourself.
DUCHESS OF YORK Then patiently hear my impatience.
RICHARD Madam, I have a touch of your condition,
    That cannot brook the accent of reproof.
DUCHESS OF YORK O, let me speak!
160 **RICHARD** Do then, but I'll not hear.
DUCHESS OF YORK I will be mild and gentle in my words.
RICHARD And brief, good mother, for I am in haste.
DUCHESS OF YORK Art thou so hasty? I have stayed for
        thee,
    God knows, in torment and in agony.
165 **RICHARD** And came I not at last to comfort you?
DUCHESS OF YORK No, by the holy rood, thou know'st it
        well,
    Thou cam'st on earth to make the earth my hell.
    A grievous burden was thy birth to me:
    Tetchy and wayward was thy infancy:
170 Thy schooldays frightful, desp'rate, wild, and furious:
    Thy prime of manhood daring, bold, and venturous:

---

140 branded i.e. branded with   **141 owed** owned   **143 villain** wicked one/servant   **148 flourish** trumpet
fanfare (usually signalling the arrival or departure of a person in authority)   **alarum** call to arms   **149 tell-
tale** prattling   **150 Rail** rant   **lord's anointed** i.e. the king, supposedly chosen by God and anointed with
holy oil at the coronation to signify this   **151 entreat me fair** plead with me courteously   **152 report** loud
noise, specifically the explosion of a gun or cannon   **156 impatience** anger   **157 condition** temperament
158 brook . . . reproof bear the language of rebuke   **163 stayed** waited   **166 rood** cross   **169 Tetchy**
fretful   **wayward** wilful, obstinate   **170 frightful** frightening   **desp'rate** reckless   **171 prime** early years

Thy age confirmed, proud, subtle, sly and bloody,
More mild, but yet more harmful, kind in hatred.
What comfortable hour canst thou name,
175 That ever graced me with thy company?
RICHARD Faith, none, but Humphrey Hour, that called
    your grace
To breakfast once forth of my company.
If I be so disgracious in your eye,
Let me march on and not offend you, madam.
180 Strike up the drum.   *Drums*
DUCHESS OF YORK I prithee hear me speak.
RICHARD You speak too bitterly.
DUCHESS OF YORK Hear me a word,
For I shall never speak to thee again.
185 RICHARD So.
DUCHESS OF YORK Either thou wilt die, by God's just
    ordinance
Ere from this war thou turn a conqueror,
Or I with grief and extreme age shall perish
And never more behold thy face again.
190 Therefore take with thee my most grievous curse,
Which in the day of battle tire thee more
Than all the complete armour that thou wear'st!
My prayers on the adverse party fight,
And there the little souls of Edward's children
195 Whisper the spirits of thine enemies
And promise them success and victory.
Bloody thou art, bloody will be thy end:
Shame serves thy life and doth thy death attend. *Exit*
QUEEN ELIZABETH Though far more cause, yet much less
    spirit to curse
200 Abides in me: I say amen to her.
RICHARD Stay, madam, I must talk a word with you.
QUEEN ELIZABETH I have no more sons of the royal blood
For thee to slaughter: for my daughters, Richard,
They shall be praying nuns, not weeping queens,
205 And therefore level not to hit their lives.

---

172 **age confirmed** maturity   173 **kind in hatred** concealing hatred in kindness (**kind** may play on the sense of 'natural')   174 **comfortable** cheerful, comforting   176 **Humphrey Hour** unclear; possibly a reference to 'dining with Duke Humphrey', which meant going hungry, or perhaps an actual person is meant   176 **grace** puns on **graced**   177 **forth** out   186 **ordinance** law (plays on the sense of 'artillery') 187 **turn** return   191 **tire** may it weigh heavy on, exhaust   192 **complete** full, well-equipped 195 **Whisper** whisper to   198 **serves** supplies/accompanies   **doth** i.e. will   205 **level** aim, set your target sights

RICHARD You have a daughter called Elizabeth,
　　Virtuous and fair, royal and gracious.
QUEEN ELIZABETH And must she die for this? O, let her
　　　live,
　　And I'll corrupt her manners, stain her beauty,
210　Slander myself as false to Edward's bed,
　　Throw over her the veil of infamy:
　　So she may live unscarred of bleeding slaughter,
　　I will confess she was not Edward's daughter.
RICHARD Wrong not her birth, she is a royal princess.
215　**QUEEN ELIZABETH** To save her life, I'll say she is not so.
RICHARD Her life is safest only in her birth.
QUEEN ELIZABETH And only in that safety died her
　　　brothers.
RICHARD Lo, at their birth good stars were opposite.
QUEEN ELIZABETH No, to their lives ill friends were
　　　contrary.
220　**RICHARD** All unavoided is the doom of destiny.
QUEEN ELIZABETH True, when avoided grace makes
　　　destiny.
　　My babes were destined to a fairer death,
　　If grace had blessed thee with a fairer life.
RICHARD You speak as if that I had slain my cousins.
225　**QUEEN ELIZABETH** Cousins, indeed, and by their uncle
　　　cozened
　　Of comfort, kingdom, kindred, freedom, life.
　　Whose hand soever lanched their tender hearts,
　　Thy head, all indirectly, gave direction.
　　No doubt the murd'rous knife was dull and blunt
230　Till it was whetted on thy stone-hard heart,
　　To revel in the entrails of my lambs.
　　But that still use of grief makes wild grief tame,
　　My tongue should to thy ears not name my boys
　　Till that my nails were anchored in thine eyes,
235　And I, in such a desp'rate bay of death,

---

209 **manners** morals/courteous habits　210 **false** unfaithful　211 **veil** shroud (usually associated with either modesty or mourning)　212 **So** provided　**of** by　216 **safest ... birth** only safeguarded by her high birth　218 **opposite** hostile, antagonistic　219 **friends** also 'relatives'　**contrary** opposed
220 **unavoided** unavoidable　**doom** decree/destined judgement/condemnation　221 **avoided grace** an absence of God's grace (i.e. Richard)　222 **fairer** better/nobler/more just　225 **cozened** cheated
227 **Whose hand soever** whoever's hand　**lanched** pierced　228 **head** brain/instigation/command　**all indirectly** through indirect means (plays on the sense of 'wrongly')　232 **But ... use** did not the constant experience　235 **bay** cove, inlet/point at which the cornered deer turns to face the hounds pursuing it

Like a poor bark, of sails and tackling reft,
Rush all to pieces on thy rocky bosom.

RICHARD Madam, so thrive I in my enterprise
And dangerous success of bloody wars,

240   As I intend more good to you and yours,
Than ever you and yours by me were harmed.

QUEEN ELIZABETH What good is covered with the face of
          heaven,
To be discovered, that can do me good?

RICHARD Th'advancement of your children, gentle lady.

245 QUEEN ELIZABETH Up to some scaffold, there to lose their
          heads?

RICHARD Unto the dignity and height of fortune,
The high imperial type of this earth's glory.

QUEEN ELIZABETH Flatter my sorrow with report of it:
Tell me what state, what dignity, what honour,

250   Canst thou demise to any child of mine?

RICHARD Even all I have; ay, and myself and all,
Will I withal endow a child of thine,
So in the Lethe of thy angry soul
Thou drown the sad remembrance of those wrongs

255   Which thou supposest I have done to thee.

QUEEN ELIZABETH Be brief, lest that the process of thy
          kindness
Last longer telling than thy kindness' date.

RICHARD Then know, that from my soul I love thy
          daughter.

QUEEN ELIZABETH My daughter's mother thinks it with
          her soul.

260 RICHARD What do you think?

QUEEN ELIZABETH That thou dost love my daughter from
          thy soul.
So from thy soul's love didst thou love her brothers,
And from my heart's love I do thank thee for it.

---

236 poor bark shabby, ill-equipped ship **tackling** rigging **reft** deprived **237 Rush** am dashed
238 thrive I may I thrive **enterprise** military undertaking **239 dangerous success** risky outcome
240 As only as far as **242 covered . . . heaven** i.e. concealed by God **243 discovered** revealed
244 Th'advancement the promotion, favouring (Elizabeth responds to the literal sense) **245 scaffold**
raised platform on which executions took place **246 dignity** honour, high rank **247 type** symbol,
emblem **248 Flatter** increase, pander to/alleviate, mollify **249 state** high rank **250 demise** convey,
transfer (legal term) **251 Even** exactly **252 endow** bestow upon/give as a dowry **253 So** if **Lethe** in
Greek mythology, the river in the underworld that induced forgetfulness in any who drank from or were
immersed in it **254 remembrance** memory **256 process** story, narrative **257 telling** in the telling
date duration, end **259 thinks** i.e. believes **261 from** Elizabeth now shifts the sense to 'away from, at
variance with'

RICHARD Be not so hasty to confound my meaning:
265   I mean that with my soul I love thy daughter
      And do intend to make her Queen of England.
QUEEN ELIZABETH Well then, who dost thou mean shall
        be her king?
RICHARD Even he that makes her queen. Who else
      should be?
QUEEN ELIZABETH What, thou?
270 **RICHARD** Even so. How think you of it?
QUEEN ELIZABETH How canst thou woo her?
RICHARD That I would learn of you,
      As one being best acquainted with her humour.
QUEEN ELIZABETH And wilt thou learn of me?
275 **RICHARD** Madam, with all my heart.
QUEEN ELIZABETH Send to her, by the man that slew her
        brothers,
      A pair of bleeding hearts: thereon engrave
      'Edward' and 'York', then haply will she weep:
      Therefore present to her — as sometime Margaret
280   Did to thy father, steeped in Rutland's blood —
      A handkerchief, which, say to her, did drain
      The purple sap from her sweet brother's body,
      And bid her wipe her weeping eyes withal.
      If this inducement move her not to love,
285   Send her a letter of thy noble deeds:
      Tell her thou mad'st away her uncle Clarence,
      Her uncle Rivers, ay, and, for her sake,
      Mad'st quick conveyance with her good aunt Anne.
RICHARD You mock me, madam: this is not the way
290   To win your daughter.
QUEEN ELIZABETH There is no other way,
      Unless thou couldst put on some other shape,
      And not be Richard that hath done all this.
RICHARD Say that I did all this for love of her.
295 **QUEEN ELIZABETH** Nay, then indeed she cannot choose
        but hate thee,
      Having bought love with such a bloody spoil.

---

264 **confound** overturn, destroy   270 **How** what   273 **humour** temperament   277 **engrave** inscribe (plays on the sense of 'place in the grave')   278 **haply** probably/perhaps   279 **sometime** once, formerly 282 **purple** blood-red   283 **withal** with it   286 **mad'st away** disposed of, killed   288 **conveyance** removal, dispatch (playing on the senses of 'stealing' and 'deceit, trickery')   292 **shape** appearance/role/ disguise   296 **spoil** booty gained from plunder

RICHARD Look what is done cannot be now amended:
Men shall deal unadvisedly sometimes,
Which after-hours give leisure to repent.
300   If I did take the kingdom from your sons,
To make amends, I'll give it to your daughter.
If I have killed the issue of your womb,
To quicken your increase, I will beget
Mine issue of your blood upon your daughter.
305   A grandam's name is little less in love
Than is the doting title of a mother;
They are as children but one step below,
Even of your mettle, of your very blood,
Of all one pain, save for a night of groans
310   Endured of her, for whom you bid like sorrow.
Your children were vexation to your youth,
But mine shall be a comfort to your age.
The loss you have is but a son being king,
And by that loss your daughter is made queen.
315   I cannot make you what amends I would:
Therefore accept such kindness as I can.
Dorset your son, that with a fearful soul
Leads discontented steps in foreign soil,
This fair alliance quickly shall call home
320   To high promotions and great dignity.
The king that calls your beauteous daughter wife
Familiarly shall call thy Dorset brother.
Again shall you be mother to a king,
And all the ruins of distressful times
325   Repaired with double riches of content.
What? We have many goodly days to see.
The liquid drops of tears that you have shed
Shall come again, transformed to orient pearl,
Advantaging their love with interest
330   Of ten times double gain of happiness.
Go then, my mother, to thy daughter go:
Make bold her bashful years with your experience,
Prepare her ears to hear a wooer's tale,

---

297 **Look what** whatever   298 **deal** act, behave (plays on the sense of 'kill')   299 **after-hours** later moments   302 **issue** offspring, children   303 **quicken** give life to **increase** descendants, children **beget** conceive   304 **upon** by   308 **mettle** substance, spirit, temperament   309 **Of all one** causing the same amount of   310 **of her** by the younger Elizabeth (Queen Elizabeth's daughter) **bid like sorrow** endured similar pain   315 **would** would like to   316 **can** am able (to offer)   322 **Familiarly** as a family member   328 **orient** shining   329 **Advantaging** adding to the value of **their love** the love that caused the tears to be shed   331 **mother** mother-in-law   332 **bold** confident, prepared (with connotations of 'sexually ready')

Put in her tender heart th'aspiring flame
335 Of golden sovereignty, acquaint the princess
With the sweet silent hours of marriage joys.
And when this arm of mine hath chastisèd
The petty rebel, dull-brained Buckingham,
Bound with triumphant garlands will I come
340 And lead thy daughter to a conqueror's bed:
To whom I will retail my conquest won,
And she shall be sole victoress, Caesar's Caesar.

QUEEN ELIZABETH What were I best to say? Her father's
brother
Would be her lord? Or shall I say her uncle?
345 Or he that slew her brothers and her uncles?
Under what title shall I woo for thee,
That God, the law, my honour and her love,
Can make seem pleasing to her tender years?

RICHARD Infer fair England's peace by this alliance.

350 QUEEN ELIZABETH Which she shall purchase with still
lasting war.

RICHARD Tell her the king, that may command, entreats.

QUEEN ELIZABETH That at her hands which the king's
king forbids.

RICHARD Say she shall be a high and mighty queen.

QUEEN ELIZABETH To vail the title, as her mother doth.

355 RICHARD Say I will love her everlastingly.

QUEEN ELIZABETH But how long shall that title 'ever'
last?

RICHARD Sweetly in force unto her fair life's end.

QUEEN ELIZABETH But how long fairly shall her sweet life
last?

RICHARD As long as heaven and nature lengthens it.

360 QUEEN ELIZABETH As long as hell and Richard likes of it.

RICHARD Say I, her sovereign, am her subject low.

QUEEN ELIZABETH But she, your subject, loathes such
sovereignty.

RICHARD Be eloquent in my behalf to her.

QUEEN ELIZABETH An honest tale speeds best being
plainly told.

---

341 **retail** relate, re-tell   342 **victoress** female victor   **Caesar's Caesar** i.e. the conqueror of the victor
344 **lord** husband   349 **Infer** allege, give as a reason   350 **purchase...war** pay for with everlasting
(personal) strife   352 **That...forbids** i.e. a relationship (uncle/niece) considered by the Church as
incestuous   **king's king** i.e. God   354 **vail** lower (in submission), yield   356 **title** claim (plays on the sense
of 'queen's title')   357 **in force** in place, active (perhaps with sinister play on 'enforce')   358 **fairly** justly/in
safety   362 **loathes** puns on **low**   363 **in** on   364 **speeds** succeeds   **plainly** honestly/in simple terms,
without adornment

365   **RICHARD** Then plainly to her tell my loving tale.
      QUEEN ELIZABETH Plain and not honest is too harsh a
         style.
      RICHARD Your reasons are too shallow and too quick.
      QUEEN ELIZABETH O no, my reasons are too deep and
         dead:
         Too deep and dead, poor infants, in their graves.
370   **RICHARD** Harp not on that string, madam: that is past.
      QUEEN ELIZABETH Harp on it still shall I till heart-strings
         break.
      RICHARD Now, by my George, my garter and my
         crown—
      QUEEN ELIZABETH Profaned, dishonoured and the third
         usurped.
      RICHARD I swear—
375   **QUEEN ELIZABETH** By nothing, for this is no oath:
         Thy George, profaned, hath lost his lordly honour;
         Thy garter, blemished, pawned his knightly virtue;
         Thy crown, usurped, disgraced his kingly glory.
         If something thou wouldst swear to be believed,
380   Swear then by something that thou hast not
         wronged.
      RICHARD Then, by myself—
      QUEEN ELIZABETH Thyself is self-misused.
      RICHARD Now, by the world—
      QUEEN ELIZABETH 'Tis full of thy foul wrongs.
385   **RICHARD** My father's death—
      QUEEN ELIZABETH Thy life hath it dishonoured.
      RICHARD Why then, by heaven—
      QUEEN ELIZABETH Heaven's wrong is most of all.
         If thou didst fear to break an oath with him,
390   The unity the king my husband made
         Thou hadst not broken, nor my brothers died.
         If thou hadst feared to break an oath by him,
         Th'imperial metal, circling now thy head,
         Had graced the tender temples of my child,
395   And both the princes had been breathing here,

---

367 quick hasty (Elizabeth plays on the sense of 'alive' when she responds with its opposite: **dead**)   **368 too** puns on 'two'   **deep** profound, learned (sense then shifts to 'deep down, buried')   **371 heart-strings** tendons or nerves supposed to brace the heart, hence intense feelings (puns on 'harp strings')   **372 my George** the image of Saint George, patron saint of England, that formed part of the insignia of the Order of the Garter, the highest order of knighthood in England   **garter** band tied around the leg to keep up hosiery; Knights of the Garter wore a blue and gold one below the left knee   **376 his** its   **382 self-misused** disgraced, abused by yourself   **389 him** i.e. God   **390 unity** i.e. reconciliation between court factions in Act 2 scene 1   **391 hadst** would have

Which now, two tender bedfellows for dust,
Thy broken faith hath made the prey for worms.
What canst thou swear by now?
RICHARD The time to come.
400 QUEEN ELIZABETH That thou hast wrongèd in the time
o'erpast,
For I myself have many tears to wash
Hereafter time, for time past wronged by thee.
The children live whose fathers thou hast
slaughtered,
Ungoverned youth, to wail it with their age:
405 The parents live whose children thou hast butchered,
Old barren plants, to wail it with their age.
Swear not by time to come, for that thou hast
Misused ere used, by time's ill-used repast.
RICHARD As I intend to prosper and repent,
410 So thrive I in my dangerous affairs
Of hostile arms. Myself myself confound.
Heaven and fortune bar me happy hours!
Day, yield me not thy light; nor, night, thy rest.
Be opposite all planets of good luck
415 To my proceeding if, with dear heart's love,
Immaculate devotion, holy thoughts,
I tender not thy beauteous princely daughter.
In her consists my happiness and thine:
Without her, follows to myself and thee,
420 Herself, the land and many a Christian soul,
Death, desolation, ruin and decay.
It cannot be avoided but by this:
It will not be avoided but by this.
Therefore, dear mother — I must call you so —
425 Be the attorney of my love to her:
Plead what I will be, not what I have been:
Not my deserts, but what I will deserve.
Urge the necessity and state of times,
And be not peevish found in great designs.
430 QUEEN ELIZABETH Shall I be tempted of the devil thus?
RICHARD Ay, if the devil tempt you to do good.

400 o'erpast past   402 Hereafter time the future   404 Ungoverned parentless, without a father's
control   wail…age lament it in their maturity/throughout their lifetime   406 with along with   410 So
thrive I to the same extent may I thrive   411 Myself myself confound may I destroy myself
414 opposite hostile, adversarial   415 proceeding course of action   417 tender not do not love, hold
dear   princely royal   425 attorney representative, pleader of a cause   426 Plead offer as a plea in court
427 my deserts what I deserve   428 times affairs/the present time   429 great designs important affairs,
the business of state (plays on the sense of 'schemes aimed at attaining power')   430 of by

QUEEN ELIZABETH Shall I forget myself to be myself?
RICHARD Ay, if yourself's remembrance wrong yourself.
QUEEN ELIZABETH Yet thou didst kill my children.
435 RICHARD But in your daughter's womb I bury them,
    Where in that nest of spicery they will breed
    Selves of themselves, to your recomforture.
QUEEN ELIZABETH Shall I go win my daughter to thy
    will?
RICHARD And be a happy mother by the deed.
440 QUEEN ELIZABETH I go. Write to me very shortly,
    And you shall understand from me her mind.
RICHARD Bear her my true love's kiss, and so, farewell. *Kisses her*
                        Exit [Queen Elizabeth]
    Relenting fool, and shallow, changing woman!—
    How now, what news?
Enter Ratcliffe [with Catesby following]
445 RATCLIFFE Most mighty sovereign, on the western coast
    Rideth a puissant navy: to our shores
    Throng many doubtful hollow-hearted friends,
    Unarmed, and unresolved to beat them back.
    'Tis thought that Richmond is their admiral,
450   And there they hull, expecting but the aid
    Of Buckingham to welcome them ashore.
RICHARD Some light-foot friend post to the Duke of
    Norfolk:
    Ratcliffe, thyself, or Catesby. Where is he?
CATESBY Here, my good lord.
455 RICHARD Catesby, fly to the duke.
CATESBY I will, my lord, with all convenient haste.
RICHARD Ratcliffe, come hither. Post to Salisbury.
    When thou com'st thither— Dull, unmindful villain, *To Catesby*
    Why stay'st thou here, and go'st not to the duke?
460 CATESBY First, mighty liege, tell me your highness'
    pleasure,
    What from your grace I shall deliver to him.
RICHARD O, true, good Catesby. Bid him levy straight
    The greatest strength and power that he can make,
    And meet me suddenly at Salisbury.

---

432 **forget . . . myself** forget my anguish and the wrongs done to me in order to be mother of a monarch
433 **if . . . yourself** if remembering yourself (i.e. collecting your wits/remembering your wrongs) compromises
your future   **436 spicery** spices   **437 recomforture** new comfort   **441 mind** opinion, intention
446 **puissant** mighty, powerful   **447 doubtful** fearful/unreliable   **hollow-hearted** false, insincere
449 **their** i.e. the attacking navy's   **450 hull** float with sails furled   **452 light-foot** swift-footed   **post** hurry
458 **unmindful** inattentive   **463 strength and power** army   **464 suddenly** immediately   **Salisbury**
town in Wiltshire, south-west England

465 CATESBY I go. *Exit*

RATCLIFFE What, may it please you, shall I do at
    Salisbury?

RICHARD Why, what wouldst thou do there before I go?

RATCLIFFE Your highness told me I should post before.

RICHARD My mind is changed.—

Enter Lord Stanley [Earl of Derby]

470   Stanley, what news with you?

DERBY None good, my liege, to please you with the
    hearing,
    Nor none so bad, but well may be reported.

RICHARD Hoyday, a riddle: neither good nor bad.
    Why need'st thou run so many miles about,

475   When thou mayst tell thy tale the nearest way?
    Once more, what news?

DERBY Richmond is on the seas.

RICHARD There let him sink, and be the seas on him!
    White-livered runagate, what doth he there?

480 DERBY I know not, mighty sovereign, but by guess.

RICHARD Well, as you guess?

DERBY Stirred up by Dorset, Buckingham and Morton,
    He makes for England, here to claim the crown.

RICHARD Is the chair empty? Is the sword unswayed?

485   Is the king dead? The empire unpossessed?
    What heir of York is there alive but we?
    And who is England's king but great York's heir?
    Then tell me, what makes he upon the seas?

DERBY Unless for that, my liege, I cannot guess.

490 RICHARD Unless for that he comes to be your liege,
    You cannot guess wherefore the Welshman comes.
    Thou wilt revolt, and fly to him, I fear.

DERBY No, my good lord: therefore mistrust me not.

RICHARD Where is thy power, then, to beat him back?

495   Where be thy tenants and thy followers?
    Are they not now upon the western shore,
    Safe-conducting the rebels from their ships?

DERBY No, my good lord, my friends are in the north.

---

472 well easily, readily   **473 Hoyday** exclamation of contemptuous impatience   **475 nearest** most
direct   **479 White-livered runagate** cowardly renegade, runaway   **484 chair** throne   **sword** official
sword of office   **unswayed** not wielded   **485 empire** kingdom   **unpossessed** not inherited/not ruled
488 makes he is he doing   **489 that** i.e. the crown   **490 for that** because   **491 the Welshman** i.e.
Richmond, grandson of the Welsh Owen Tudor and Katherine of Valois (widow of Henry V)   **494 power**
army   **495 tenants** who would have been required to undertake military service for their lord

RICHARD Cold friends to me: what do they in the north,
500   When they should serve their sovereign in the west?
DERBY They have not been commanded, mighty king.
    Pleaseth your majesty to give me leave,
    I'll muster up my friends and meet your grace
    Where and what time your majesty shall please.
505 RICHARD Ay, thou wouldst be gone to join with
    Richmond.
    But I'll not trust thee.
DERBY Most mighty sovereign,
    You have no cause to hold my friendship doubtful:
    I never was nor never will be false.
510 RICHARD Go then and muster men, but, leave behind
    Your son, George Stanley. Look your heart be firm,
    Or else his head's assurance is but frail.
DERBY So deal with him as I prove true to you.
                 Exit Stanley [Earl of Derby]
Enter a Messenger
MESSENGER My gracious sovereign, now in Devonshire,
515   As I by friends am well advisèd,
    Sir Edward Courtney and the haughty prelate,
    Bishop of Exeter, his elder brother,
    With many more confederates, are in arms.
Enter another Messenger
SECOND MESSENGER In Kent, my liege, the Guildfords
    are in arms,
520   And every hour more competitors
    Flock to the rebels, and their power grows strong.
Enter another Messenger
THIRD MESSENGER My lord, the army of great
    Buckingham—
RICHARD Out on ye, owls! Nothing but songs of death?
                      He striketh him
    There, take thou that, till thou bring better news.
525 THIRD MESSENGER The news I have to tell your majesty
    Is that by sudden floods and fall of waters
    Buckingham's army is dispersed and scattered,
    And he himself wandered away alone,
    No man knows whither.

---

499 **Cold** unfriendly, distant (plays on the fact that the north of England often undergoes cold weather)
502 **Pleaseth** if it please   508 **hold** consider, deem   511 **Look** make sure   512 **assurance** safety
515 **advisèd** informed   520 **competitors** associates, allies   523 **owls** thought to be birds of ill omen,
whose cry portended death   526 **fall of waters** i.e. heavy rain, storms

530 **RICHARD** I cry thee mercy:
There is my purse to cure that blow of thine.   *Gives money*
Hath any well-advisèd friend proclaimed
Reward to him that brings the traitor in?
THIRD MESSENGER Such proclamation hath been made,
my lord.
Enter another Messenger
535 **FOURTH MESSENGER** Sir Thomas Lovell and Lord
Marquis Dorset,
'Tis said, my liege, in Yorkshire are in arms.
But this good comfort bring I to your highness:
The Breton navy is dispersed by tempest.
Richmond, in Dorsetshire, sent out a boat
540 Unto the shore, to ask those on the banks
If they were his assistants, yea or no,
Who answered him they came from Buckingham
Upon his party: he, mistrusting them,
Hoised sail and made his course again for Brittany.
545 **RICHARD** March on, march on, since we are up in arms.
If not to fight with foreign enemies,
Yet to beat down these rebels here at home.
Enter Catesby
CATESBY My liege, the Duke of Buckingham is taken:
That is the best news. That the Earl of Richmond
550 Is with a mighty power landed at Milford
Is colder news, but yet they must be told.
RICHARD Away towards Salisbury! While we reason
here,
A royal battle might be won and lost.
Someone take order Buckingham be brought
555 To Salisbury. The rest march on with me.
                                        Flourish.   Exeunt

[Act 4 Scene 5]   *running scene 17*

Enter [Stanley, Earl of] Derby and Sir Christopher

DERBY Sir Christopher, tell Richmond this from me:
That in the sty of the most deadly boar
My son George Stanley is franked up in hold.

---

530 cry thee mercy beg your pardon **532 well-advisèd** prudent **541 assistants** supporters **543 his party** Richmond's faction **544 Hoised** hoisted **548 taken** captured **550 Milford** Milford Haven, on the coast of south-west Wales **551 colder** less welcome **552 reason** talk **4.5** *Location: unspecified; possibly Stanley's home in the north of England, to which Richard sent him to muster troops, or his London residence* **2 sty** pen **boar** i.e. Richard **3 franked** penned **hold** custody

    If I revolt, off goes young George's head:
5   The fear of that holds off my present aid.
    So get thee gone: commend me to thy lord.
    Withal say that the queen hath heartily consented
    He should espouse Elizabeth her daughter.
    But tell me, where is princely Richmond now?
10 **CHRISTOPHER** At Pembroke, or at Ha'rfordwest, in
      Wales.
    DERBY What men of name resort to him?
    CHRISTOPHER Sir Walter Herbert, a renownèd soldier,
    Sir Gilbert Talbot, Sir William Stanley,
    Oxford, redoubted Pembroke, Sir James Blunt,
15 And Rice ap Thomas with a valiant crew,
    And many other of great name and worth:
    And towards London do they bend their power,
    If by the way they be not fought withal.
    DERBY Well, hie thee to thy lord: I kiss his hand,
20 My letter will resolve him of my mind. Farewell.
                                    Exeunt

Act 5 Scene 1   *running scene 18*

Enter Buckingham with [Guards bearing] halberds [and the
Sheriff], led to execution

BUCKINGHAM Will not King Richard let me speak with
    him?
SHERIFF No, my good lord: therefore be patient.
BUCKINGHAM Hastings, and Edward's children, Grey and
    Rivers,
    Holy King Henry, and thy fair son Edward,
5 Vaughan, and all that have miscarrièd
    By underhand corrupted foul injustice,
    If that your moody discontented souls
    Do through the clouds behold this present hour,
    Even for revenge mock my destruction!—
10 This is All Souls' day, fellow, is it not?
SHERIFF It is.

---

8 **espouse** marry 10 **Pembroke** town in south-west Wales, just south of Milford Haven **Ha'rfordwest**
Haverfordwest, a town north of Milford Haven 11 **name** rank/reputation **resort** gather 14 **redoubted**
revered/feared **Pembroke** Earl of Pembroke (Richmond's uncle) 15 **Rice** i.e. Rhys 17 **bend** direct
18 **by** on 20 **resolve . . . mind** explain my intentions 5.1 *Location: Salisbury* 5 **miscarrièd** come to
harm, died 7 **moody** angry 10 **All Souls' day** 2 November, the day in the Church calendar devoted to
prayer for the souls of the dead

BUCKINGHAM Why, then All Souls' day is my body's
      doomsday.
      This is the day which, in King Edward's time,
      I wished might fall on me, when I was found
15   False to his children and his wife's allies:
      This is the day wherein I wished to fall
      By the false faith of him whom most I trusted:
      This, this All Souls' day to my fearful soul
      Is the determined respite of my wrongs.
20   That high all-seer which I dallied with
      Hath turned my feignèd prayer on my head
      And given in earnest what I begged in jest:
      Thus doth he force the swords of wicked men
      To turn their own points in their masters' bosoms.
25   Thus Margaret's curse falls heavy on my neck:
      'When he', quoth she, 'shall split thy heart with
         sorrow,
      Remember Margaret was a prophetess.'
      Come lead me, officers, to the block of shame.
      Wrong hath but wrong, and blame the due of blame.
                 Exeunt Buckingham with Officers

Act 5 Scene 2   *running scene 19*

*Enter Richmond, Oxford, Blunt, Herbert and others, with
Drum and Colours*

RICHMOND Fellows in arms, and my most loving friends
      Bruised underneath the yoke of tyranny,
      Thus far into the bowels of the land
      Have we marched on without impediment;
5   And here receive we from our father Stanley
      Lines of fair comfort and encouragement.
      The wretched, bloody, and usurping boar —
      That spoiled your summer fields and fruitful vines,
      Swills your warm blood like wash, and makes his
         trough
10   In your embowelled bosoms — this foul swine

13 This . . . allies Buckingham refers to his speech in Act 2 scene 1, in which, following the formal reconciliation of court factions, he wished to be punished with treacherous friends if he was ever disloyal to Elizabeth and her allies   **19 determined respite of** ordained end to the postponement in punishing   **20 all-seer** i.e. God   **dallied with** trifled with, mocked   **21 feignèd** insincere, pretend   **22 in jest** in pretence   **28 block** execution block   **5.2** *Location: Tamworth, in the East Midlands*   **3 bowels** centre, inmost part   **5 father** stepfather   **8 spoiled** stripped, despoiled   **9 Swills** gulps   **wash** pig food   **10 embowelled** disembowelled

Is now even in the centre of this isle,
Near to the town of Leicester, as we learn.
From Tamworth thither is but one day's march.
In God's name, cheerly on, courageous friends,
15   To reap the harvest of perpetual peace
By this one bloody trial of sharp war.
OXFORD Every man's conscience is a thousand men,
To fight against this guilty homicide.
HERBERT I doubt not but his friends will turn to us.
20 **BLUNT** He hath no friends but what are friends for fear,
Which in his dearest need will fly from him.
RICHMOND All for our vantage. Then, in God's name,
march.
True hope is swift, and flies with swallow's wings:
Kings it makes gods and meaner creatures kings.

Exeunt

[Act 5 Scene 3]   *running scene 20*

*Enter King Richard in arms, with Norfolk, Ratcliffe and the
Earl of Surrey [with Soldiers, who pitch Richard's tent]*

RICHARD Here pitch our tent, even here in Bosworth
Field.
My lord of Surrey, why look you so sad?
SURREY My heart is ten times lighter than my looks.
RICHARD My lord of Norfolk—
5 **NORFOLK** Here, most gracious liege.
RICHARD Norfolk, we must have knocks, ha? Must we
not?
NORFOLK We must both give and take, my loving lord.
RICHARD Up with my tent! Here will I lie tonight,
But where tomorrow? Well, all's one for that.
10   Who hath descried the number of the traitors?
NORFOLK Six or seven thousand is their utmost power.
RICHARD Why, our battalia trebles that account:
Besides, the king's name is a tower of strength,
Which they upon the adverse faction want.
15   Up with the tent! Come, noble gentlemen,
Let us survey the vantage of the ground.

---

12 Leicester chief town of Leicestershire, east of Tamworth   **14 cheerly** cheerfully, hopefully   **16 sharp**
harsh, merciless   **18 homicide** murderer   **22 vantage** advantage   **24 meaner** humbler
5.3   *Location: Bosworth Field, to the east of Leicester*   **2 sad** solemn, grave   **6 knocks** hard blows
9 all's...that it doesn't matter, it makes no difference   **10 descried** discovered, seen   **12 battalia**
army   **account** number   **14 want** lack   **16 vantage...ground** best position for military action

Call for some men of sound direction:
Let's lack no discipline, make no delay,
For, lords, tomorrow is a busy day.

Exeunt [into the tent]

Enter Richmond, Sir William Brandon, Oxford, [Blunt] and
Dorset [with Soldiers, who pitch Richmond's tent]

20 RICHMOND The weary sun hath made a golden set,
And by the bright tract of his fiery car,
Gives token of a goodly day tomorrow.
Sir William Brandon, you shall bear my standard.
Give me some ink and paper in my tent:
25 I'll draw the form and model of our battle,
Limit each leader to his several charge,
And part in just proportion our small power.
My lord of Oxford, you, Sir William Brandon,
And you, Sir Walter Herbert, stay with me.
30 The Earl of Pembroke keeps his regiment;
Good Captain Blunt, bear my goodnight to him,
And by the second hour in the morning
Desire the earl to see me in my tent.
Yet one thing more, good captain, do for me:
35 Where is Lord Stanley quartered, do you know?
BLUNT Unless I have mista'en his colours much —
Which well I am assured I have not done —
His regiment lies half a mile at least
South from the mighty power of the king.
40 RICHMOND If without peril it be possible,
Sweet Blunt, make some good means to speak with
      him,
And give him from me this most needful note.
BLUNT Upon my life, my lord, I'll undertake it.
And so, God give you quiet rest tonight.   *[Exit]*
45 RICHMOND Goodnight, good Captain Blunt. Come
      gentlemen,
Let us consult upon tomorrow's business;
Into my tent: the dew is raw and cold.

They withdraw into the tent

Enter Richard, Ratcliffe, Norfolk and Catesby [and other
Soldiers]

17 sound direction good tactical judgement   21 tract traces, streaks   car chariot (which in classical
mythology was driven by the sun god)   23 standard flag, military banner   25 form and model
arrangement and ground-plan   26 Limit appoint, designate   several separate, respective   charge duty
27 part . . . proportion distribute evenly   30 keeps stays with   35 quartered encamped   36 colours
identifying battle flags   42 needful urgent

RICHARD What is't o'clock?

CATESBY It's supper-time, my lord: it's nine o'clock.

50 RICHARD I will not sup tonight.

    Give me some ink and paper.

    What, is my beaver easier than it was?

    And all my armour laid into my tent?

CATESBY It is, my liege, and all things are in readiness.

55 RICHARD Good Norfolk, hie thee to thy charge:

    Use careful watch, choose trusty sentinels.

NORFOLK I go, my lord.

RICHARD Stir with the lark tomorrow, gentle Norfolk.

NORFOLK I warrant you, my lord.   *Exit*

60 RICHARD Ratcliffe!

RATCLIFFE My lord?

RICHARD Send out a pursuivant at arms

    To Stanley's regiment: bid him bring his power

    Before sun-rising, lest his son George fall

65 Into the blind cave of eternal night.—

    Fill me a bowl of wine. Give me a watch.   *To other Soldiers*

    Saddle white Surrey for the field tomorrow.

    Look that my staves be sound, and not too heavy. *Exit some Soldiers*

    Ratcliffe!

70 RATCLIFFE My lord?

RICHARD Saw'st the melancholy Lord Northumberland?

RATCLIFFE Thomas the Earl of Surrey and himself,

    Much about cockshut time, from troop to troop

    Went through the army, cheering up the soldiers.   *Enter a Soldier*

75 RICHARD So, I am satisfied.— Give me a bowl of wine:—

    I have not that alacrity of spirit,

    Nor cheer of mind, that I was wont to have.—

    Set it down.— Is ink and paper ready?

RATCLIFFE It is, my lord.

80 RICHARD Bid my guard watch. Leave me.

    Ratcliffe, about the mid of night come to my tent

    And help to arm me. Leave me, I say.

                    Exeunt Ratcliffe [and Soldiers]

                    Richard withdraws to his tent, writes, and then sleeps

Enter Derby to Richmond in his tent

---

52 **beaver** helmet's visor   **easier** looser, moving more efficiently   53 **into** in   55 **hie** hasten   **charge** duty/post   59 **warrant** assure, guarantee   62 **pursuivant at arms** officer attendant on a herald, i.e. messenger   66 **watch** watch light, a slow-burning candle or one marked at regular divisions to measure the passing of time/guard, watchman   67 **Surrey** the name of a horse   68 **staves** staffs used as weapons   **sound** in good condition   73 **cockshut time** dusk, twilight (when poultry are cooped up)   74 **cheering up** encouraging, rallying   76 **alacrity** readiness, sharpness   77 **wont** used, accustomed   78 **it** presumably the wine   82 **arm me** put on my armour

DERBY Fortune and victory sit on thy helm!

RICHMOND All comfort that the dark night can afford

85   Be to thy person, noble father-in-law!
       Tell me, how fares our noble mother?

DERBY I, by attorney, bless thee from thy mother
       Who prays continually for Richmond's good.
       So much for that. The silent hours steal on,

90   And flaky darkness breaks within the east.
       In brief — for so the season bids us be —
       Prepare thy battle early in the morning,
       And put thy fortune to th'arbitrement
       Of bloody strokes and mortal-staring war.

95   I, as I may — that which I would I cannot —
       With best advantage will deceive the time,
       And aid thee in this doubtful shock of arms.
       But on thy side I may not be too forward
       Lest, being seen, thy brother, tender George,

100   Be executed in his father's sight.
       Farewell. The leisure and the fearful time
       Cuts off the ceremonious vows of love
       And ample interchange of sweet discourse
       Which so long sundered friends should dwell upon:

105   God give us leisure for these rites of love!
       Once more, adieu. Be valiant, and speed well!

RICHMOND Good lords, conduct him to his regiment:
       I'll strive with troubled noise to take a nap,
       Lest leaden slumber peise me down tomorrow,

110   When I should mount with wings of victory.
       Once more, good night, kind lords and gentlemen.

                              Exeunt. Richmond remains

       O thou, whose captain I account myself,   *Kneels*
       Look on my forces with a gracious eye:
       Put in their hands thy bruising irons of wrath,

115   That they may crush down with a heavy fall
       Th'usurping helmets of our adversaries!
       Make us thy ministers of chastisement,

---

83 **helm** helmet   85 **father-in-law** stepfather   87 **attorney** proxy   90 **flaky** streaked with light
91 **season** time of day   93 **th'arbitrement** the decision, final judgement   94 **mortal-staring** deathly-
faced, with fatal gaze   95 **that...would** what I would like to do (i.e. fight openly on your side)
96 **With...time** with every opportunity I get, I will be strategically duplicitous (towards Richard)
97 **doubtful shock** clash of forces, the outcome of which is uncertain/frightening military encounter
98 **forward** eager   99 **brother** stepbrother   **tender** young   101 **leisure** time available   103 **ample
interchange** full exchange   **sweet discourse** pleasant conversation   104 **sundered** separated
108 **with** against   109 **peise** weigh   112 **account** consider   113 **gracious** filled with divine grace/
favourable   114 **irons** swords

That we may praise thee in thy victory!
To thee I do commend my watchful soul,
120   Ere I let fall the windows of mine eyes:
Sleeping and waking, O, defend me still!   *Sleeps*

Enter the Ghost of Prince Edward, son to Henry VI

GHOST OF PRINCE EDWARD Let me sit heavy on thy soul
    tomorrow!   *To Richard*
Think how thou stab'st me in my prime of youth
At Tewkesbury: despair therefore, and die!—
125   Be cheerful, Richmond, for the wrongèd souls
    To Richmond
Of butchered princes fight in thy behalf.
King Henry's issue, Richmond, comforts thee. [*Exit?*]
    The Ghosts either exit individually or remain onstage

Enter the Ghost of Henry the Sixth

GHOST OF KING HENRY VI When I was mortal, my   *To Richard*
    anointed body
By thee was punchèd full of holes;
130   Think on the Tower and me: despair and die!
Harry the Sixth bids thee despair and die!—
Virtuous and holy, be thou conqueror! *To Richmond*
Harry, that prophesied thou shouldst be king,
Doth comfort thee in sleep: live and flourish! [*Exit?*]

Enter the Ghost of Clarence

135   **GHOST OF CLARENCE** Let me sit heavy in thy soul   *To Richard*
    tomorrow!
I, that was washed to death with fulsome wine,
Poor Clarence, by thy guile betrayed to death!
Tomorrow in the battle think on me,
And fall thy edgeless sword: despair and die!—
    To Richmond
140   Thou offspring of the House of Lancaster,
The wrongèd heirs of York do pray for thee.
Good angels guard thy battle! Live and flourish!
    [*Exit?*]

Enter the Ghosts of Rivers, Grey and Vaughan

GHOST OF RIVERS Let me sit heavy in thy soul tomorrow,   *To Richard*
Rivers that died at Pomfret: despair and die!

---

119 watchful wakeful   ***Prince Edward*** son of Margaret and Henry VI   **124 despair** experience spiritual hopelessness (thought to precede suicide)   **127 issue** child, offspring   **128 anointed** marked with holy oil, the sign of monarchy   **129 punchèd** punctured, pierced   **130 Tower** of London, where Henry was murdered (see *3 Henry VI*, Act 5 scene 6)   **136 washed** i.e. drowned (in a butt of malmsey, a strong sweet wine)   **fulsome** nauseating/an abundant quantity of   **139 fall** drop, let fall   **edgeless** blunt, useless   **142 battle** army

145 **GHOST OF GREY** Think upon Grey, and let thy soul   *To Richard*
    despair!
GHOST OF VAUGHAN Think upon Vaughan, and, with   *To Richard*
    guilty fear,
    Let fall thy lance: despair and die!   *To Richmond*
ALL Awake, and think our wrongs in Richard's bosom
    Will conquer him! Awake, and win the day!
                     [Exeunt Ghosts?]
Enter the Ghost of Lord Hastings
150 **GHOST OF HASTINGS** Bloody and guilty, guiltily awake   *To Richard*
    And in a bloody battle end thy days!
    Think on Lord Hastings: despair and die!
    Quiet untroubled soul, awake, awake!   *To Richmond*
    Arm, fight, and conquer, for fair England's sake!
                        [Exit?]
Enter the Ghosts of the two young Princes
155 **GHOSTS OF PRINCES** Dream on thy cousins smothered in   *To Richard*
    the Tower:
    Let us be laid within thy bosom, Richard,
    And weigh thee down to ruin, shame, and death!
    Thy nephews' souls bid thee despair and die!—
                      To Richmond
    Sleep, Richmond, sleep in peace and wake in joy:
160   Good angels guard thee from the boar's annoy!
    Live and beget a happy race of kings!
    Edward's unhappy sons do bid thee flourish.
                   [Exit Ghosts?]
Enter the Ghost of Anne, his wife   *To Richard*
GHOST OF ANNE Richard, thy wife, that wretched Anne
    thy wife,
    That never slept a quiet hour with thee,
165   Now fills thy sleep with perturbations.
    Tomorrow in the battle think on me,
    And fall thy edgeless sword: despair and die!—
    Thou quiet soul, sleep thou a quiet sleep: *To Richmond*
    Dream of success and happy victory!
170   Thy adversary's wife doth pray for thee.   *[Exit?]*
Enter the Ghost of Buckingham   *To Richard*
GHOST OF BUCKINGHAM The first was I that helped thee
    to the crown:
    The last was I that felt thy tyranny.

156 laid buried   **160 annoy** injury, harm   **164 quiet** peaceful

O, in the battle think on Buckingham,
And die in terror of thy guiltiness!
175   Dream on, dream on, of bloody deeds and death:
Fainting, despair; despairing, yield thy breath!—
I died for hope ere I could lend thee aid; *To Richmond*
But cheer thy heart, and be thou not dismayed:
God and good angels fight on Richmond's side,
180   And Richard fall in height of all his pride.   [*Exit?*]
         If the Ghosts have not exited individually, they all vanish at this point
Richard starts out of his dream
RICHARD   Give me another horse! Bind up my wounds!
Have mercy, Jesu! — Soft, I did but dream.
O coward conscience, how dost thou afflict me!
The lights burn blue. It is not dead midnight.
185   Cold fearful drops stand on my trembling flesh.
What? Do I fear myself? There's none else by.
Richard loves Richard: that is, I am I.
Is there a murderer here? No. Yes, I am.
Then fly. What, from myself? Great reason why:
190   Lest I revenge. What? Myself upon myself?
Alack, I love myself. Wherefore? For any good
That I myself have done unto myself?
O no! Alas, I rather hate myself
For hateful deeds committed by myself!
195   I am a villain: yet I lie, I am not.
Fool, of thyself speak well: fool, do not flatter.
My conscience hath a thousand several tongues,
And every tongue brings in a several tale,
And every tale condemns me for a villain.
200   Perjury in the high'st degree,
Murder, stern murder, in the direst degree,
All several sins, all used in each degree,
Throng all to th'bar, crying all, 'Guilty! Guilty!'
I shall despair. There is no creature loves me;
205   And if I die, no soul shall pity me.
Nay, wherefore should they, since that I myself
Find in myself no pity to myself?
Methought the souls of all that I had murdered

---

176 Fainting staggering, losing consciousness/losing heart   **yield** give up   **180 Richard** may Richard **182 Soft** wait   **184 lights burn blue** thought to be a sign of the presence of ghosts   **185 drops** i.e. of sweat   **191 Wherefore?** Why?   **197 several** different, separate   **198 brings in** introduces (as evidence) **202 used . . . degree** committed at every degree of severity   **203 th'bar** i.e. of the court   **204 creature** person/minion created through favour, i.e. not a genuine supporter

Came to my tent, and every one did threat
210 Tomorrow's vengeance on the head of Richard.
Enter Ratcliffe
RATCLIFFE My lord?
RICHARD Who's there?
RATCLIFFE Ratcliffe, my lord, 'tis I. The early village cock
Hath twice done salutation to the morn.
215 Your friends are up and buckle on their armour.
RICHARD O Ratcliffe, I fear, I fear—
RATCLIFFE Nay, good my lord, be not afraid of shadows.
RICHARD By the apostle Paul, shadows tonight
Have struck more terror to the soul of Richard
220 Than can the substance of ten thousand soldiers
Armèd in proof, and led by shallow Richmond.
'Tis not yet near day. Come, go with me:
Under our tents I'll play the eavesdropper,
To hear if any mean to shrink from me.
Exeunt Richard and Ratcliffe
Enter the Lords to Richmond, sitting in his tent
225 **LORDS** Good morrow, Richmond!
RICHMOND Cry mercy, lords and watchful gentlemen,
That you have ta'en a tardy sluggard here.
LORDS How have you slept, my lord?
RICHMOND The sweetest sleep, and fairest-boding dreams
230 That ever entered in a drowsy head,
Have I since your departure had, my lords.
Methought their souls, whose bodies Richard
    murdered,
Came to my tent and cried on victory:
I promise you my heart is very jocund
235 In the remembrance of so fair a dream.
How far into the morning is it, lords?
LORDS Upon the stroke of four.
RICHMOND Why, then 'tis time to arm and give
    direction.—   *His oration to his Soldiers*
More than I have said, loving countrymen,
240 The leisure and enforcement of the time
Forbids to dwell upon. Yet remember this:
God and our good cause fight upon our side,

---

209 **threat** threaten   217 **shadows** something insubstantial (Richard shifts the sense to 'ghosts')
221 **proof** impenetrable armour   224 **shrink from** i.e. desert   226 **Cry mercy** forgive me   **watchful** alert/
protective, guarding   227 **ta'en** caught   233 **cried on** invoked, called out to   234 **jocund** lively,
joyful   239 **said** already said, said before   240 **leisure** time available   **enforcement** constraints

The prayers of holy saints and wrongèd souls,
Like high-reared bulwarks, stand before our faces,
245 Richard except, those whom we fight against
Had rather have us win than him they follow
For what is he they follow? Truly, gentlemen,
A bloody tyrant and a homicide:
One raised in blood, and one in blood established;
250 One that made means to come by what he hath,
And slaughtered those that were the means to help
    him:
A base foul stone, made precious by the foil
Of England's chair, where he is falsely set:
One that hath ever been God's enemy.
255 Then if you fight against God's enemy,
God will in justice ward you as his soldiers:
If you do swear to put a tyrant down,
You sleep in peace, the tyrant being slain:
If you do fight against your country's foes,
260 Your country's fat shall pay your pains the hire:
If you do fight in safeguard of your wives,
Your wives shall welcome home the conquerors:
If you do free your children from the sword,
Your children's children quits it in your age.
265 Then, in the name of God and all these rights,
Advance your standards, draw your willing swords.
For me, the ransom of my bold attempt
Shall be this cold corpse on the earth's cold face:
But if I thrive, the gain of my attempt
270 The least of you shall share his part thereof.
Sound drums and trumpets boldly and cheerfully.
God and Saint George, Richmond and victory!
                                    [*Exeunt*]
Enter King Richard, Ratcliffe and Catesby [*with Attendants
and Soldiers*]
RICHARD What said Northumberland as touching
    Richmond?
RATCLIFFE That he was never trainèd up in arms.

244 **bulwarks** fortifications   245 **except** excepted   249 **raised** promoted (to the throne)   **established** confirmed in power   250 **made means** contrived, grasped opportunities, used any resource   252 **stone** jewel   **foil** setting for a jewel (designed to highlight the jewel's beauty)   253 **chair** throne   **falsely** wrongfully, treacherously/artificially   256 **ward** protect   260 **fat** wealth, prosperous growth   **hire** recompense   264 **quits** requites, repays   **age** old age   266 **Advance your standards** raise your battle flags   267 **the . . . face** i.e. if I fail the only ransom to be paid for me shall be my death (noblemen captured in war were often released on payment of a ransom)   269 **thrive** succeed/live   272 **Saint George** patron saint of England   273 **as touching** regarding

275 **RICHARD** He said the truth: and what said Surrey then?
RATCLIFFE He smiled and said, 'The better for our
purpose.'
RICHARD He was in the right, and so indeed it is.
Clock strikes
Tell the clock there. Give me a calendar.
Who saw the sun today?
280 **RATCLIFFE** Not I, my lord.
RICHARD Then he disdains to shine, for by the book
He should have braved the east an hour ago
A black day will it be to somebody. Ratcliffe!
RATCLIFFE My lord?
285 **RICHARD** The sun will not be seen today:
The sky doth frown and lour upon our army.
I would these dewy tears were from the ground.
Not shine today? Why, what is that to me
More than to Richmond? For the selfsame heaven
290 That frowns on me looks sadly upon him.
Enter Norfolk
NORFOLK Arm, arm, my lord: the foe vaunts in the field.
RICHARD Come, bustle, bustle. Caparison my horse.   *He arms*
Call up Lord Stanley, bid him bring his power.
I will lead forth my soldiers to the plain,
295 And thus my battle shall be orderèd:
My foreward shall be drawn in length,
Consisting equally of horse and foot:
Our archers shall be placèd in the midst;
John Duke of Norfolk, Thomas Earl of Surrey,
300 Shall have the leading of the foot and horse.
They thus directed, we will follow
In the main battle, whose puissance on either side
Shall be well wingèd with our chiefest horse.
This, and Saint George to boot! What think'st thou,
Norfolk?
305 **NORFOLK** A good direction, warlike sovereign.
This found I on my tent this morning: *Shows a paper*

---

278 **Tell** count (the chimes of)   **calendar** almanac, containing astrological predictions that dealt with
meteorology   281 **book** almanac   282 **braved the east** i.e. risen   **braved** made splendid/
challenged   283 **black** dark, gloomy/evil, disastrous   286 **lour** glower, threaten darkly
287 **from** not on   290 **sadly** solemnly   291 **vaunts** flaunts itself proudly   292 **Caparison** harness,
equip   296 **foreward** vanguard, front line of troops   **drawn** extended   297 **horse and foot** cavalry and
infantry, horsemen and foot soldiers   301 **directed** positioned, deployed   302 **puissance** power
303 **wingèd** flanked   **chiefest horse** best cavalry   304 **to boot** (to support us) as well

'Jockey of Norfolk, be not so bold,   *Reads*
For Dickon thy master is bought and sold.'
RICHARD A thing devisèd by the enemy.
310 Go, gentleman, every man to his charge
Let not our babbling dreams affright our souls:
For conscience is a word that cowards use,
Devised at first to keep the strong in awe.
Our strong arms be our conscience, swords our law.
315 March on, join bravely, let us to't pell-mell:
If not to heaven, then hand in hand to hell.—
What shall I say more than I have inferred?   *His oration to his army*
Remember whom you are to cope withal:
A sort of vagabonds, rascals and runaways,
320 A scum of Bretons and base lackey peasants,
Whom their o'er-cloyèd country vomits forth
To desperate adventures and assured destruction.
You sleeping safe, they bring you to unrest:
You having lands, and blest with beauteous wives,
325 They would restrain the one, distain the other.
And who doth lead them but a paltry fellow,
Long kept in Bretagne at our mother's cost?
A milksop, one that never in his life
Felt so much cold as over-shoes in snow?
330 Let's whip these stragglers o'er the seas again,
Lash hence these overweening rags of France,
These famished beggars, weary of their lives,
Who, but for dreaming on this fond exploit,
For want of means, poor rats, had hanged
      themselves.
335 If we be conquered, let men conquer us,
And not these bastard Bretons, whom our fathers
Have in their own land beaten, bobbed and thumped,
And on record, left them the heirs of shame.

---

307 **Jockey** contraction of 'John-kin', a nickname for 'John' (Norfolk's first name)   308 **Dickon** diminutive of Dick, i.e. Richard   **bought and sold** betrayed for a bribe   315 **join** join battle   **pell-mell** with headlong haste/at close quarters, with hand-to-hand combat   317 **inferred** stated   318 **cope** fight, grapple 319 **sort** gang   321 **o'er-cloyèd** over-full and sickened   325 **restrain** deprive you of   **distain** defile, soil, rape   326 **fellow** with lower-class connotations   327 **Bretagne** Brittany   **mother's** an error (for 'brother's') that appears in the second edition of Shakespeare's major source, Holinshed's *Chronicles*; just conceivably 'mother' might refer to 'mother England'   328 **milksop** weak, cowardly person/infant still on a milk diet   329 **over-shoes in snow** when snow is above the level of one's shoes   330 **whip these stragglers** i.e. as vagabonds were whipped out of the parish by a local official   331 **Lash hence** whip away from here   **overweening** ambitious, overreaching   **rags** vagrants/old scraps   333 **but** were it not for **fond exploit** foolish military undertaking   334 **want** lack   337 **land** with connotations of 'sexual territory', i.e. wives and daughters   **bobbed and thumped** beaten, pounded/had sex with, raped (their women)   338 **on record** as is officially recorded   **the ... shame** in disgrace/illegitimate children

Shall these enjoy our lands? Lie with our wives?
340 Ravish our daughters?   *Drum afar off*
                              Hark! I hear their drum.
Fight, gentlemen of England! Fight boldly, yeomen!
Draw, archers, draw your arrows to the head!
Spur your proud horses hard, and ride in blood:
Amaze the welkin with your broken staves!

Enter a Messenger

345 What says Lord Stanley? Will he bring his power?
MESSENGER My lord, he doth deny to come.
RICHARD Off with his son George's head!
NORFOLK My lord, the enemy is past the marsh
         After the battle let George Stanley die.
350 RICHARD A thousand hearts are great within my bosom.
         Advance our standards, set upon our foes.
         Our ancient word of courage, fair Saint George,
         Inspire us with the spleen of fiery dragons!
         Upon them! Victory sits on our helms.   [*Exeunt*]

Alarum, excursions. Enter Catesby

355 CATESBY Rescue, my lord of Norfolk, rescue, rescue!
         The king enacts more wonders than a man,
         Daring an opposite to every danger:
         His horse is slain, and all on foot he fights,
         Seeking for Richmond in the throat of death.
360 Rescue, fair lord, or else the day is lost!

Alarums. Enter Richard

RICHARD A horse! A horse! My kingdom for a horse!
CATESBY Withdraw, my lord: I'll help you to a horse.
RICHARD Slave, I have set my life upon a cast,
         And I will stand the hazard of the die.
365 I think there be six Richmonds in the field:
         Five have I slain today instead of him.
         A horse! A horse! My kingdom for a horse! [*Exeunt*]

Alarum. Enter Richard and Richmond: they fight. Richard is
slain. Retreat and flourish. Enter Richmond, Derby bearing
the crown, with divers other Lords

---

339 Lie have sex   **340 Ravish** rape   **341 yeomen** property-owning men below the level of gentlemen
343 proud splendid/rearing   **blood** i.e. the blood drawn from spurring the horses so hard
344 Amaze terrify, alarm, bewilder   **welkin** sky   **broken** i.e. shattered from energetic use   **346 deny**
refuse   **348 past the marsh** i.e. advancing   **350 great** full of emotion   **352 word of courage** i.e. battle
cry   **353 spleen** fury   **dragons** Saint George was famed for the legendary killing of a dragon   *Alarum,*
excursions trumpet call to arms and bouts of fighting across the stage   **356 a man** is humanly possible
357 Daring an opposite defying an enemy   **363 set ... cast** gambled my life on the throw of a **die**
364 stand await, endure   **hazard** chance   **die** singular of dice (with connotations of death)   **365 six**
Richmonds probably refers to the military precaution of disguising other soldiers as their commander

RICHMOND God and your arms be praised, victorious
    friends!
    The day is ours, the bloody dog is dead.

370 **DERBY** Courageous Richmond, well hast thou acquit
    thee.
    Lo, here, these long-usurpèd royalties
    From the dead temples of this bloody wretch
    Have I plucked off, to grace thy brows withal:
    Wear it and make much of it.

375 **RICHMOND** Great God of heaven, say 'Amen' to all!
    But, tell me, is young George Stanley living?

DERBY He is, my lord, and safe in Leicester town,
    Whither, if you please, we may withdraw us.

RICHMOND What men of name are slain on either side?

380 **DERBY** John Duke of Norfolk, Walter Lord Ferris,
    Sir Robert Brackenbury, and Sir William Brandon.

RICHMOND Inter their bodies as become their births:
    Proclaim a pardon to the soldiers fled
    That in submission will return to us:

385   And then, as we have ta'en the sacrament,
    We will unite the white rose and the red.
    Smile heaven upon this fair conjunction,
    That long have frowned upon their enmity!
    What traitor hears me and says not 'Amen'?

390   England hath long been mad, and scarred herself;
    The brother blindly shed the brother's blood,
    The father rashly slaughtered his own son,
    The son, compelled, been butcher to the sire:
    All this divided York and Lancaster,

395   Divided in their dire division.
    O, now let Richmond and Elizabeth,
    The true succeeders of each royal house,
    By God's fair ordinance conjoin together.
    And let thy heirs — God, if thy will be so —

400   Enrich the time to come with smooth-faced peace,
    With smiling plenty and fair prosperous days!
    Abate the edge of traitors, gracious Lord,

---

370 acquit thee acquitted yourself   **371 royalties** emblems of sovereignty, i.e. the crown   **379 name** rank   **382 become their births** befits their social standing   **385 ta'en the sacrament** confirmed an oath by taking Holy Communion   **386 unite…red** i.e. unite the Houses of Lancaster (symbolized by a red rose) and York (a white rose) by marrying Elizabeth, daughter of Edward IV   **387 conjunction** union (literally, proximity of planets)   **393 sire** father   **397 succeeders** inheritors, heirs   **398 ordinance** decree   **402 Abate** blunt **edge** sword edge

That would reduce these bloody days again,
And make poor England weep in streams of blood;
405 Let them not live to taste this land's increase
That would with treason wound this fair land's
    peace.
Now civil wounds are stopped, peace lives again:
That she may long live here, God say 'Amen'! *Exeunt*

403 **reduce** bring back   405 **increase** growth, harvest, prosperity   407 **stopped** staunched, stopped from
bleeding/no longer inflicted

TEXTUAL NOTES

Q = First Quarto text of 1597
F = First Folio text of 1623
F2 = a correction introduced in the Second Folio text of 1632
Ed = a correction introduced by a later editor
SD = stage direction
SH = speech heading (i.e. speaker's name)

List of parts = Ed

1.1.1 SH RICHARD = Ed. *Not in* F **77 was...his** = Q. F = was, for her
1.2.209 SH RICHARD = Q. F *assigns line to Lady Anne*
1.3.6 If...me? *accidentally printed twice in* F **17 come the lords** = Q. F = comes the Lord **158 of** *spelled* off *in* F **305 on** = Q. F = an **310 SH QUEEN ELIZABETH** = Q. F = *Mar.* **343 SH FIRST MURDERER** = Ed. F = *Vil. (for Villain)*
2.1.108 at = Q. F = and
2.2.1 SH BOY = Q. F = *Edw.* **3 you** = Q. *Not in* F **47 I** = Q. *Not in* F **83 weep** = Q. F = weepes **84–5 and...they** = Q. F = so do not they *(i.e. one line omitted due to eyeskip)* **87 Pour** *spelled* Power *in* F **121 Ludlow** = Q. F = London **146 God's** = Q. F = God **153 Ludlow** = Q. F = London
3.1.124 as = Q. F = as, as,
3.4.26 cue *spelled* Q *in* F
3.5.104 Penker = Ed. F = *Pevker*
4.1.16 SH BRACKENBURY = Ed. F = *Lieu.*
Act 4 Scene 4 = Ed. F = *Scena Tertia* **36 seniory** = Q. F = signeurie **44 holp'st** *spelled* hop'st *in* F **289 this is not** = Q, F2. F = this not **370 Harp...past** *mistakenly printed after the following line in* F **442 SD Exit [Queen Elizabeth]** = Ed. F = *Exit (directly after her last speech)* **457 Ratcliffe** = Ed. F = *Catesby* **519 SH SECOND** = Ed. *Not in* F **522 SH THIRD** = Ed. *Not in* F **535 SH FOURTH** = Ed. *Not in* F **538 Breton** *spelled* Brittaine *in* F **544 Brittany** *spelled* Brittaine *in* F
Act 4 Scene 5 = Ed. F = *Scena Quarta* **10 Ha'rfordwest** = Ed. F = Hertford West
5.2.11 centre = Q. F = Centry
5.3.29 you = F2. F = your **122 SH GHOST OF PRINCE EDWARD** = Ed. F = *Gh* **128 SH GHOST OF KING HENRY VI** = Ed. F = *Ghost* **135 SH GHOST OF CLARENCE** = Ed. F = *Ghost* **143 SH GHOST OF RIVERS** = Ed. F = *Riu* **145 SH GHOST OF GREY** = Ed. F = *Grey.* **146 SH GHOST OF VAUGHAN** = Ed. F = *Vaugh.* **150 SH GHOST OF HASTINGS** = Ed. F = *Gho.* **155 SH GHOSTS OF PRINCES** = Ed. F = *Ghosts.* **158 souls bid** = Q. F = soule bids **163 SH GHOST OF ANNE** = Ed. F = *Ghost* **171 SH GHOST OF BUCKINGHAM** = Ed. F = *Ghost* **225 SH LORDS** = Q. F = *Richm.* **317 SD His...army** = Q. *Not in* F **341 Fight** = Q. F = Right **354 helms** = Q. F = helpes

QUARTO PASSAGES THAT DO NOT APPEAR IN THE FOLIO

Lines are numbered continuously, for ease of reference.

Following 4.2.102:

BUCKINGHAM My lord!

RICHARD How chance the prophet could not at that time
Have told me, I being by, that I should kill him?

BUCKINGHAM My lord, your promise for the earldom,—

5   **RICHARD** Richmond! When last I was at Exeter,
The mayor in courtesy showed me the castle,
And called it Rougemont: at which name I started,
Because a bard of Ireland told me once
I should not live long after I saw Richmond.

10   **BUCKINGHAM** My lord!

RICHARD Ay, what's o'clock?

BUCKINGHAM I am thus bold to put your grace in mind
Of what you promised me.

RICHARD Well, but what's o'clock?

15   **BUCKINGHAM** Upon the stroke of ten.

RICHARD Well, let it strike.

BUCKINGHAM Why let it strike?

RICHARD Because that, like a Jack, thou keep'st the stroke
Betwixt thy begging and my meditation.
20   I am not in the giving vein today.

Following 5.3.215:

RICHARD O Ratcliffe, I have dreamed a fearful dream!
What thinkest thou, will our friends prove all true?

RATCLIFFE No doubt, my lord.

---

2 prophet i.e. Henry VI   **3 by** nearby   **him** Henry VI/Richmond   **5 Exeter** town in the county of Devon, south-west England   **7 Rougemont** puns on **Richmond**   **8 bard** (prophetic) poet   **18 Jack** small figure of a man that struck the clock bell every hour (plays on the sense of 'knave, base fellow')   **keep'st the stroke** observe the hour by striking the bell, i.e. regularly interrupt   **19 meditation** thoughts, reflection   **22 true** loyal

SCENE-BY-SCENE ANALYSIS

ACT 1 SCENE 1

Lines 1–41: The play opens with a soliloquy by Richard, revealing his skilful use of language. He outlines recent history, emphasizing that the action of this play is part of a wider series of events. The civil war between the royal Houses of York and Lancaster has ended, and Yorkist Edward IV is king, creating a 'glorious summer' of peace in contrast to the previous 'winter' of 'discontent'. Richard's speech moves away from matters of state towards himself, creating links and tensions between political and personal. Richard describes how men who were soldiers are now lovers. He claims that his own physical deformities prevent him from courting, describing himself bitterly as 'Deformed' and 'unfinished'. His apparent preoccupation with his looks establishes the play's interest in appearance and identity (genuine and feigned). He declares that since he 'cannot prove a lover' he will 'prove a villain' and outlines his plans against his brothers, the king and the Duke of Clarence. He has set about rumours of a prophecy, 'which says that "G" / Of Edward's heirs the murderer shall be', the first in a series of references to prophecies, dreams and omens. Richard sees Clarence being led in, guarded, and cuts short his soliloquy, urging his thoughts to 'Dive' down to his 'soul', emphasizing his ability to conceal his true self and the disparity between appearance and reality.

Lines 42–147: Richard asks why Clarence is being taken to the Tower. Clarence reveals that it is because his name 'is George', showing that Richard's false prophecy has had an effect on Edward who 'hearkens after prophesies and dreams' (although, ironically, being Duke of Gloucester, Richard himself is also 'G'). Richard feigns sympathy and suggests that Clarence's downfall is the result of the influence of the queen. Various political undercurrents are revealed: we also learn that the Lord Chamberlain, Hastings, has been freed from the Tower, apparently due to the influence of the king's mistress, Jane Shore. Lord Brackenbury claims that he has been charged with ensuring that 'no man shall have private conference' with Clarence, but Richard argues that they are discussing 'no treason' and assures Clarence that he will speak to the king. Clarence is led away as Hastings arrives, vowing revenge on the 'kites and buzzards' who have had him arrested, establishing the animal imagery that recurs through the play. Hastings reports that the king is 'sickly, weak and melancholy'. Richard feigns sadness, saying that he will follow Hastings to see the king.

Lines 148–165: Richard fears that Edward will die before Clarence has been executed. He plans to see that Clarence is 'packed with post-horse up to heaven' by stirring up Edward's hatred. Once Clarence and Edward are dead, he will 'bustle in'. He reveals his plan to marry Lady Anne Neville. Although the specific reasons for this remain a 'secret close intent', it is clearly a political move. Despite acknowledging that he killed both Anne's husband and Henry VI (her father-in-law), Richard seems confident that he will achieve this, suggesting a confidence with the opposite sex that his earlier speech denied and illustrating the complexities of his characterization.

ACT 1 SCENE 2

Lines 1–232: The guarded coffin of Henry VI is brought on, attended by Anne. She laments the fall of the House of Lancaster and the death of Henry, and curses Richard. She wishes him a worse fate than 'spiders' and 'toads', reinforcing the animal imagery introduced in the previous scene. She instructs the men carrying Henry's coffin to carry him to Chertsey Monastery. Richard enters and commands the men to put the coffin down. Anne compares his entrance to that of a 'fiend' conjured up by a 'black magician', introducing a series of images associating Richard with hell. She uncovers Henry's body and invites everyone to look at 'dead Henry's wounds', calling on God to revenge his death. Richard appeals to be allowed to explain. He describes Anne as an angel and 'divine perfection', which aims at flattery but also contrasts with the hellish images she uses for him, establishing them as opposing representatives of good and evil. The balance of imagery is reflected in the stichomythic structure of their argument. Initially, Anne seems to be a worthy opponent in what Richard calls their 'keen encounter of . . . wits'. Richard's mastery over language and ability to manipulate become evident, however, as he overcomes Anne's anger. He claims that he killed Anne's husband because he loves her. He praises her beauty and offers her his sword, saying that if her 'vengeful heart cannot forgive' she must kill him. She cannot, and, despite fearing that both Richard's tongue and heart are false, she softens. He places a ring on her finger, claiming his heart is hers, and begs to be allowed to take Henry's body to Chertsey so that he may 'wet his grave' with 'repentant tears'. Pleased that he has 'become so penitent', she agrees.

Lines 233–271: Richard instructs the men to take Henry to Whitefriars, not Chertsey. Any vicarious belief the audience may have had in his sincerity is destroyed as he marvels at his ability to manipulate Anne (and, perhaps, us) and comments that he has her, but 'will not keep her long'. He appears surprised that Anne finds him 'a marv'llous proper man', despite his physical appearance, and resolves to employ 'a score or two of tailors / To study fashions to adorn my body'. The clothing imagery reinforces the obsession with appearance and identity, as do repeated references to looking glasses.

ACT 1 SCENE 3

Lines 1–109: Lord Rivers and Lord Grey try to reassure Queen Elizabeth, who worries about what will 'betide' her after Edward's death. They remind her that her son, Prince Edward, will be her 'comforter', but she is concerned that his youth means that he will be under the protection of Richard. Derby and Buckingham report that the king wishes to make peace between Richard and the queen's brothers, and between the queen's brothers and Hastings, and has summoned them all. Richard arrives with Hastings and Dorset, complaining that people have been telling the king 'dissentious rumours' about him. He argues, ironically, that he 'cannot flatter and look fair' and asks the assembled company to tell him how he has 'injured' them and caused them to trouble the king 'with lewd complaints'. The queen retorts that it is his own behaviour that has caused the king to send for him. Richard accuses the queen of using her power to achieve status and positions in court for her family, and complains that his brother Clarence is imprisoned by Elizabeth's 'means'. She denies this and their argument escalates, with Elizabeth declaring that she has 'Small joy' in being queen and being constantly 'bated, scorned and stormed at'. Queen Margaret, the widow of Henry VI, enters unnoticed.

Lines 110–324: Elizabeth and Richard argue as Margaret watches, making comments aside. Her presence as an 'audience' reinforces our sense of Richard as an actor. Margaret's observations show her hatred of Richard and Elizabeth: she wishes Elizabeth that even her 'Small joy' be lessened and observes that Richard is a 'cacodemon' (evil spirit) whose kingdom is hell, reinforcing Anne's previous imagery. She steps forward and accuses them of being 'wrangling pirates' who argue over what has been 'pilled' from her. The following exchange, which centres on past struggles for the kingdom, reminds us that the events of the play are part of wider history, and of the violent nature of the struggle for power. Margaret invokes a series of prophetic curses, as Richard calls her 'witch' and 'withered hag'. Margaret hopes that Elizabeth's son, Edward, will 'Die in his youth' by 'untimely violence', as her own son did, and that Elizabeth will 'Die neither mother, wife, nor England's queen'. Elizabeth remains silent during Margaret's outburst, but Richard argues. Margaret warns that Richard will soon suspect his friends 'for traitors' and 'take deep traitors' for his 'dearest friends'. She abuses Richard's appearance, invoking the images of animals and hell that have previously been associated with him. Her comparison of Richard to a 'bottled spider' with a 'deadly web' shows her awareness of his manipulative nature. Buckingham urges Margaret to 'have done' and she warns him against Richard and his 'venom tooth' before leaving, saying that they will remember her words and think of her as a 'prophetess'. Richard assumes an air of forgiveness and says that Margaret 'hath had too much wrong' and that he repents of any part he has had in this. He adds that he hopes God will pardon those who have wronged Clarence. Rivers comments that this is 'virtuous and . . . Christian-like'. Catesby summons them to the king's presence.

Lines 325–357: Richard stays and considers how he has convinced Derby, Hastings and Buckingham that the queen and her family are plotting against himself and Clarence. He is pleased with the effectiveness of his 'piece of scripture', saying that he uses 'old ends stol'n forth of holy writ' to 'clothe' his villainy, so that he can 'seem a saint' when in reality he 'play[s] the devil'. Once again we see opposing images of heaven and hell, and of clothing, suggesting Richard's ability to disguise his true self. Two Murderers enter and Richard gives them a warrant to be admitted to Clarence. Richard warns them to be 'sudden in the execution' and not to let Clarence plead with them, as he is 'well-spoken', showing the play's concern with the power of language.

ACT 1 SCENE 4

Lines 1–98: Clarence describes a dream to his Keeper in vivid and poetic language, demonstrating that Richard was right: he is 'well-spoken'. Clarence recounts how, in his dream, he had escaped and was sailing to Burgundy with Richard. As they stood on deck, looking back at England, Richard stumbled and knocked Clarence overboard. He describes the sights and sounds as he drowned, including 'gold', 'pearls' and 'jewels' all 'scattered in the bottom of the sea . . . in dead men's skulls', a reminder of the link between death and the desire for wealth and power. He goes on to describe nightmarish visions of the afterlife and acknowledges his own guilt for past deeds before asking the Keeper to sit by him 'awhile' as he goes to sleep. As Clarence sleeps, Brackenbury, the Lieutenant of the Tower, arrives. He watches Clarence and considers how all men are the same, regardless of rank. The Murderers bring Brackenbury the warrant, ordering him to leave them. Brackenbury does so, observing that he will not 'reason what is meant hereby, / Because I will be guiltless from the meaning', lines symptomatic of a recurrent exploration of guilt and innocence.

Lines 99–287: In a darkly humorous exchange, the Murderers contemplate what they are about to do, weighing spiritual consequences against monetary reward. Clarence wakes and stalls them with powerful speeches, but they insist that they have been commanded to kill him by the king. Clarence asks them to go to Richard, but they reveal that Richard actually sent them. Clarence refuses to believe this, describing how Richard loves him and how he 'hugged [him] in his arms, and swore, with sobs' to gain his 'delivery', a testament to Richard's acting skills and ambiguity in language. Clarence shows his own powers of persuasion as the Second Murderer decides that he cannot go through with the deed. The First Murderer, however, stabs Clarence and takes his body to be drowned in a butt of malmsey wine. He returns and threatens to tell Richard how 'slack' his companion was, but the Second Murderer says he can tell Richard and take the entire fee, as he repents.

ACT 2 SCENE 1

The king expresses satisfaction that, although he is very ill, he has achieved peace among the quarrelling factions and so his soul 'shall part to heaven' in peace. Hastings and Rivers shake hands and Edward warns that they must mean it or God will 'Confound' their 'hidden falsehood', emphasizing the recurring deceptions of the play but also suggesting a justice beyond the human court. Richard arrives and praises Edward for his 'blessèd labour' and begs to be reconciled in 'friendly peace' with everyone. The queen asks her husband to pardon Clarence, but Richard accuses her of mocking him, saying 'Who knows not that the gentle duke is dead?' Edward, shocked, claims that he reversed the order to execute Clarence. Richard explains that the 'countermand' was not delivered in time. Derby enters and kneels before Edward, asking that Edward spare the life of his servant. Edward grows angry, bitter that he can 'give pardon to a slave', but could not do so for his own brother. He blames the assembled company for not pleading hard enough on Clarence's behalf and has to be helped away. Richard takes the opportunity to provoke dissent, observing to the remaining courtiers that 'the guilty kindred of the queen' had obviously urged Edward to execute Clarence.

ACT 2 SCENE 2

Lines 1–33: Clarence's children question the Duchess of York about the death of their father. Despite her denials, Clarence's son tells her that 'good uncle Gloucester' has told them that King Edward was responsible for their father's death, 'provoked to it by the queen'. He describes how Richard wept as he told him the news and asked the boy 'to rely on him'. The duchess observes that Richard hides his 'deep vice' 'with a virtuous visor', another image of clothing and concealment. Once more, it is a woman who appears to have insight into Richard's true character: so far only Anne, Elizabeth and the duchess have directly expressed their distrust.

Lines 34–100: The queen arrives, clearly distressed, and announces that King Edward has died. The duchess sympathizes: she too has lost a husband. Sustaining the association between images of mirrors and the theme of identity, she adds that until now she had comfort in two of her sons, 'two mirrors' of their father's 'princely semblance'. Now, however, she claims that she only has 'but one false glass', Richard. Clarence's children declare that they cannot share in their aunt's grief, as she 'wept not' for their father, another example of events of the past reinforcing divisions in the present. Both of the women and the children then exclaim in grief over their losses. In contrast to these personal emotions, Rivers and Dorset focus on the political circumstances, urging Elizabeth to send for the young Prince Edward and 'Let him be crowned.'

Lines 101–153: Richard arrives, offering comfort to the queen and asking his mother's blessing, although his brief aside reminds us of the disparity between his words and true feelings/intentions. Buckingham smoothly suggests that Prince Edward be brought to London, accompanied 'with some little train' in case 'the new-healed wound of malice should break out'. Rivers and Hastings agree and Richard asks his mother and Elizabeth to go and give their 'censures in this business'. He remains behind with Buckingham and they plot to 'part the queen's proud kindred from the prince'.

ACT 2 SCENE 3

In a contrast to the court-based action so far, and demonstrating the important link between king and kingdom, three citizens discuss the current circumstances. While one remains optimistic, the others express their fears about a 'land that's governed by a child'. They show distrust of Richard and worry what the struggles between Richard and the queen's relatives will do to the kingdom.

ACT 2 SCENE 4

The archbishop, the queen, the duchess, and young York wait for the prince's arrival. The intimate and domestic discussion between mother and grandmother concerning the comparative heights of Edward and York contrasts with the political arguments that have dominated so far. York reports that his 'uncle Gloucester' said that 'Small herbs have grace, great weeds do grow apace', an image that evokes the destructive nature of Richard's speedy rise to power. The family exchange is gently humorous, although once again the duchess expresses doubt over Richard's character, until a messenger brings the news that Rivers, Grey and Vaughan have been imprisoned on the command of Richard and Buckingham. Elizabeth sees that Richard has begun the 'ruin' of her family, comparing him to a hunting 'tiger', and foresees 'as in a map, the end of all'. She decides to take York into sanctuary, and the duchess offers to go with them. The archbishop gives them the king's seal of authority that he carries and takes them to safety.

ACT 3 SCENE 1

Lines 1–94: Prince Edward enters London, accompanied by Richard, Buckingham and the Lord Cardinal. Edward asks why none of his 'uncles' on his mother's side are there to greet him and asks where his mother and brother are. As he does so, Hastings arrives with the news that the queen and York have 'taken sanctuary' and that Elizabeth prevented York from coming to greet his brother. Buckingham, annoyed, sends the Lord Cardinal to 'persuade' Elizabeth to send York to Prince Edward, and orders Hastings that, if she will not give in, to 'pluck him perforce' from his mother's arms. When the Cardinal objects, Buckingham cleverly argues that York is too young to 'have the wit' to claim sanctuary and therefore to take him is to 'break no privilege nor charter'. It is interesting that here, as in the rest of this scene, it is Buckingham, not Richard, who is making decisions and giving orders, demonstrating his increasing power. The Cardinal and Hastings depart and the prince asks where he is to stay until his coronation. Richard suggests the royal residence at the Tower, but Edward is not keen. We see that Edward has a similar control over language to Richard's and that he is not fooled by his uncle's clever arguments.

Lines 95–201: York is brought in and the brothers show that they are a match for Richard verbally, but they are still powerless to prevent him, as 'Lord Protector', from sending them to stay in the Tower. When the brothers have gone, Richard, Buckingham and Catesby discuss their plans to place Richard on the throne. Buckingham argues that they will find it difficult to convince Hastings and sends Catesby to 'summon him tomorrow to the Tower' under the pretext of discussing the coronation, so that they can test his loyalty. Richard adds that Catesby should tell Hastings that the queen's relatives are to be executed the next day, as this will please him. Buckingham asks Richard what they will do if Hastings will not join their conspiracy and Richard answers simply 'Chop off his head'. He promises Buckingham 'the earldom of Hereford' once he is king.

ACT 3 SCENE 2

Lines 1–34: Hastings is woken in the early hours by a messenger from the Earl of Derby. He reports that Derby has had a prophetic dream in which a boar (Richard's heraldic emblem) 'razèd off his helm'. Derby is worried about the 'two councils' that Richard intends to hold, a technique clearly intended to create political division. He asks if Hastings will join him in escaping north to 'shun the danger that his soul divines'. Demonstrating his own lack of perception, Hastings replies that there is nothing to fear from the 'separated council'.

Lines 35–123: Catesby arrives and Hastings asks for news of the 'tott'ring state', evoking the country's turmoil. Catesby comments that he thinks the world will not 'stand upright' again until Richard is king. Shocked, Hastings asks if this is Richard's intention and learns that it is, and that Richard hopes for his backing. Catesby adds that Hastings' enemies, 'the kindred of the queen', 'must die at Pomfret'. Apparently oblivious to the danger he is placing himself in, Hastings declares that he is glad of this, but that he will not help Richard to the throne. Derby arrives in person and Hastings jokingly asks where his 'boar-spear' is. Derby insists that the 'several councils' bode ill, but Hastings is unmoved. As Derby and Catesby head to the Tower, Hastings jokes with a Pursuivant and shows his pleasure that his enemies are to be executed. Buckingham arrives to escort Hastings to the Tower.

ACT 3 SCENE 3

Ratcliffe escorts Rivers, Grey and Vaughan to their executions. They proclaim their loyalty to the prince and remember Margaret's earlier curses upon them. Rivers reminds them that she also cursed Richard and Buckingham.

ACT 3 SCENE 4

Lines 1–57: The council assembles. Hastings announces that they are there to 'determine of the coronation', asking 'when is the royal day?' The bishop suggests the next day, and Buckingham asks if anyone knows Richard's mind on the subject. The bishop suggests that Buckingham should, but Buckingham's response is ambiguous. He suggests that Hastings might know, and, although Hastings denies this, he offers to speak on Richard's behalf. Richard arrives and Buckingham informs him that Hastings was about to pronounce his 'part' on the coronation, implying that Hastings aspires to Richard's power, and creating an awareness of theatre and performance, also emphasized by the word 'cue'. Richard seems cheerful and asks the bishop to send for a bowl of strawberries. Richard draws Buckingham aside and reports that Catesby 'hath sounded Hastings' and found that he 'will lose his head' rather than help depose Prince Edward. They withdraw. Hastings comments on Richard's good humour and ironically suggests that Richard can never 'hide his love or hate'.

Lines 58–106: Richard returns in a changed mood. He angrily claims that people are conspiring his death 'with devilish plots / Of damnèd witchcraft' and have placed 'hellish charms' on his body. Hastings suggests that the penalty for such an action must be death. Richard shows them the withered arm he has had since birth, claiming that he has been bewitched by Elizabeth, 'that monstrous witch', and 'that harlot, strumpet Shore'. Hastings is uncertain, and Richard immediately accuses him of treachery and conspiracy with Mistress Shore and orders his execution. Too late, Hastings realizes his blindness and recounts the omens that he has ignored, including Margaret's curses. He makes his own prophecy that England is about to enter 'the fearful'st time', before being led away.

ACT 3 SCENE 5

Richard and Buckingham are dressed in damaged armour, a deliberate choice of 'costume' for the events they are about to stage. This theatrical self-awareness is emphasized by Richard asking if Buckingham can pretend to be 'distraught and mad with terror' and Buckingham's assurance that he can 'counterfeit the deep tragedian'. Catesby arrives as arranged, bringing the Mayor. Richard and Buckingham feign confusion and appear to be defending the Tower. Lovell and Ratcliffe bring in Hastings' head and Richard sets about convincing the Mayor that Hastings was a traitor. Buckingham helps, reporting that Hastings, in league with 'Mistress Shore', had plotted to kill Richard. He expresses regret that Lovell and Ratcliffe have already carried out the execution, as he would have liked the Mayor to hear Hastings' confession so as to reassure the citizens that his execution was necessary. It becomes clear that this episode has been to further Richard's cause with the English people and to prevent 'the censures of the carping world'. After the Mayor has left, Richard sends Buckingham to talk to the citizens of London, slurring the reputation of the old king and suggesting that his children are illegitimate. Buckingham assures him that he will 'play the orator'. Richard goes to make secret arrangements 'To draw the brats of Clarence out of sight'.

ACT 3 SCENE 6

The opinion of England's subjects is represented by a Scrivener, who comments that the execution of Hastings is a 'palpable device' by Richard.

ACT 3 SCENE 7

Lines 1–93: Buckingham reports on his speech, in which he undermined the reputation of King Edward and his children and praised Richard, rallying the crowds to shout 'God save Richard, England's royal king!' In response to this, however, the people 'spake not a word' and their silence provides a powerful contrast to the abundance of language so far. Richard is perplexed and angry. Buckingham tells him that the Mayor is coming, advising him to 'get a prayer-book' and 'stand between two churchmen'. Richard leaves and the Mayor arrives, as does Catesby. Catesby pretends that Richard refuses to see any of them as he is 'Divinely bent to meditation' and Buckingham sends him back to ask again. He observes to the Mayor that Richard is 'virtuous', unlike 'lewd' Edward, and pretends to be concerned that Richard will not accept the crown, commenting on how difficult it is to draw 'holy and devout religious men' from their 'zealous contemplation'.

Lines 94–245: Richard appears with two clergymen. Buckingham apologizes for interrupting his devotion and begs that he will listen to their requests. He urges Richard to accept the crown. Initially Richard refuses, allowing Buckingham to repeat all of the persuasive arguments for him and against Edward and his children. The Mayor tells Richard that his citizens 'entreat' him to accept, but Richard still feigns reluctance. Finally, he piously accepts the 'burden' of kingship.

ACT 4 SCENE 1

Elizabeth, Dorset, and the duchess meet Anne, now Richard's wife, with a little girl (probably Clarence's daughter). They are all going to the Tower to visit 'the gentle princes', but Brackenbury refuses them entry on the orders of 'the king'. Confused, they question him and he corrects his phrasing to 'the Lord Protector'. Elizabeth asserts her right as a mother to see her children and Anne supports her, saying that she will 'bear the blame', but Brackenbury refuses. Derby arrives, bringing the news that Richard is to be crowned and that Anne is to become queen. She is dismayed at these 'Despiteful tidings!' Elizabeth instructs her son Dorset to 'cross the seas, / And live with Richmond' (the Lancastrian heir). The duchess curses her own womb for bringing forth Richard, a 'cockatrice'. Derby urges Anne to go with him, but she would rather die than become queen.

As Elizabeth sympathizes, Anne regrets her weakness in believing Richard's 'honey words' and expresses her belief that he means to kill her. As they part, Elizabeth encourages everyone to 'look back' at the Tower, and asks that the 'ancient stones' will pity her 'tender babes'.

ACT 4 SCENE 2

King Richard ascends his throne with the assistance of Buckingham, a visual metaphor of events so far. Establishing the scene's quick shifts between public and private and demonstrating the increasingly thin margin between Richard's personal and public personae, he and Buckingham speak aside from the rest of the court. Richard fears his kingship is not safe while Prince Edward lives. Announcing that he will 'be plain', in direct contrast to his usual linguistic style, he asks Buckingham to kill the princes, but Buckingham asks for 'some pause' to think. Buckingham leaves. Aside, Catesby observes that Richard is angry; Richard clearly feels that Buckingham is no longer trustworthy. He calls his Page and asks quietly if he knows of anyone whom 'corrupting gold / Will tempt unto a close exploit of death'. The Page suggests a man called Tyrrell. Richard sends the page to fetch him and resolves to himself that Buckingham will 'No more' be 'neighbour to [his] counsels'. Derby brings the news that Dorset has fled to join Richmond. Drawing Catesby aside, Richard sends him to put about the rumour that Anne is ill 'and like to die'. He contemplates his next plan: to marry Elizabeth's daughter and secure his kingship, which 'stands on brittle glass'. The Page brings Tyrrell, who agrees to kill the princes. Buckingham returns and claims the 'earldom of Hereford', as promised, but Richard ignores him and continues discussing Richmond with Derby. This division between the two men marks a turning point in the play: Richard becomes increasingly isolated by his desire to retain power and has lost an ally through distrust, recalling Margaret's curse of Act 1 scene 3. Realizing that he is out of favour, and therefore in danger, Buckingham flees to Wales.

ACT 4 SCENE 3

Tyrrell reveals that the 'bloody act is done'. He is shaken, and describes the remorse of the men he hired to do the killing, 'fleshed villains, bloody dogs', who nonetheless 'Melted with tenderness' and wept when they reported to him. He gives a moving description of the princes, 'girdling one another / Within their alabaster innocent arms'. Richard arrives and questions Tyrrell: did Tyrrell see the princes' bodies? Did he see them buried? Richard's inhumanity is heightened by the contrast with Tyrrell and the hired men, who, despite their harsh natures, still felt remorse for their actions. Tyrrell leaves and Richard contemplates the latest developments in his plans: Clarence's son is imprisoned, his daughter is 'meanly matched' in marriage, and Anne is dead. He leaves to 'woo' the young Princess Elizabeth. Ratcliffe brings news that 'Morton is fled to Richmond' and that Buckingham is increasing his armies. Richard resolves to act: in direct contrast to his earlier reliance on language, he declares that 'fearful commenting / Is leaden servitor to dull delay' and prepares to do battle.

ACT 4 SCENE 4

Lines 1–134: Margaret has remained concealed in England, watching the 'waning' of her enemies. She hears the duchess and Queen Elizabeth approaching, and again withdraws to watch. As the two women mourn the princes, she comments with satisfaction on their grief, seeing it as revenge for her own losses. She comes forward and points out that her curses have come true: Elizabeth is 'a most distressed widow', has lost her sons and is 'queen of sad mischance'. She starts to leave, but Elizabeth begs her to teach her to curse her enemies. Margaret says that the way to do this is to 'Compare dead happiness with living woe' and her grief and therefore her words will pierce like Margaret's. Margaret leaves and Elizabeth and the duchess vow to smother Richard 'in the breath of bitter words'.

Lines 135–442: Richard arrives and the two women launch a bitter attack on him, directly accusing him of killing the princes and Clarence. Reinforcing the attention to disguise, Elizabeth suggests that his 'golden crown' conceals a 'branded' forehead, a reference to Cain that also emphasizes the accusations of fratricide. Richard calls for trumpets and drums to drown out 'these tell-tale women', saying that he will only listen if they speak courteously. The duchess asserts her right as his mother to speak to Richard, and accuses him of making the earth her 'hell'. She curses him, hoping that he will die shamed in battle, and leaves. Elizabeth is about to follow, but Richard detains her. She bitterly comments that she has 'no more sons' for Richard to 'slaughter', but he is only interested in her 'royal and gracious' daughter. He explains that he wishes to make her his queen and asks how to win her. Queen Elizabeth bitterly suggests that he sends her the bleeding hearts of her brothers. Richard attempts to persuade her in a speech that shows his old command over language, but his charming imagery is juxtaposed by the repellent idea of what he is suggesting, which he is either choosing to ignore or genuinely cannot see. Elizabeth points this out, asking if she should say to her daughter that 'Her father's brother / Would be her lord?' Echoing the argument with Anne in Act 1 scene 2, Elizabeth verbally matches Richard, defeating his every move, but he persists until she apparently gives in, although her final words to Richard are ambiguous. However, he chooses to see her as defeated and describes her as a 'Relenting fool'.

Lines 443–555: Ratcliffe and Catesby report that Richmond's navy is approaching the coast, with the intention of joining Buckingham and his army. Richard orders Catesby to go the Duke of Norfolk, and grows angry when he does not leave. Catesby explains that he has not been given any message for Norfolk, the first sign of genuine weakness in Richard. Derby brings confirmation that Richmond intends 'to claim the crown'. Angry, Richard questions Derby's loyalty and, despite Derby's assurances, holds his son George hostage until he has mustered his forces to join Richard in battle. A series of messengers bring bad news, until Richard strikes one man before he can even speak, suggesting his increasing loss of self-control. The man reports that Buckingham's army has been dispersed by floods and that Buckingham is missing. The confusion continues as it is reported first that Richmond is returning to France, and then that he has landed at Milford, but Buckingham has been taken prisoner by Richard's forces. Richard heads for Salisbury to do battle.

ACT 4 SCENE 5

Derby sends word to Richmond of his support, but explains that Richard is holding his son hostage. He also reveals that Queen Elizabeth has consented to Richmond marrying her daughter.

ACT 5 SCENE 1

Buckingham, under guard, asks to speak to Richard, but is refused. He knows that it is his 'doomsday', and recalls the words of Margaret's prophecy.

ACT 5 SCENE 2

Richmond's army marches towards Leicester.

ACT 5 SCENE 3

The action shifts quickly between events and the opposing camps, building pace and tension.

Lines 1–19: Richard and his followers pitch his tent in Bosworth Field. The mood is sombre, but Richard is cheered by news that the 'traitors' number only 'six or seven thousand', a third the size of his own army. They go to survey the battleground.

Lines 20–47: Richmond and his followers pitch his tent on the opposite side of the battlefield, a visual representation of their conflict. Richmond is optimistic, seeing the 'golden' sunset as a good omen for the following day. The solar imagery returns us to the opening lines of the play and associated ideas of 'summer' replacing a 'winter of discontent'. Richmond draws up his battle plans and sends Blunt with a 'needful note' to Derby.

Lines 48–82: Richard also sends a message to Derby, instructing him to 'bring his power / Before sun-rising' or his son will die. He then commands that his horse, 'white Surrey', is saddled for the next day, but complains that he lacks 'cheer of mind'. He writes, then sleeps.

Lines 83–121: Derby secretly visits Richmond to assure him of his loyalty, but tells him that he 'may not be too forward' because Richard has his son. He leaves, and Richmond prays before sleeping.

Lines 122–224: As both men sleep, a series of Ghosts appears on stage, all victims of Richard. In turn, they approach Richard and curse him for his role in their deaths, repeating that he will 'despair and die'. Each Ghost also addresses Richmond, blessing him and wishing him victory. When the last Ghost, that of Buckingham, has spoken, Richard awakes suddenly, crying out: 'Give me another horse! Bind up my wounds!' His self-doubt is evident in marked contrast to his earlier confidence and his confusion is clear as he asserts 'I am I', then argues 'I am not'.

Lines 225–272: Richmond wakes from 'the sweetest sleep'. He reports his 'fairest-boding' dream and then addresses his soldiers. His patriotic speech reminds them that 'God' and their 'good cause' are on their side. He condemns Richard's tyranny.

Lines 273–354: Richard, observing that the sun 'distains to shine', issues orders that Derby and his men are to be summoned. He addresses his troops, focusing on the weaknesses of the enemy and describing Richmond as 'a paltry fellow'. A messenger informs Richard that Derby has defected, but he has no time to kill his son: the battle has begun.

Lines 355–408: Catesby reports that Richard is fighting on foot, having lost his horse, and is determined to kill Richmond. Richard enters, calling for a horse, but will not withdraw when Catesby asks him to, focusing only on Richmond and sustaining his single-minded desire to retain power until the last. Richmond appears. They fight, and Richard is killed. Richmond declares that 'the bloody dog is dead' and claims the throne. He announces his intention to marry Princess Elizabeth, thus uniting 'divided York and Lancaster'. As Henry VII, he will restore peace to the long-fractured kingdom.

RICHARD III IN PERFORMANCE: THE RSC AND BEYOND

The best way to understand a Shakespeare play is to see it or ideally to participate in it. By examining a range of productions, we may gain a sense of the extraordinary variety of approaches and interpretations that are possible – a variety that gives Shakespeare his unique capacity to be reinvented and made 'our contemporary' four centuries after his death.

We begin with a brief overview of the play's theatrical and cinematic life, offering historical perspectives on how it has been performed. We then analyse in more detail a series of productions staged over the last half-century by the Royal Shakespeare Company. The sense of dialogue between productions that can only occur when a company is dedicated to the revival and investigation of the Shakespeare canon over a long period, together with the uniquely comprehensive archival resource of promptbooks, pro-gramme notes, reviews and interviews held on behalf of the RSC at the Shakespeare Birthplace Trust in Stratford-upon-Avon, allows an 'RSC stage history' to become a crucible in which the chemistry of the play can be explored.

Finally, we hear the voices of an array of practitioners via interviews with a distinguished actor who has played Richard, the director of a highly successful production, and the designer of a complete cycle of Shakespeare's history plays. After the interviews, there is a brief essay by Richard Eyre on the experience of directing the play and touring it in Eastern Europe.

FOUR CENTURIES OF *RICHARD III*: AN OVERVIEW

To judge by the number of contemporary references to the play and reprints of the 1597 Quarto, *Richard III* was an immediate popular success from its first performances in the early 1590s – it did much to make the names of both Shakespeare as playwright and Richard Burbage as leading actor. In his commonplace book, *Palladis Tamia* (1598), Francis Meres cites it as an example of Shakespeare's excellence as a writer of tragedies. The success of Burbage's performance is evidenced in a well-known anecdote recorded in the diary of a law student, John Manningham:

> Upon a time when Burbage played Richard III there was a citizen grew so far in liking with him, that before she went from the play she appointed him to come that night unto her by the name of Richard III. Shakespeare overhearing their conclusion went before, was entertained, and at his game ere Burbage came. Then message being brought that Richard III was at the door, Shakespeare caused return to be made that William the Conqueror was before Richard III.[1]

Apart from the light cast upon the relationship between Shakespeare and Burbage, the story, if true, attests to the success of Richard's seductive onstage persona.

A performance at court was recorded in November 1633 after the birth of Queen Henrietta Maria's son, the Duke of York (later James II), suggesting that the play remained in the repertoire of the King's Men until the closure of the theatres when the country collapsed into civil war in 1642.

After the reopening of the theatres with the Restoration of the monarchy in 1660, *Richard III* was assigned to Thomas Killigrew's company and revived briefly with a new prologue. Thomas Betterton, the best-known actor in the period, played Richard, not in Shakespeare's play, but in an adaptation by John Caryll, *The English Princess* (1666). This was based on events leading up to the Wars of the Roses and Lady Elizabeth's choice of Richmond over Richard. When Shakespeare's play was revived, Betterton played

King Edward IV and Richard was played by Samuel Sandford, who specialized in villains. It was with Sandford in mind that Colley Cibber wrote his own immensely successful adaptation, first performed at Drury Lane in 1699.

Cibber's play is little more than half the length of Shakespeare's, with Richard's part even more dominant: the number of his soliloquies is increased whereas the roles of characters such as Buckingham are cut. Hastings, Clarence, Edward and Margaret are eliminated altogether. There is a concomitant simplification of other characters: Derby (Stanley) and the queen are less ambiguous and Henry Richmond is idealized and given lines from Shakespeare's *Henry V*. Supposing the audience to have a less intimate knowledge of English history and the identity of the various characters than the original Shakespearean playgoers, he invents scenes with Henry VI at the beginning to clarify the politics and history and to demonstrate Richard's past evil-doings. Cibber stages the murder of the princes, although this short scene is unique to the edition of 1700 and it is generally believed that it was cut in performance. In the printed version Shakespeare's lines are in italics while Cibber's are in Roman type. In his introduction Cibber relates how he was obliged to cut the first act in performance on the grounds that the plight of King Henry VI might remind people of the banished James II. The overall effect of Cibber's revisions is two-fold: to simplify the plot to make the play more easily understood and to enhance the role of Richard. Cibber's play dominated the stage until 1821 and was, as the critic Stanley Wells points out, 'for a couple of centuries probably the most popular play on the English stage'.[2] Innovations such as the inclusion of Richard's self-revelatory soliloquy from *3 Henry VI* and the adapted line 'Off with his head! So much for Buckingham' continued to be used even in the Laurence Olivier film version of 1955.

There was a change of plan and Cibber, a natural comedian, took the part himself, giving a performance which was almost universally derided. The eighteenth-century theatre historian Thomas Davies records how finally 'the public grew out of patience and fairly hissed him off the stage'.[3] It was David Garrick making his acting debut as Richard in the 'illegitimate' theatre in Goodman's Fields in 1741 who made the role his own. Garrick's performance and 'naturalistic' acting style drew instant acclaim. Recognizing the significance of his performance, fellow-actor James Quin commented 'if the young fellow was right, he and the rest of the players had all been wrong'.[4] In his biography of Garrick, Davies describes the effect of his first performance:

> Mr Garrick's easy and familiar, yet forcible style in speaking and acting, at first threw the critics into some hesitation concerning the novelty as well as propriety of his manner. They had been long accustomed to an elevation of the voice, with a sudden mechanical depression of its tones, calculated to excite admiration, and to intrap applause. To the just modulation of the words, and concurring expression of the features from the genuine workings of nature, they had been strangers, at least for some time. But after he had gone through a variety of scenes, in which he gave evident proofs of consummate art, and perfect knowledge of character, their doubts were turned into surprise and astonishment, from which they relieved themselves by loud and reiterated applause.[5]

John Philip Kemble played the part but it hardly suited his scholarly, dignified persona, whereas the eccentric George Frederick Cooke at Covent Garden at the beginning of the nineteenth century won considerable acclaim. In her study of the play in performance, Julie Hankey says that 'Cooke's Richard was neither subtle and protean like Garrick's, nor lofty like Kemble's; it seems to have been joyfully, gloatingly horrible.'[6] The Romantics admired the individualism, if not the villainy of Richard. Of Edmund Kean's performance, William Hazlitt said: 'If Mr Kean does not completely succeed in concentrating all the lines of the character, as drawn by Shakespear [sic], he gives an animation, vigour, and relief to the part which we have never seen surpassed. He is more refined than Cooke; more bold, varied and original than Kemble in the same character.'[7] Junius Brutus Booth modelled his performance on Kean's and achieved some success, despite the efforts of Kean's supporters to drown him out. Booth later emigrated to America and became a successful actor-manager there. His performance as Richard was noted for its physicality, especially in the concluding battle scenes, as were those of his American successor in the role, Edwin Forrest. The Cibber text was still being used in these performances, though the play was billed as Shakespeare's.

In England, meanwhile, William Charles Macready attempted to restore Shakespeare's text:

> Though he used Cibber's adaptation, this was a Richard more Shakespearian than most, and his own briefly performed adaptation of Shakespeare, while not successful, demonstrated his aims. His Richard was intellectually supple, witty, proud, and commanding. He was less bitter than Kean, full of an organizing energy, with a passionate enjoyment of his vengeance. The performance was thus witty and controlled, with much evidence of suppressed power.[8]

Henry Irving was praised for finally eliminating Cibber in his production at the Lyceum in 1877. He managed to restore even more of Shakespeare's text in a subsequent revival of 1896. Gone with Cibber's text, though, was his fundamental conception of the role and Irving was blamed for this change of approach. As a reviewer explained in the *Athenaeum*:

> All that is conventional in tragedy is gone, leaving us musing whether after all we were wise in demanding its removal ... We have no 'sawing of the air with your hand thus' [*Hamlet*, 3.2.4–5], and we have no search for the flea in the actor's bosom, as was irreverently described a favourite gesture of Charles Kean, Macready, and Phelps. We have, on the contrary, a polished presentment of Court manners, in which nothing offends and is as nearly as possible real. Where, however, is tragedy? It is gone. Richard III is not now a tragic role. It is what is conventionally called 'a character part'. Very fine is some of the acting, and the character of Richard is charged with a ferocity that is impressive and we dare say original. We are, however, never scorched or electrified. We are gratified, tickled, amused.[9]

The old-style melodrama was still in evidence, for example in John Barrymore's 1920 performance at the Plymouth Theater in New

York, a production which incorporated even more of *3 Henry VI* than Cibber had done. The show lasted until one o'clock in the morning, but still had a rapturous reception. Tyrone Guthrie at the Old Vic in London in 1937 offered, by contrast, an ironic modern production. As the London *Times* reviewer explained:

> Mr Emlyn Williams might have attempted the difficult return to full-blooded stage tradition and sought to carry conviction by storm. Instead he wisely took oblique means to the same end. By giving Richard a humorous relish of his own excesses he did what he could to prevent the audience from smiling at them in the wrong way ... if we were amused, so in his own devilish way was the royal murderer. The actor had cleverly outflanked our criticism of a demoded tragic villain, and at the same time had contrived to make of him an arresting theatrical figure – a figure of stealthy, cat-like cunning, with more perhaps of the poisoner than the soldier in his composition but formidably, relentlessly dominant and consistently exciting.[10]

The Second World War changed attitudes to the play and saw the start of productions which related more or less obliquely to Fascism. Donald Wolfit confessed that his study of Richard in the 1942 production at the Strand Theatre had been influenced by Hitler.[11] The most famous post-war Richard, indeed the most famous Richard of all time thanks to his later film version, was Laurence Olivier. His acclaimed performance reconciled different facets of Richard, as the critic J. C. Trewin recognized:

> A Richard must make his theatrical effects boldly; at the same time he must expose the man's brain. It is the marriage of intellect and dramatic force, of bravura and cold reason, which so distinguishes Mr Laurence Olivier's study at the New Theatre.[12]

Kenneth Tynan analysed Olivier's performance in detail:

> From a sombre and uninventive production this brooding, withdrawn player leapt into life, using the circumambient gloom as his springboard. Olivier's Richard eats into the memory like

acid into metal, but the total impression is one of lightness and deftness. The whole thing is taken at a baffling speed when one recalls how perfectly, even finically, it is articulated: it is Olivier's trick to treat each speech as a kind of plastic vocal mass, and not as a series of sentences whose import must be precisely communicated to the audience: the method is impressionistic. He will seize on one or two phrases in each paragraph which, properly inserted, will unlock its whole meaning: the rest he discards, with exquisite idleness. To do this successfully he needs other people on the stage with him: to be ignored, stared past, or pushed aside during the lower reaches, and gripped and buttonholed when the wave rises to its crested climax. For this reason Olivier tends to fail in soliloquy – except when, as in the opening speech of Richard, it is directed straight at the audience, who then become his temporary foils... Olivier the actor needs reactors: just as electricity, *in vacuo*, is unseen, unfelt, and powerless.[13]

Actors since the 1950s have inevitably felt the burden of Olivier's performance as they have sought to offer their own representations of the role. Despite this a number of actors have succeeded in thoughtful, original and exciting productions of the play; for example, Antony Sher in Bill Alexander's 1984 production, Simon Russell Beale in that of Sam Mendes and Ian McKellen for Richard Eyre at the National Theatre in London in 1992.

The play was edited to form part of Peter Hall and John Barton's radical analysis of power politics, *The Wars of the Roses*, for the RSC in 1963, a production that received great acclaim and that was shown (in much abridged form) on television.

David Wheeler's production at the Cort Theater, New York, starring Al Pacino in 1979, received mixed reviews; Pacino's quest for the essence of the character was further developed in his idiosyncratic film *Looking for Richard* (1996), in which he explores the text and the rehearsal process in a series of workshops while attempting to relate the plot to the world around him. The Rustaveli Company of Soviet Georgia created a highly politicized production in 1979–80. Directed by Robert Sturua, it received rave reviews, especially for physical inventiveness of a kind that also characterized a production by the Odeon Theatre of Bucharest that toured internationally in 1994, making particularly strong use of masks suggestive of Richard's animal crest, the boar. In 2003 Barry Kyle directed the play at the Globe Theatre with an all-female cast. Katherine Hunter's engagingly 'ironic and humorously amoral Richard'[14] was generally admired, as was Linda Bassett's powerful Queen Margaret.

The most notable films have been Laurence Olivier's (1955) and Ian McKellen's (1995). Olivier's was set in the Middle Ages and is theatrical in its use of long shots, which give it a static feel. The diction, especially Olivier's famously clipped tones, now seems dated. For the McKellen film, which was developed out of Richard Eyre's stage production for the National Theatre in London, director Richard Loncraine updated the period and set, relating the play to the 1936 British abdication crisis and the rise of Oswald Mosley's British Union of Fascists. Both movies open spectacularly and employ what film critics call the 'forbidden look': in soliloquy, Olivier and McKellen stare straight into the camera, engaging the audience in a similar manner to the stage actor speaking directly into the auditorium.

AT THE RSC

Richard: A Discovery of Evil

In the last fifty years *Richard III* in performance has come to symbolize evils particularly relevant to our times. When performed as part of a history play cycle involving the three parts of *Henry VI*, the play and the character's significance become part of a wider examination of socio-political concerns. When performed in isolation, the character of Richard becomes dominant, and the play usually delves into psychological territory encompassing modern beliefs on the nature of evil in man. In creating the early RSC landmark production *The Wars of the Roses* in 1963, directors Peter Hall and John Barton edited and rewrote the three parts of *Henry VI* so they could be played in conjunction with *Richard III* as a trilogy. *Richard III* was subsequently performed as part of a sequence involving the *Henry VI* plays in 1988, 2001 and 2006–08.

The Wars of the Roses, strongly influenced by the politically charged, 'alienating', 'epic theatre' of Bertolt Brecht and the work of the Berliner Ensemble, took the play away from an acting tradition which had revolved around the star actor/director. It was a conscious repudiation of the 'Olivier tradition', which, in the words of theatre historian Hugh Richmond, 'was largely marked by an extremely naïve moral structure supposedly excusing a delight in the portrait of melodramatic evil incarnate'. 'We can', Richmond continues, 'find a far greater range of sociological interests in Hall's production than any before it.'[15]

Peter Hall's examination of the tragedy of kingship in the programme note pointed to the dilemma of whether a ruler can remain moral when the instincts which placed him in a position of power are essentially selfish and amoral, animalistic:

> Man in action is basically an animal . . . To hunt better, men unite into packs. Then the man who kills the beast becomes the king, and must kill his rivals to remain king . . . The tension between man the animal in action, murdering to protect, or lying to save, and the moral man trying to rule by a developed human ethic is what makes history tragic. I believe this is still the dilemma of power.[16]

Short in stature and boyish in appearance, Ian Holm cut a remarkably different figure from the likes of Olivier and Christopher Plummer, who played the part for the RSC in 1961. Critics seemed to miss the point of this new-look Richard, commenting on how his physicality diminished his domination of the play. This deliberate choice on the part of the director emphasized that Richard was only one in a long line of pretenders to the throne. What the designer referred to as the 'great steel cage of war' portrayed the battle between the Yorkists and the Lancastrians as a disintegration of the country from feudal to fascist, its protagonists crushed or shaped by the processes of history, and the warring ethos of their families:

'Richard, once on the throne [rules] by police-state methods. The barons supporting him are dressed in the black helmets and jackboots of bully-boy Fascists and tramping in unison to his every command.'[17]

Connecting *Richard III* with the major experience of evil in political form during the twentieth century – the rise of Fascism in Germany, resulting in the election of Hitler and the horrors which followed – demonstrated how the play could be taken away from medieval melodrama and conferred with contemporary relevance. It also pointed to a more nihilistic vision of the play, reminding the audience while they were watching that, although this tyrant was stopped, many more were to follow who were far worse.

In 1974 Barry Kyle's production at The Other Place studio theatre took place in 'an asylum with all the characters dressed in costumes vaguely reminiscent of concentration camps'.[18] Ian Richardson, who played Richard, was fascinated by what he called:

> The schizophrenia . . . in the very last soliloquy, the nightmare one where he seems to be two people talking to each other. The one is some horrid, monstrous spectre, the other what is left of the good soul of Richard, if anything is left at all. Any examination of that soliloquy will show that Richard's mind has completely gone, in much the same way as some of the monsters of our own lifetime – Stalin, Hitler, Idi Amin all spring to mind. This is total schizophrenia born out of megalomania.[19]

In order to make the psychology behind his Richard something recognizable, Henry Goodman (2003) found a parallel for Richard's deranged mind with modern fictional serial killers, such as Hannibal Lecter. Similarly, actor Antony Sher described how he looked at the behaviour of recent real-life serial killers in order to get a handle on Richard's completely amoral behaviour. Dennis Nilsen was a British serial killer who lived in London; during a murderous spree which started in 1978 and lasted five years, he killed more than a dozen men in his home and disposed of the bodies in his garden, attic and other rooms about his house. Reading up on the case in preparation to play Richard, Sher became fascinated by the banal normality of elements of the psychopath's character sitting alongside the perversity.

Richard's 'unnatural' tendencies are linked in the text with animal imagery. In Elizabethan times man was held to be the highest of creatures and exhibiting animalistic behaviour was seen as a fall from grace, a sin against the order of the universe, which rendered the sinner somehow subhuman. In Shakespeare, characters who upset the natural order of things, whether turning against their family members or against the state, are often referred to as predatory or poisonous animals. Richard is referred to as a 'poisonous bunch-backed toad', a 'bottled spider'. In productions of *Richard III* these beliefs about 'unnatural' behaviour are embodied in Richard's deformity, physically demonstrating his twisted nature and his closeness to the animal world. In 1970 Norman Rodway repulsed many a critic by his resemblance to swine: 'He lumbers onstage at Stratford, blinking at the sun: his great pig-head appears to have been crew-cut, and some animal's skin is slung over his hump.'[20] Antony Sher (1984) paid more attention to the spider-like qualities of Richard as he weaved his web of deception around the court: 'The central image of his Richard he built on the "bottled spider," the assumption being that here was a creature too venomous to be set free.'[21]

The most dominant characteristic of the Sher portrayal was his use of crutches to give Richard an extraordinary mobility: 'huge black arachnid-legs which flew him across the stage in giant leaps, and which he used as extension limbs to fight off attackers, beat lackeys and, in one famous moment, lift Lady Anne's skirt and probe between her legs'.[22] Dressed entirely in black throughout most of the production he appeared for the opening soliloquy like a black spider emerging through the finely-wrought gothic screen which covered the stage, from the tombs of the dead, which lay behind in darkness. The *Sunday Times* critic described the effect:

> The opening lines are spoken quietly, almost didactically; but with 'But I, that am not framed for sportive tricks' [1.1.14], Sher advances menacingly on the audience, his body swinging like a

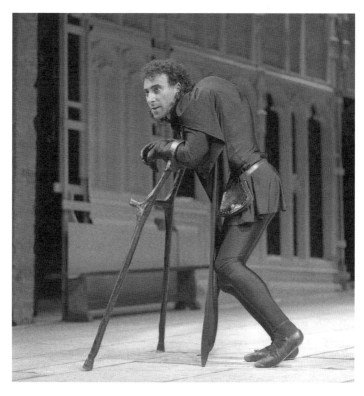

2. Bottled spider with crutches – Antony Sher, 1984.

missile on the adeptly manipulated callipers that support it, his hump displayed with a kind of inverted pride . . . we are spellbound by a sense of fiendish energy and huge physical strength.[23]

Simon Russell Beale (1992) admitted: 'I haven't the physical dexterity to play him as a spider, as Tony Sher did. I'm the "bunchbacked toad".'[24] This was another performance much admired by the critics:

He supremely shows physical self-hatred rebounding into social revenge . . . Shrouded in ankle-length cloaks hiding who knows what deformities, small flat head rocking with reptilian cunning on a roll of neck fat, he outdoes even Queen Margaret's catalogue of bestial comparisons.[25]

We are first aware of him not as a body, however, but as an undefined threat, a sinister creaking noise as he paces about shrouded in darkness.[26]

A stick is heard tapping across the stage, the lights go up, and there he is with his scrubbed skull, pink jowls and vast hump: a depraved blend of Mr Punch and A. A. Milne's Piglet, gloating over the havoc he will wreak.[27]

Many actors have found Richard's deformity a pitiable circumstance, motivating his decision to 'prove a villain' and take the path of evil. Like Iago, he despises the beauty in other people's lives that makes him seem ugly by comparison. Unlike Iago, he is outwardly marked and this sets him apart: 'I am myself alone'. Deformity lay at the centre of Alan Howard's performance in 1980. This is how various newspaper critics described the performance:

Howard's Gloucester is not an unfathomable monster; still less a scourge of God visited upon a sacrilegious land. He is a cripple getting even with those who have the use of their legs . . . Besides the surgical boot, Mr Howard is encumbered with a chain round the left thigh which he has to tug to get the leg moving.[28]

His dangling right arm seems to contain a built-in dagger ever ready to point at people's throats.[29]

Where all recent Richards have limped and scuttled efficiently round the stage, this one is uncomfortable, liable to stumble, often in pain . . . while Buckingham talks to the citizens, he practises a straight walk with slow agonized concentration, a performance he repeats at his coronation. . . . As this Richard's preoccupation with his grotesque body grows, so does his suspicious isolation from those around him. When Buckingham lightly says that he would play the orator 'as if the fee were for myself', he eyes him with real suspicion . . . This is no Mr Punch, but the bitter self-hating Richard of an earlier tradition.[30]

David Troughton, who played Richard in the manner of a sinister clown in Steven Pimlott's 1995 production, was helped in his performance by relating Richard's deformity to a genuine medical condition:

> According to history, Richard had come into the world feet first, a breach birth ... As Richard was dragged out by his feet, one of his hips might have been displaced causing extreme discomfort all his life. As he grew up, because of the pain of walking, a severe limp would develop, forcing his spine to grow crooked, giving the appearance of one shoulder being higher than the other ... His arm could also have been deformed at birth or through an illness such as polio. In pain all his life? What an insight into a character. Here was one very simple explanation for Richard's malevolence.[31]

In modern productions Richard is also often associated with childishness, exhibiting the selfish amorality of a young child who only sees his own needs. This might be the arrested development of a man of war in a domestic, social world. Anton Lesser (1988) described how, in the first half of the play, Richard 'is entirely concerned with getting':

> 'I want that, I want that' and then 'I've got it, I've got it ... Oh, I'm bored now.' So I decided to rush to the throne with a scream of possessive delight and leap into it ... they all go and just leave him sitting there on his own in a throne that is miles too big for him, his legs dangling down like a little child's, quite unable to reach the floor. The pathos of that image is important at this pivotal point in the play, the wild excitement of leaping into that seat followed in a second or two by the loneliness and stillness of the little figure dwarfed by it.[32]

In Sean Holmes' 2003 production childhood became an essential theme and part of the scenic design, even extending to the throne, which looked like an outsized high chair:

> [A] rocking-horse became connected with the young Duke of York, Richard's namesake ... it provided a link with Richard's own childhood ... on a horse, even a rocking horse, he is freed of his deformity and becomes big and grown-up and cured of his illness ... at the end, the rocking horse would reappear when ... the

ghosts were revealed, young York now riding it with terrible energy, and Richard's cry 'My kingdom for a horse' taking on a disturbing sense of the need to escape again into childhood innocence.[33]

The production also featured inclusion of an unscripted character, 'a page, a young boy in his own image . . . a frequent, silent presence near Richard, his only companion'.[34]

In 1970 Norman Rodway's performance verged on that of the naughty adolescent. When sealing Hastings' fate at the council meeting, he 'fairly shrieks with delight as he jumps away from Hastings, leaving him holding what's supposed to be a withered arm'.[35] As reviewer D. A. N. Jones put it:

We are in a haunted nursery, with a toy-box full of sharp swords and real skulls . . . Richard, himself puerile, likes playing with children; he has a dressing-up box, with wigs and rusty armour, which he uses when stage-managing his coups. There's a fascinating sequence, while he is awaiting news from the Lord Mayor, when he simply fidgets and makes faces, like a bored and repulsive toddler.[36]

The other side of Richard is the side he shows to the audience, the actor, the comedian, the arch-manipulator. By use of humour Richard gets the audience on his side, so that, in the first half of the play, when he commits some hideous act, the audience cannot help but laugh with him. This humour is of the blackest kind, also making the audience complicit, a fact that, if the production is done well, they should later regret. This black comedy, 'pushing the extremes of horror and farce',[37] is very modern and in tune with contemporary tastes, the technique having been adopted by many directors of horror films.*

---

* In *Man Bites Dog* (Belgium, 1992, dir. Rémy Belvaux) and *The Last Horror Movie* (UK, 2003, dir. Julian Richards), the serial killer, like Richard, talks to the audience directly about his actions, plots and feelings (or lack of them) about what he does, often comically. These films, including others such as *Funny Games* (Austria, 1997, dir. Michael Haneke), act as an indictment against media violence and the viewers' ability to watch violent acts without appropriate emotion. Ultimately, they shock the audience back into a sense of their own humanity. As with *Richard III* there is a breaking point between the audience and the protagonist where laughter dies and creeping horror takes hold, not least because of their earlier complicity through humour.

Many productions have emphasized Richard the self-conscious actor. In 2003 Henry Goodman emerged through a traditional red curtain for his soliloquy and was picked out by a spotlight. Goodman's intention was to:

> make absolutely clear was that Richard has to dress up for this new summer of opportunity . . . And it sickens him . . . In performance, I became so debonair and deft as the opening character, audiences thought I was playing an actor who strips off his clothes and plays Richard – but that is never what I intended.[38]

3. Richard the showman – Henry Goodman, 2003.

Observer critic Susannah Clapp described the effect:

> Cock-eyed, hobble-legged, leering with scorn, Henry Goodman gives us Richard III as angry showman. As he nuzzles into Queen Anne's breast, he rolls a knowing eye at the audience . . . From the beginning, Sean Holmes's Edwardian production underlines the idea of Richard as the manic trickster . . . He delivers the

winter of discontent speech as a rapid music-hall turn, garishly snickering and capering.[39]

The horror of the violence on stage is often relieved by moments of nervous laughter. On the line about dogs barking at him, Goodman's Richard 'limps into the wings and stabs some poor yelping cur to death'.[40] The beheading of Hastings has provided ample opportunity for 'horrid laughter'. In 1995 David Troughton explained how:

> During the mock siege of London, Hastings's severed head ... covered in a white, blooded cloth, is brought on by Ratcliffe, invariably causing a laugh of revulsion from the audience as it is hurled into the air, landing on stage with a heavy thud. This is perfectly in keeping with the humorous charade that Richard is perpetrating, and indeed, I heighten the moment by stabbing my knife through it, then presenting the skewered head to the Mayor of London. More laughter follows. The blade, however, gets stuck and only comes free with a struggle ... which heightens the audience's gleeful horror.[41]

In 2003, Hastings' head was accidentally trodden on and tripped over by Richard. Likewise, in Bill Alexander's 1984 production the head of Hastings was thrown from one character to another like a rugby ball, testing the Mayor's loyalty to Richard when he is obliged to join in the game:

> When the head was tossed about, the audience froze; but seconds later they were thawed by laughter ... He was, flat-out, a man obsessed with power, a man who wanted to attain the throne as quickly as possible, and a man who wanted to have fun along the way ... and he demands that we engage in it with him.[42]

Simon Russell Beale (1992) was so repulsive in appearance that when he came onto the stage, the sound of barking dogs heralded his entrance. The historian David Starkey, doubling as a theatre reviewer, gave a good account:

He is wearing Doc Martens, dark pegtop trousers, a long scruffy coat and an open-necked shirt.... This is Richard the alternative comedian ... The head is shaven; the eyes pop; the lips stretch hungrily; the body distends like an air-cushion with a spring inside ... The effect is grotesque and horribly funny; pure slapstick, when Richard squashes a dish of strawberries on his forehead to simulate a wound to persuade the Lord Mayor the reality of the plot against him.[43]

The idea of Richard as 'jester' or comedian was built into the costume design of the 1992 production, with David Troughton donning an 'Elizabethan-looking doublet together with very odd short culottes', giving Richard 'a mischievous "Mr Punch" feel ... not only was he a joker, he was an evil joker, bent on mass destruction for his own ends which made him very dangerous indeed – the funny man in red whom no-one suspects ... smiling as he stabs his victims in the back'.[44]

Cursing Women

Richard's lack of understanding with regard to women proves his downfall. Actor Henry Goodman noted that 'there is a real misogyny about Richard as he fantasizes about love but is incapable of giving or receiving it. In his deformity he reasons ... that love is something he will never receive because of the world's love of beauty.'[45]

The cursing of Richard by his mother is often performed as the moment which undoes him, shakes him out of his bravura, unsettles him and seals his fate. For David Troughton's Richard, the twisted relationship between mother and son was central to the character. His hatred of the world was derived from the Duchess of York's complete absence of love for him. For his meeting with his mother in the fourth act he placed himself, with great awkwardness, on the ground, his head in her lap. Wanting her blessing he received only her curse. Director Steven Pimlott identified it as 'a peculiarly terrible scene, a mother cursing her child in a way that is unique in Shakespeare'. Open-mouthed with horror (Troughton was influenced by Edvard Munch's famous painting *The Scream*), Richard 'hurled himself away from her and towards the crown which he had placed on the ground'.[46]

Anton Lesser described the devastating effect the mother's curse had on his Richard:

> She needs to express the horror at what she has given birth to ... to make it terminal. 'I shall never speak to thee again.' ... In our production Richard's response was punctuated by his rhythmically wounding himself in the hand with his dagger. The idea I wanted to express was that he feels he must hurt, must mutilate himself because if he doesn't he will kill his mother in his rage at what, in his eyes, she has been responsible for.[47]

The curse on Alan Howard's Richard (1980) created a mental disturbance from which he never recovered: 'His mother's curse leaves him so shattered that he plays the next scene with Elizabeth in earnest, as though he might really find in her a new mother. From then on he is on the edge of madness.'[48]

The duchess' lack of motherly love has an impact on how Richard relates to other women in the play. The 'wooing' scene of Lady Anne reveals much but, often heavily cut in performance, is a particularly difficult scene to make convincing. Actor Anton Lesser explains:

> Richard must not be seen by Anne to be 'acting'. The more she is confused about how genuine his feelings are, the more unbalancing it will be for her ... Richard bases his strategy on attack: everything she accuses him of he accepts, with the proviso that everything he has done he has done for her. He makes her, quite specifically, an 'accessory' ... producing a sense of guilt ... she is forced into the belief that it was her body, her physicality, all that she as a devout Christian is trying to rise above, which provoked his behaviour. The idea we were aiming for was that guilt about her own sexuality, rather than any particular attraction towards his, is what governs her behaviour here.[49]

Lisa Stevenson, who played Lady Anne in 2003, found a truth to the scene through this guilt, and through the belief in the centrality of cursing to the structure of the play:

> A lot of women suffer from guilt when they're grieving ... So when Richard comes along and tells Anne that it is her fault that her husband and father-in-law died, she was so vulnerable that on some weird level she believed it. I think that's why she doesn't kill him ... I had an idea for the play that the sickness might be pregnancy-related ... when she returns as a ghost, she says 'thy wife, that wretched Anne ... That never slept a quiet hour with thee'. I think Richard has been raping her and I think that it's been horrific ... Her prophecy about Richard's marriage comes true: 'If ever he have wife, let her be made / ... miserable'. And she says 'If ever he have child, abortive be it / Prodigious and untimely brought to life'. I had an idea that I was going to know that I was pregnant and the baby (Richard's baby) was going to have died in my womb, but still be there, which would lead to terrible blood poisoning.[50]

In other productions Lady Anne has been portrayed as slightly more resistant and knowing than the text suggests. Although Aislin McGuckin (2000) put up 'a particularly dignified resistance to his wooing', she seemed 'grimly aware that in doing so she has signed her own death warrant'.[51] Annabelle Apsion as Lady Anne in 1992 'calls his bluff to the extent of actually nicking his proffered breast with his sword. For a split second, Richard is disoriented by the drawn blood, but then his cold, appraising eyes flick back to Anne, keenly monitoring how this upset may work to his advantage.'[52]

However, there have also been productions where Lady Anne's desperate state has made her a more willing conquest. Of Terry Hands' 1980 production one critic wrote:

> 'Did you not kill this King?' 'I grant ye.' I have never heard this cheeky exchange without it raising a laugh until last night when it was lost in the high-speed passionate crescendo between [Alan] Howard and Sinead Cusack, which is played towards her capitulation with the drive of an orgasm.[53]

Lady Anne (Sinead Cusack)...throws off her black gown at the moment of her submission to reveal a warm red dress beneath.[54]

For his production in 1970 Hands' direction suggested that:

her attraction is a kind of kinkiness...One moment she is self-righteously whacking him over the back with a large cross, in a naïve attempt to exorcise him; the next, she is giggling and dabbling lips with him, notwithstanding the corpse of her husband nearby. The hand-maiden of the Lord is abruptly revealed as the Devil's concubine.[55]

In 1984 and 2001 Queen Elizabeth became the prime target of Richard's misogynistic rage. The *Times Literary Supplement* reviewer of Michael Boyd's production (2001) commented:

His wooing of her – as mother-in-law, rather than as wife... seems almost more of a showdown than the one soon to ensue on Bosworth Field...At first traumatized into shaking incoherence by her husband's death, she discovers reserves of strength and eloquence that make her, theatrically, Richard's most potent antagonist. As a tall, intelligent, determined woman of non-royal birth, she embodies all that Richard finds most threatening.[56]

In 1984 the tussle between the two of them was played as more physical than verbal. The critic Chris Hassel wrote in the *Shakespeare Quarterly* that:

[Antony] Sher is brutal with Elizabeth from the start. He forces her face to him with his sceptre. He pulls her around by the bodice to make her face him again on the throne. Once he throws her to the ground. But she is not without her own weapons against this intimidation. She has those withering words of irony...also...a venomous kiss for Richard at the end, from which he recoils as from an adder's sting.[57]

Like a primeval spirit conjured by both grief past and grief to come, Margaret emerges as the embodiment of female revenge. Her curses on the court prophesy the play's events and, almost too late, the distressed wives and mothers desire knowledge of her powers in order to stop Richard. Margaret's evocation of ancient tribalism is often emphasized in modern productions by representations of witchcraft. In 2001, Fiona Bell, who also played Queen Margaret in the three parts of *Henry VI*, carried the bones of her dead son around with her in a sack, taking them out and arranging them as a human skeleton when conjuring her curses on the court. Penny Downie, who played Margaret in 1988, explained how:

> one could see her as this ageless figure of moral nemesis, who brings on to the stage the entire Wars of the Roses and who has herself been purified by suffering to play this final moral role . . . People have to hear the curse if it is to work . . . Like an aborigine pointing the bone – you have to believe you are going to die if you are going to die. And the fact is that they all do believe in these curses, none more so than Richard.[58]

In 1992, Cherry Morris as Margaret 'intoned from a chalk circle',[59] and appeared at the death of each of Richard's victims:

> The almost ritual manner in which all of Margaret's prophetic curses are fulfilled is brought out by the simple but powerful way [Sam] Mendes has her stand aloft each time in one of the doors of the back-screen and reintone the curse over the last speeches of Richard's various victims.[60]

At the battle of Bosworth Field, when Richard was on the point of victory, the appearance of Margaret 'mesmerises him and seals his doom'.[61]

Providence and the Supernatural

> It is interesting that Shakespeare doesn't write 'The Battle', as he does in other History plays. He writes 12 or 14 pages on the night before the Battle of Bosworth and about a page on the battle. Which means that, in a way, Richard's battle is lost the night before it has begun.[62]

Traditional religious imagery of good and evil often permeates modern productions, making powerful statements on the nature of providence. For Adrian Noble's 1988 production Anton Lesser described how:

> The goblet in which Ratcliffe brought the wine ... has something of symbolic potency for Richard in his dream, so that the cup of wine becomes the communion cup, the blood of Christ ... here is a symbol of retribution, deliverance, sin, forgiveness, ceremony, final judgement ... when he snaps back into consciousness, and realizes it was all a dream, the power of all those curses hits him: 'I shall despair' – and die. The impact of that was increased, we felt, by having Richard also hear what is said to Richmond ... During [the soliloquy that follows the dream] he continues verbally the action of stabbing himself, which in our production, had followed his mother's curse. He pins himself like a butterfly to a board ... he cannot escape the truth ... It is as though a veil has been taken away from Richard; he has been in a state of deep illusion, not just through the dream but through his life, and the curtain has now been drawn back and he looks in the mirror and sees every line on his own face – like the picture of Dorian Gray.[63]

David Troughton described something similar in his 1995 rendition of the role:

> Alone at last, Richard attempts a final reconciliation with the audience and God. I take both the bread and the wine and set up a simple altar on the rubble-strewn stage, using my cross-handled dagger as a primitive crucifix. But instead of finding a restored friendship and possible redemption in this act of the Last Sacrament, on drinking the blood of Christ I conjure up a manifestation of the audience's hatred; the ghosts of all Richard's past victims who sit beside him at a large oblong table, surrounding the beatific Richmond, praying for Richard's defeat and the future King Henry's success. The image of Jesus and his disciples looms large but this time it is Richard, the devil, and not Richmond, the Son of God, who has certainly had his Last Supper.[64]

This approach has continuity with William Hogarth's famous painting of David Garrick at the same moment, in which the crucifix in prominent.

The Ghosts are also effective representatives of the force of providence. In 1984 they emerged from behind four large tombs which dominated the gothic set:

> Each ghost holds a single candle. Smoke swirls around their feet...Some, of course, have been buried there since Tewkesbury. Each prophesies with the stillness of truth; each remains on stage as the others appear. Occasionally all echo key words of prayer and prophecy, like participants in a supernatural ritual.[65]

Michael Boyd in 2001, and again when his production was revived and adapted in 2007–08, populated his stage with the Ghosts of the dead, 'emphasising the mad futility of the endless cycle of revenge killings, which only ends with the arrival of the future Henry VII at the end of Richard III'.[66] The Shakespearean scholar Barbara Hodgdon provides an excellent account:

> At Richard III's coronation...the huge upstage doors opened, revealing a procession of ghostly victims...Among them...was Margaret, leading her dead son, and then Henry VI, robed in white, entered to prostrate himself on the floor, hands outstretched as though crucified. Last of all was York, and it was he who proclaimed 'God save King Richard, of that name the third!' echoed by the others...the line between the dead and the living began to blur: apparitions all, caught momentarily in the 'bottled spider's' web...[Following the battle and Richard's demise]... With Richard's body lying alone on stage, all drew back: standing in the exits and aisles, they watched him rise...and prepare to leave. But as he turned upstage to go, the doors of the fortress opened: there stood Henry VI, all in white. For an instant, the two faced one another, double faces of kingship: Richard, symptomatic of the tyranny of the individual...Henry, his complete opposite...Richard's mantra – 'I am myself alone' – seemed to apply equally to them both.[67]

The Ghosts almost always appear in the final battle in order to oversee the working out of the curse, and sometimes to actively assist in Richard's execution. In 1980, Terry Hands 'pull[ed] out all the stops at the end with the ghosts of all Richard's victims lining up at Bosworth and crowding round him in clusters while Richmond puts the sword in...it certainly gives you the sense that England has been purged of evil'.[68] In 1998:

> Instead of visiting Richard in a dream in his tent on the eve of Bosworth, the ghosts of his casualties wait to intervene and distract him with counsels of despair in his climactic sword fight with Jo Stone-Fewing's squeaky-clean Richmond. The spectres of the young princes jump with demonic playfulness on Richard's shoulder and pop up between his legs. The transpositions give graphic emphasis to the idea that it is the recognition of what he has done, rather than Richmond that defeats him.[69]

Terry Hands' first (1970) production omitted the final battle, and instead Richard was 'encircled by ghosts of his murdered victims, who perform a dance of death'[70] and then lead him off stage.

In 1995 the Ghosts of Richard's victims had occupied a specific area of the stage during the production. At the end of the play the battle again was omitted and Richard was not murdered but, aware of the inevitability of his death, put down his sword and made his way to the Ghosts' area, watch by them from above. After Richmond's final speech he gave him a slow ironic handclap.

ACTOR, DIRECTOR AND DESIGNER: INTERVIEWS WITH SIMON RUSSELL BEALE (Richard, 1992), BILL ALEXANDER (director, 1984) and TOM PIPER (designer, 2006)

The Actor: Simon Russell Beale, born in 1961, studied at Cambridge University. He came to prominence as a Shakespearean actor with the RSC in the early 1990s, when he played Thersites in *Troilus and Cressida*, Ariel in *The Tempest* and Richard III in the production discussed here, which toured the country in an intimate, mobile auditorium set up in sports halls in towns that generally lacked access to professional theatre. All three productions were directed by Sam Mendes, with whom Beale has continued to work in Shakespearean and other classical roles, including Iago at London's National Theatre and Malvolio at Mendes' Donmar Warehouse. Also a notable Hamlet at the National, he is especially admired for the intelligence of his verse-speaking.

The Director: Bill Alexander, born in 1948, trained as a theatre director at the Bristol Old Vic. He joined the RSC as an Assistant Director in 1977 and then became a resident Director in 1980. His reputation was strongly established through three productions starring Sir Antony Sher: *Tartuffe* and a play about its author Molière, and then the *Richard III* of 1984, which he talks about here. The experience of being in this famous production, which transferred to London's Barbican Theatre in 1985 and then toured internationally the following year, was recorded by Sher in his book *The Year of the King*. From 1992 to 2000, Bill Alexander was Artistic Director of the Birmingham Repertory Theatre.

The Designer: Tom Piper was appointed Royal Shakespeare Company Associate Designer in 2003. He graduated from Trinity College, Cambridge, before training at the Slade School of Art. He has designed productions from pantomime to opera, staged in every kind of theatre including the Royal National Theatre, Abbey Theatre Dublin, Lyric Hammersmith Studio and the Royal Albert Hall. His sets are characterized by striking uncluttered designs which allow imaginative use of the stage space. Materials tend to be stylish but undecorated: wood, metal, plain coloured cloth. He designed RSC Artistic Director Michael Boyd's tetralogy of the three parts of *Henry VI* and *Richard III* in both their small-scale versions in the intimate Swan Theatre (2000) and their larger-scale reincarnation in the Stratford Courtyard Theatre and the London Roundhouse (2006–08).

In terms of Shakespeare's vision of the Wars of the Roses and the eventual resolution at Bosworth Field, with Henry Richmond becoming king and inaugurating the Tudor dynasty, the world of the play is very medieval, very fifteenth century. At the same time, the rise and fall of a tyrant is a perennial historical theme, and there have been very successful productions set in, say, 1930s Germany or the Baghdad of Saddam Hussein. What sort of a setting did you and your designer choose, and why?

BA: We chose a medieval setting. Our starting point was the relationship between this early play of Shakespeare's and the great cycles of mystery and miracle plays that were fading memories during the writer's youth. Richard seemed to me a direct descendant of the Vice figure in these plays – wicked yet beguiling; fascinating, seductive and deadly. At least this is his starting point, but his tragedy is to develop a conscience, or at least a terrifying sense of self-consciousness that also forms a bridge from the ritualistic, allegorical past to the emergent psychologically realistic present that Shakespeare was helping to create. The set was modelled on the interior of the chapter house in Worcester Cathedral, linking the play to the roots of medieval religious drama. The central character's mental progress from mythical mask of evil to vulnerable self-awareness for me shaped the play. Analogies with figures such as Hitler or Saddam seemed pointlessly superficial, nor did I want to lose the significance of the *actual* historical moment – late medieval to early modern – and *its* relevance to now.

TP: The designer works with the director through discussions, sketches and models to create the world of the play – an environment in which the actors can tell the story dressed in clothes that reflect their nature, wealth and status within that world. That world may alter over time as characters and their situations change. With a Shakespeare play especially, where so much of the sense of location is given by the language, the design needs only to be suggestive and does not have to slavishly create a real location. As *Richard III* moves swiftly from street to tower to court to battle, the set design needs to be a springboard for the imagination of the audience, to transport them instantly from place to place. The director then works with the actors through rehearsal

4. Tom Piper's set design for Michael Boyd's history cycle at Stratford-upon-Avon: a bare platform with a cylindrical metallic tower behind. Entrances could be made through the clanging doors or down ladders and ropes. Ghosts and overhearers could appear in the recess above the doors.

to discover the meaning of the text, and how best to tell the story in the created world.

I tend to believe that there are broadly three periods in which you can set a play: the period it is set in, the time it was written, or now. Any other time setting risks adding another layer of interpretation; for example, seeing the play set in 1930s Germany has all the layers of our twenty-first-century interpretation of that time and place imposed on a play written in the sixteenth century.

Our production was in effect *Henry VI Part 4*, as it played on the back of the earlier trilogy and, for practical changeover reasons between one play and the next, had to be played in the same basic environment. Those *Henry VI* plays were definitely medieval in feel, with clothes influenced by medieval references. But at the end of *Henry VI Part 3* King Edward calls for an end to bloodshed – the dawning of a glorious summer is promised and the past will be left behind. So for *Richard III* we decided to break with the past and create a contemporary world influenced by, but not directly copying, Eastern European political situations.

Where did you start with Richard, from a physical/stylistic point of view? With prosthetics? With changing attitudes to bodily difference (we no longer regard physical disability as a sign of divine disapproval…)? Or perhaps with the play's imagery: he's variously described as a spider, boar, wolf and 'poisonous bunch-backed toad'?

BA: In the first week of rehearsal Tony Sher (who played Richard) and I were taken to the Wardrobe Department to find that all previous humps had been lined up for our inspection, and we were invited to choose between Ian Holm's hump, Alan Howard's lump, Norman Rodway's hump, etc. etc. We politely said we'd like our own hump. In fact there were three humps used in performance: one worn for the majority of scenes; one under the armour for the battle with a specially designed slit for Richmond's sword as he ritualistically plunged it deep into Richard's back as he knelt praying; and a third hump (very detailed and realistic, and very expensive!) as he and Lady Anne knelt, backs to the audience, during their wedding, stripped naked to the waist as was the custom. I inserted the wedding ceremony, which is not in the play, asking our composer Guy Woolfenden to write a dramatic piece of wedding music closely modelled on *Carmina Burana*. He never stopped worrying about being sued by Carl Orff!

SRB: Unusually for me I was very keen to get a visual image for him early on. I'm not usually concerned that early on about how I look, but in this case I did want to get an image of him. I suppose that's the nature of the part because you've got to face the question of his disability. I didn't actually use so much of the spider, boar, wolf, toad imagery as the nature of his job. I had this idea that he should look like a retired American footballer. A soldier who had gone to seed. It was his job before that was important for me – that he should look massive and muscled, old muscle. I had a body suit with a hump put in, as a lot of Richards do, and gradually realized that it was looking like a toad. We just happened to slip into one of the images for him, which was quite interesting. And it was picked up on by people that I looked like a toad. But it came from his work as a soldier rather than anything from the imagery of the play. I knew that we were going to do a broadsword fight – although it wasn't a period production in the design sense, they fought with broadswords at the end – so I wanted the heavy look of someone who was used to wielding a broadsword, with huge shoulders. The hump just became a continuation of those muscles on his back.

TP: The starting point really had to be with the actor (Jonathan Slinger) and how he wanted to approach the part, rather than imposing any ideas of how he might be disabled. Jonathan was keen to explore a journey in the character through his route from third son of York to eventual king. There is a brilliant monologue in *Henry VI Part 3*, where Richard first talks to the audience directly, in which he accepts his disabilities, which up to that point he has been keen to cover up, and starts almost to celebrate his deformity. We began by assuming that the young Richard would not have had any special clothes made, but at the same time would try to be quite dandyish and youthful, thrilled by the violence around him. He sported a wolfish fur coat over a basic black robe, which did come from the bottled spider line, and a wig to cover a large birthmark over his temple. At the end of the monologue he ripped off the wig, exposing the vivid stain: 'I am myself alone'. I did some research into spinal deformities and we created a hump that would be appropriate. It is dangerous to actually build up a foot to create a limp, so the limping and the withered arm is created through Jonathan's movement. In *Richard III* he was in a contemporary black suit and polo neck (a reference to [Russian President] Putin), with a leg brace strapped over his trousers.

And psychologically? 'Since I cannot prove a lover ... I am determinèd to prove a villain' sounds like a 'compensation' theory of character, doesn't it? In defence of my client, m'lud, he may be a serial killer but you see he was a misfit as a child ... that sort of thing? – or emphatically not?

SRB: That was inevitably part of the psychological make-up, although I suspect that compensation behaviour, which is what I probably did alight on, was as much to do with his relationship with his parents. I remember being very keen that in Richard's mind his father was an adored figure, a hero figure. We ignored the *Henry VI* plays, but I just had the image of him as having had a relationship with a strong and powerful father who didn't acknowledge his disabilities, but treated him as an equal with his other sons. That is in contrast of course with his mother. The scene when she lambasts him was about her revealing, consciously or unconsciously, what she has always felt about him, and what he, consciously or unconsciously, perhaps unconsciously, knew that she thought about him. It was a question of him realizing that she has always regarded him as some sort of diseased, malformed creature, as opposed to his brothers, and his father never thought that. That was what was going through my mind. He was hurt by it, but it wasn't unexpected. It just confirmed what he'd always thought about his mother. So I think it was as much to do with the mother and the father as with him compensating for being deformed, although that is obviously an element of it. It's a bit of simple bravado at the beginning. 'I can do this, you just watch me.' I remember during another production the director Roger Michell saying something to me that I always use now, which is to cast the audience in a role for the soliloquy. For instance Iago couldn't give a shit about what the audience thinks, and that's their role. Hamlet wants friends, somebody to help him. Richard is the leader of the gang. It's like he's saying 'You wait till you see me do this. I'm going to do something so unexpected, like woo Lady Anne, and I will do it, I promise.' I think that's part of the compensation theory too.

The sheer quantity of 'back story' is a problem for the audience of this play, isn't it? Did you have particular ways of dealing with that? There's a venerable tradition, going back to Colley Cibber in the eighteenth century, of importing large chunks from *Henry VI Part 3*.

BA: I think *Richard III* stands alone well as a story even when detached from the three parts of *Henry VI*. There would perhaps be an argument for cutting large chunks, or indeed all, of the Queen Margaret scenes, as the play does need cutting anyway, but even in those the vividness of the psychological conflict carries its own explanatory narrative. He changed a lot as a writer between *Henry VI* and *Richard III* and it has a completely different feel from the earlier plays. It stands alone without great knowledge of the back story. *Henry VI* 1, 2 and 3 are Chronicle plays, almost pageant-like in their parade of incident. *Richard III*, on the other hand, is on the way to becoming a full-blown psychodrama of the type finally perfected with *Macbeth* a decade later. It doesn't really feel like the fourth part of tetralogy. But it is a strange hybrid in some ways with some scenes that verge on the ritualistic.

TP: The set was the same but the characters were now in a stylized modern dress. For those actors who were playing the same character as they had in *Henry VI Part 3*, I tried to create a look that reflected their period costumes in silhouette and colour, yet were contemporary in feel. So, for example, Edward and Elizabeth end *Henry VI Part 3* in white coronation robes, and in *Richard III* they were both dressed in long cream coats. Some characters, like Margaret, we deliberately left in a broken-down version of their period look from *Henry VI*. As we had the same actress playing both the young, sexy Margaret in *Henry VI Part 1* and the old Margaret in *Richard III*, it was a way of suggesting that she had aged, without applying prosthetics – she became a more stylized, mythic character. The great advantage of doing the tetralogy of plays together is that the back story is so much clearer, and the audience have seen how Richard's personality has been forged in the brutality of the Wars of the Roses. Margaret's cycles of curses, and Richard's hatred of her, have a greater resonance when you have seen her stab his father York in the back.

What was the journey that you went on with regard to Richard's relationship with Buckingham? That's crucial, isn't it?

BA: Yes, it certainly is a central relationship. Our starting point was to make the audience believe it would last. Or *could* last. We have to believe in Richard's capacity to generate a sense of security in someone who thinks of themselves as a friend. Most of his immediate male colleagues seem to regard him as loyal, honest, funny and friendly. Most of them seem to actually like him as he is so effective

5. Jonathan Slinger as Richard in Michael Boyd's production.

at portraying himself as one of the blokes. A good egg. Only the women suspect him. Only the women ever refer to his deformity. From the assumption that Buckingham was an ambitious politician we wanted to go one stage further and have him regard Richard as not only trustworthy but innocent, and therefore potentially *gullible*. We imagined that it was at the back of Buckingham's mind that he may be able to double-cross Richard in the future.

SRB: In our production Buckingham was smooth, educated; a class political act with a class political brain. In a way he was the brains behind the operation. One of my favourite moments in the play was the scene when the princes return to London. I was waiting there with balloons for them, and the Prince of Wales says of the Tower, 'Did Julius Caesar build that place, my lord?' Buckingham answers, but in our version 'my lord' went to me. Richard gave a face to suggest 'I don't know and I care less.' Buckingham had to step in and reply. In other words, Richard's political instinct was to do with a deep-seated psychological need to prove himself, but with no real political sophistication behind it. It was just brute desire. Whereas Buckingham was much more subtle. He has the idea of pretending to be religious, he's the PR man, he can spin. Of course what is so fantastic about it is that in the end brute force wins.

When I was crowned, I was very keen that Richard should want to make it a fabulous occasion. Originally I wore very obvious make-up, because I'd read that George VI had to wear make-up and that these were very staged events. The make-up was cut eventually, but Richard was dressed in a glorious, very long, blue cloak and as he went towards the throne he got tangled in the cloak and fell. The sheer biting humiliation of that sent him into a fury. The person he reached for was Buckingham, and quite precisely, because he had to rely on Buckingham to help him up, that meant that he had to go. That was the immediate psychological reaction to having been humiliated in front of everybody – that he would have to get rid of the man who helped him. That was a mini-version of the bigger version, which is that he had to be got rid of anyway as he'd served his purpose and become too dangerous. There is a part of Buckingham's psychology which is that help is humiliation in the political sphere.

And the development of Richard's language, especially in soliloquy? Is there a huge change as the play unfolds, beginning from the astonishing confidence of the opening monologue and culminating in the fragmentation of the nightmare before the battle?

BA: Absolutely. The language reflects the change from theatrical and impish self-confidence to terrified self-awareness. It also reflects

6. Simon Russell Beale (*right*) as a sinisterly jovial Richard with balloons for the princes.

a change in his relationship with the audience, from confiding in a huge crowd of assumed admirers to a deserted man, bereft of an audience, with no one to talk to but himself; trying to find the feedback that once sustained him but finding only his own echo.

SRB: He doesn't soliloquize after his crowning, except for that last battle scene. He starts with this fantastic bravado, this fantastic relationship with the audience, and as soon as he's crowned, and especially – and this, in my mind, is the turning point for

Richard – after the murder of the children, from then on he simply does not. He has a line after the Elizabeth scene, which is almost muttered to himself. I think it is always fascinating with Shakespeare *when* people stop soliloquizing. Hamlet stops after the boat. He doesn't need his friends in the audience any more. He's gone to a different place. Iago stops simply because things get too busy. He can barely speak to us in the first place because he is spinning a whole load of lies that he doesn't believe either. Richard stops because the crown is not what he expected it to be and he doesn't know how to cope with that. And then you have the death of the children. He can kill grown-ups in this play. Most grown-ups seem prepared to kill any other grown-up, they all seem to be on that level of ruthlessness, but you don't kill children. Even the Murderer says this is beyond the pale. I had this package brought on, which I'd based on [the soap opera] *Coronation Street* actually. When Stan Ogden died, Hilda Ogden got his glasses and his remaining bits and bobs – the last bit of him, if you like – in a brown paper packet delivered to her house and she opened it over the credits with no music. It was a fantastically moving performance. I wanted to do something like that. In our production Richard received a brown paper packet with the boys' pyjamas in it and he smelt the pyjamas, which smelt of talc and children. That I think is the moment when he switches off. He has no desire or need to communicate any more to people outside the play. And so consequently that last soliloquy at Bosworth is fiendishly difficult and also comes at slightly the wrong time. I can understand why people cut it because that late on is the last moment you want a soliloquy. It's a completely different beast.

Richard loves play-acting, doesn't he? As in the scene with the prayer-book. Presumably that dramatic self-conscious-ness is one of the keys to his charisma in the theatre?

BA: Richard loves acting because he has fully absorbed the idea that one may smile and smile and be a villain. It seems amusing and hilarious to him how easy it is to dupe people, to experience up close their vanity leading directly to their gullibility. This dramatic self-consciousness makes him charismatic to audiences because he realizes they are more entertained by audacious, immoral and downright wicked behaviour than they would be by someone spouting pieties and lecturing them on goodness or the art of sanctity. I wanted Tony to think of the audience as one thousand selves, or an audience of Richard fans, near-clones needing only that particular soliloquy to be perfect clones: not talking to himself but to a mass of near-selves close to the perfect him. But it withers to horrifying loneliness with 'I am I' and 'When I die no man will pity me'. Charisma is nothing without love.

SRB: Less so than the question implies. He wasn't a very good play-actor in the religious scene in my version. I think he can don a persona, as he does with Anne, but I don't think the Richard that I played was particularly conscious of play-acting. He just adapted himself to the situation that he was in and the objective that he needed to achieve. I think he believes things from the moment he has said them. I don't remember play-acting being particularly impor-tant. He liked his relationship with the audience. He liked being able to achieve something in public view, which I suppose is play-acting in a way. He liked the audience to see how the cogs were moving.

The initial set-up of the wooing of Lady Anne seems unpromising: Richard has stabbed her first husband (Edward Prince of Wales) to death in *Henry VI Part 3* and now he's courting her over the corpse of her father-in-law (Henry VI), whom he's also killed. And yet he wins her over. Did your rehearsal process reveal the secret of his success?

BA: He makes her believe her loves her and, despite everything, she's moved by that. He makes her believe he's a good man and misunderstood. Besides, these are dangerous times and she needs a powerful protector.

SRB: No! I don't think I ever cracked that one. I know Annabelle Apsion, who played Lady Anne, felt uncomfortable a lot of the time, both when I played it and when Ciaran Hinds took over from me after I slipped a disc in my back. I don't know what the secret of it is. It was always the scene that was the most difficult for me. It doesn't play to my particular strengths. If I were a sexier actor perhaps it would, but I couldn't really use that part of the man's armoury in my dealings with her. I also think there is some mystery there, that I'm sure a lot of Richards have unlocked, but that I found very hard indeed. I was in Milton Keynes [a commuter town in the English Midlands] and somebody suggested playing it extremely slowly, against all the technical rules, which perhaps we should have tried. But I can't pretend I ever got that one.

The women eventually play a big part in bringing Richard down: there's a definite shift in the power structure when his mother (the Duchess of York) and sister-in-law (Queen Elizabeth) gang up on him in the fourth act. Did that feel like a turning point to you?

BA: The trinity of women, Anne, Margaret and Elizabeth, are a very, very potent presence in the play, so you have no choice but to make them a strong focus in any production. The fact that they *all* initially see through him in a way the men apparently don't offers him an intriguing challenge the men don't present. He defeats Margaret simply by giving voice to what all the men feel. He turns Anne by the brilliance of his acting and survives the encounter with Elizabeth through pure determination, although you can feel the strain that he has put himself under gradually taking effect.

SRB: The most important scene in the whole play was for me the one with Elizabeth. I had this feeling that it is Richard at his most genuine and desperate, and that is why it doesn't work for him. This is a man who is tired, he's older, kingship isn't as much fun as he thought it would be. He's on the road, half way through the campaign, and he meets a woman who is the key to stability and he genuinely wants it. And when he says about marrying her daughter 'It cannot be avoided but by this; / It will not be avoided but by this', it is absolutely a genuine statement. There is no other answer that he can see out of the mess that they have got themselves into. What she does is something that he's never thought about, which is to talk about grief. And to say, 'Do you realize that there are parents up and down this country who are weeping for their dead children, and children who are weeping for their dead parents? And that it is you who has done that.' I don't think Richard has ever thought about the personal consequences of killing somebody, it has never occurred to him. He has a moment after killing the children, realizing that he has stepped over a line, but I don't think he stops to consider how their mother feels. I think he genuinely finds it disturbing that he is responsible for mass misery, because I don't think it had ever occurred to him before. He just wanted the crown because he felt he needed and deserved it, but I don't think he realizes that in doing so he has made a whole country miserable. And in our version, as I think in most productions, he doesn't win the argument with Elizabeth at all, but he has that funny little line at the end of it: 'Relenting fool, and shallow, changing woman!' He tries to fool himself into believing that he's been dealing with a stupid and weak woman, rather than the full-length soliloquy 'Was ever woman in this humour wooed?' which is somebody who has succeeded and is at the top of his deceptive powers. This is the genuine Richard laying his heart on the line, what little heart he has at any rate, and is faced with something that is implacably stronger than that, which is a mother's grief. I think it is the absolute turning point for Richard. He essentially dies. I don't think he's amoral. Iago I think is amoral, a very small and mean man, without a sense of beauty or love or life. But I think Richard does have a sense of these things. He is a moral man, brought up with moral codes, but they have distorted beyond recognition. Otherwise he couldn't wake up before Bosworth. Otherwise he wouldn't stop eating. At the end of scenes there's quite a lot about food, people arranging to meet after dinner, 'I saw good strawberries in your garden there.' And then just before Bosworth he no longer wants to eat or drink, and I think the people around him think 'Oh my God!' when he's lost his appetite. I mentioned this to a Shakespeare scholar when I did it and they told me there had just been a production on Lyon entirely based on that!

How did you approach the technical problem of the scene with the Ghosts the night before the battle? It seems to require

some theatrical equivalent of a cinematic split-screen effect –
that maybe worked especially well on the wide, shallow stage
of the Elizabethan Rose. How did you make it work in your
space?

BA: The fact that the whole of the action was set in a cathedral
made it fairly obvious that by parking Richard and his tent stage-
right and Richmond and his tent stage-left simultaneously, we were
in the setting of a medieval Mystery Play with heaven on one
side and hell's mouth on the other. In fact, in a way, it was the
culminating image of the whole scenic concept.

TP: We were working in a thrust stage so it made it very easy
to divide the space with Richmond asleep downstage and Richard
mid-stage. The Ghosts entered in a steady stream from double
doors in the upstage tower, which dominated the space. Thus they
encountered Richard first and then went on to Richmond, before
exiting through the audience.

And for all the blood, the murders, the choreographed
onstage fighting: I suppose there's a basic choice between
'stylization' (slow-motion battles, red silk for blood) and
'realism' (the clash of metal, lashings of mud and Kensington
Gore): where did you aim to find yourselves on that spectrum?

TP: We were fairly realistic, and as it was contemporary we used
guns, including a very brutal shot to the head in Pomfret. The
mumming to the Mayor was a mock terrorist attack and Hastings'
head was delivered in a clear plastic bag. The fights, however, were
stylized, especially the final section in Bosworth which involved all
the Ghosts as abstract combatants. The final encounter between
Richmond and Richard took place on a swivelling set of metal steps
with Richard trapped at the top, firing rapidly to try and hit the
whirling Richmond as he spun them around.

Most of Shakespeare's history plays are ensemble pieces, but
Richard is a huge solo part – he speaks a third of the entire
play and has more than three times as many lines as anybody

else. The role was clearly written to showcase the rising star of Richard Burbage. For a director, there must be an unusually difficult task of balancing the work that must be done with Richard and with the rest of the cast? Are there enough rewards for the other actors?

BA: Yes. Buckingham, Anne, Clarence and Margaret are all good parts, but it's a very valid point; the play is unbalanced in that sense. It's one of the reasons it needs careful cutting. Tony was always saying that Shakespeare learns later in his career how to give the central actors decent rests with large sections of the action in which they don't appear. Lear, Macbeth, Othello, Antony, Cleopatra, Coriolanus, etc., all have a significant amount of time offstage. The physical demands on the actor playing Richard are huge, and if one sees it as a star vehicle then you certainly need a star who is a modest soul and a company person. A vain and self-centred actor would be death to company spirit – rather as Richard is death to those who try to support him.

Which murder did your Richard enjoy the most? And the least?

SRB: I've answered that about the least with the princes. I don't think he ever enjoys a murder to be honest. I think he thinks killing Clarence is quite funny. He never does the deed himself anyway, and it's a more functional thing, getting rid of people who are in the way. I think he quite enjoys terrifying Hastings. I think he enjoys the terror in people's faces, but as for the killing I think that's entirely functional.

Would you say it was physically the most demanding part you've ever played? Quite apart from the hunchback, the limp or whatever, he speaks one-third of the play, three times as much as anyone else, and doesn't really get that extended fourth act feet-up-in-the-dressing-room-before-the-big-climax that even Hamlet and Lear are allowed. And then to go so quickly from the nightmare speech to the battle itself . . . how did you survive?!

SRB: Well I didn't survive. It was physically exhausting, but I don't know whether it is any more exhausting that Hamlet, or indeed Iago, which probably takes as much as Richard. I remember Sam [Mendes, the director] saying to me beforehand, 'You must be careful, it's a ball-breaker.' Although I had prosthetics on my back and a raised shoe, inevitably I fed my body into the prosthetic. I did a run at The Other Place and then a twelve-week tour and I came to London and on the very first night I slipped my disc so badly I couldn't move, and then had to have an operation. It was quite a serious injury and I was out for about three months. Funnily enough one of the best performances I think I gave of it was a week after I'd slipped the disc and I refused to admit that I was that badly injured, although I literally couldn't walk! I had to stay on all fours in the wings and then pull myself up and get onto the stage and I did one performance, which was almost completely stationary, with people moved around me, and we didn't do the fight obviously, I just fell over! But I was so angry that I think in a way it was one of the best performances that I gave of it.

RICHARD AND TYRANNY: REFLECTIONS BY RICHARD EYRE

Sir Richard Eyre was Artistic Director of Britain's National Theatre from 1987 to 1997, where his Shakespearean productions included *Hamlet* with Daniel Day-Lewis and *King Lear* with Ian Holm. His 1990 production of *Richard III*, with Ian McKellen in the title role, toured the world, and its transposition of the play to a world suggestive of 1930s Fascism inspired the McKellen film version of 1996. Eyre reflects here on the play's enduring political power.

I came to know tyranny at first hand through visiting Romania. Over a period of nearly thirty years I watched their dictator, Ceaucescu, graduate from being a malign clown to a psychotic ogre. His *folies de grandeur* consisted of razing villages to the ground in order to rehouse peasants in tower blocks, sweeping aside boulevards because the streets from his residence to his office were insufficiently straight, building miles of preposterously baroque apartment blocks which echoed in concrete the lines of Securitate men standing beneath them, and led the eye towards a gigantic palace which made Stalin's taste in architecture look restrained. They ran out of marble to clad the walls and the floors, and had to invent a process to make a synthetic substitute out of marble dust; and there was never enough gold for all the door handles of the hundreds of rooms, or the taps of the scores of bathrooms. It was a palace of Oz, built for a demented wizard, costing the lives of hundreds of building workers who, numbed by cold, fell from the flimsy scaffolding and were brushed away like rubble, to be laid out in a room reserved solely for the coffins of the expendable workforce. There was a photograph of Ceaucescu that showed only one ear, and there's a Romanian saying that to have one ear is to be mad. So another ear was painstakingly painted on the official photograph. Such are the ways of great men.

The language of demagoguery in modern times has a remarkable consistency: Ceaucescu, Stalin, Mao Tse Tung and Bokassa shared a predilection for large banners, demonstrations and military choreography, and the same architectural virus; totalitarianism consistently distorts proportion by eliminating human scale. Mass becomes the only consideration in architecture, armies and death. The rise of a dictator and the accompanying political thuggery are the main topics of Shakespeare's *Richard III*, which could be said to be a handbook for tyrants – and for their victims. I directed the play with Ian McKellen as Richard in 1990 for the National Theatre and took it to its spiritual home in Bucharest early in 1991.

We have to keep rediscovering ways of doing Shakespeare's plays. They don't have absolute meanings. There is no fixed, frozen way of doing them. Nobody can mine a Shakespeare play and discover a 'solution'. And to pretend that there are fixed canons of style, fashion and taste, is to ignore history. When there is talk of 'classical acting', what is often meant is an acting style that instead of revealing the truth of a text for the present day, reveals the bombast of yesterday.

How do we present the plays in a way that is true to their own terms, and at the same time bring them alive for a contemporary audience? It's very much easier to achieve this in a small space, and it's no coincidence that most successful Shakespeare productions of recent years have been done in theatres seating a couple of hundred people at most, where the potency of the language isn't dissipated by the exigencies of voice projection, and the problems of presentation – finding a physical world for the play – become negligible. It's hard at one end of the spectrum to avoid latching on to a visual conceit which tidies up the landscape of a Shakespeare play, and, at the other end of the spectrum, to avoid imposing unity through a rigorously enforced discipline of verse-speaking. Verse-speaking should be like jazz: never on the beat, but before, after, or across it.

The life of the plays is in the language, not alongside it, or underneath it. Feelings and thoughts are released at the moment of speech. An Elizabethan audience would have responded to the pulse, the rhythms, the shapes, sounds, and above all meanings, within the consistent ten-syllable, five-stress lines of blank verse. They were an audience who listened. To a large extent we've lost that priority; nowadays we see before we hear. Verse drama places demands on the audience, but a greater demand still on the actors, habituated by naturalistic speech, and to private, introspective, emotional displays. 'You should be able to feel the language', says the poet and dramatist Tony Harrison, 'To taste it, to conscript the whole body as well as the mind and the mouth to savour it.'

For a director, working with a designer can often be the most satisfying and enjoyable part of a production. You advance slowly, day by day, in a kind of amiable dialectic, helped by sketches, anecdotes, photographs and reference books. The play starts as a tone – of voice, or colour, and a shape as formless as the shadow of a sheet on a washing line; through reading and discussion and illustration, it acquires a clear and palpable shape. When I started working on *Richard III* with Ian McKellen and the designer, Bob Crowley, I had no definite plan about the setting. We never sought to establish literal equivalents between medieval and modern tyrants. We worked simply, day by day, reading the play aloud to each other, and refusing to jump to conclusions.

Some actors start with trying to establish the details of how the character will look, some with how they will think or feel. It was said of Olivier that he started with the shoes; with Ian McKellen it's the face and the voice. I have a postcard he sent me when we were working on *Richard III* – a droll cartoon of a severe face, recognizable as his own, with sharply receding hair, an arrow pointing to a patch of alopecia; at the throat is a military collar, above the shoulder the tip of a small hump. He is a systematic, fastidious and exacting actor; each word is picked up and examined for its possible meanings, which are weighed, assessed, discarded or incorporated. In rehearsals he is infinitely self-aware, often cripplingly so. His waking, and perhaps sleeping, dreams are of how he will appear on stage – his position, his spatial relationships with the other actors. But in performance that inhibition drops away like a cripple's crutches and he is pure performer. All the detail that has been so exhaustively documented becomes a part of an animate whole. In sport, in a great performance, there must always be an element of risk, of danger. The same must be true of the theatre. I wouldn't say there is not a good or even effective actor without this characteristic, but there is certainly no celebrated one.

As Ian, Bob and I talked, a story emerged: Richard's occupation's gone. He's a successful soldier who, in the face of great odds, has welded a life together in which he has a purpose, an identity as a military man. His opening speech describes his depression at the conclusion of war, his bitterness at the effeminacy of peace. He's a man raging with unconsummated energy, needing a world to 'bustle' in. This hunger to fill the vacuum left by battle is the driving force of the play. It has a deep resonance for me. When I made *Tumbledown,* a film about the Falklands War, I saw this sense of unfulfilled appetite at first hand in people who had fought in the war and were unable to come to terms with peace. The experience of battle is a profound distillation of fear, danger, and exhilaration; nothing in peacetime will ever match it, and those who are affected by it are as traumatized as those who have been wounded, who at least have the visible signs of trauma to show for it. Soldiers are licensed to break the ultimate taboo against killing; some of them get the habit.

Richard has had to fight against many odds; he is the youngest son, coming after two very strong, dominant, assertive, brothers – and he is deformed, 'unfinished'. His eldest brother, Edward, is a profligate, and the spectacle of his brother's success with women is a sharp thorn in his flesh. The age, no less than today, worshipped physical prowess, and Richard is accustomed, though certainly not inured, to pejorative terms like 'bunch-backed toad'; he has heard them all his life. We know that he is deformed, but the text repeatedly tells us he is a successful professional soldier. We have to reconcile the two demands of the text. Olivier's interpretation has become central to the mythology of the play, but the deformity that he depicts has never seemed to me plausibly compatible with what Shakespeare wrote. Ian McKellen played Richard with a small hump, he had chronic alopecia, and he was paralysed down one side of his body. These three handicaps taken together were sufficient to account for all the abuse he attracts and [yet he could] still serve as a professional soldier. Experience shows that even slight deformities are enough to inspire repulsion; modern reactions to disability haven't changed very much in this respect.

It is clear that Richard has been rejected from birth by his mother; she says so unequivocally to Clarence's children, and her words of contempt spoken to her son in front of his troops confirm this. It is impossible to escape the conclusion that Shakespeare is attempting to give some history, some causality, to Richard's evil.

The design of the production emerged empirically. We started with an empty model box, and put minimal elements into it – rows of overhead lamps to create a series of institutionalized public areas, a world of prisons and cabinet rooms and hospital corridors; palaces and areas of ceremonial display, set off against candle-lit areas of private pain. We drew some parallels with the rise of Hitler, but these were forced by Hitler himself; his rise shadows that of Richard astonishingly closely, as [Bertolt] Brecht showed in [his play] *The Resistible Rise of Arturo Ui*. Specific elements of Hitler's ascent to power, or [Sir Oswald] Mosley's to notoriety, were echoes that bounced off a timeless sounding board. The play is set in a mythological landscape, even if it draws on an apparently historically precise period; I say 'apparently' because Shakespeare treats historical incident with little reference to fact – incidents are conflated, characters meet whose paths never crossed, Tudor myths prevail.

Tyrants always invent their own ritual, synthetic ceremonies borrowed from previous generations in order to dignify the present and suggest an unbroken continuum with old traditions. Hitler played up all the themes of historical restitution. Napoleon, the little man from Corsica, designed the preposterous Byzantine ceremony which is represented in David's painting. Most of the English ritual, our so-called time-honoured ritual, is not very old either. The order of the last British Coronation, in 1953, had been almost wholly invented by Queen Victoria. Putting Richard in medieval costume in the Coronation, as we did, was a way of showing how tyrants, the authors of the Thousand Year Reich, would have us believe that medievalism and modern time co-exist; the past is consistently made to serve the needs of the present.

Richard III is so much a one-man show in our acting tradition that the miseries visited on woman by the male appetite for power tend to be ignored or obscured. The female characters are as strong as in any of Shakespeare's plays. The legacy of men's cruelty is swept up by women who have been educated by the experience of grief. They have caused pain to Richard and they are taught by him to suffer: Elizabeth – proud, arrogant, and abusive of him – loses her brother and her sons; the Duchess of York – sealed in her own self-importance, openly contemptuous of her son – loses another son and grandchildren at his hands; Lady Anne – blinded by her grief and her hatred and seduced by him – loses her self-respect and, finally, her life. Only Queen Margaret needs no education at his hands; 'Teach me how to curse my enemies', says Elizabeth to her. Their models in our times are only too obvious: the women who wait in Chile and in Argentina for news of their sons who have 'disappeared', and the mothers I saw in Romania shortly after the Revolution, putting candles and flowers in the streets on the spots where their sons had been killed. The play is called *The Tragedy of Richard III*, and it is the tragedy of the women that is being told.

The crude villain of melodrama has managed to overrule a play of considerable political subtlety. Richard does not appear in an untainted Eden; his England is the world of realpolitik. Clarence and Edward have both committed crimes in the civil wars, Clarence even admitting his guilt to the Keeper; Queen Elizabeth's family are greedy parvenus; Buckingham, Stanley and Ely are all morally ambiguous. At the beginning of the play Clarence has just been capriciously arrested; such behaviour may be exceptional and outrageous, but not unprecedented. What right have any of the characters to call Richard a villain?

Hastings, the Prime Minister, is a politician's politician, expedient, and amoral – when he is told of the impending execution of his political enemies, he can't fault this transparent abuse of justice; within minutes he is himself under sentence of execution. 'The rest that love me, rise and follow me', says Richard, and at this point self-preservation takes over from courage, morality, or political expediency. We all hope that we will never have to face this choice; it takes formidable courage to say 'No' when the consequence is imprisonment or worse, and, where there is a crying need for reform, it's easy enough to agree that minor infringements of liberty are a small price to pay for the benefit of an able leader. We are comfortably insulated in our unchallenged, liberal, all-too-English assumptions.

The play ends with the triumph of Richmond – a young man, almost a boy, in the hands of mature soldier-politicians who are promoting him. It is essential for their purposes that he succeed, and he is equally determined to show that he can succeed. I set his first entrance against a backdrop of a peaceful country village, in Devon in fact, near where I was born, the England of 'summer fields and fruitful vines'. If I were asked what I thought Richmond was fighting for, it would be this idealized picture of England. It was more than a metaphor for me; it was a heartland.

When I took my production of *Richard III* to Romania a year after their Revolution, familiar landmarks in Bucharest were obscured entirely by the snow and the people were unrecognizably changed from the years of oppression. Though some claimed that nothing had altered, the mere fact of being able to say this openly contradicted what they were saying. A stagehand said he wasn't at all frightened of being killed in the Revolution; after all, better to be dead than how it was. A small pixie-like woman was helping at the theatre; she was slightly retarded but had some English. 'Are you happy? I am happy' was her refrain. Like many others she was homeless, and lived in the theatre, where at least she could get hot water. Outside it was often one hour of hot water a day.

At the end of the last performance I went onstage with the actors and made a speech, starting through an interpreter. She was shouted off: 'English! English!' they chanted and I continued in English. I told them the production had come to its spiritual home, that this sort of cultural exchange was the only true diplomacy, and thanked them for their hospitality. They didn't want us to go, clapping rhythmically and incessantly, but we walked offstage slowly, blinking back tears. As we left the stage a man walked up to us and handed a note and a bouquet to one of the actors. The note read: 'Nobody can play Sir William Shakespeare's plays better than his English people. I've seen with your remarkable help that somewhere in England Sir William Shakespeare is still alive. Thank you. Signed: a Simple Man.'

SHAKESPEARE'S CAREER
IN THE THEATRE

BEGINNINGS

William Shakespeare was an extraordinarily intelligent man who was born and died in an ordinary market town in the English Midlands. He lived an uneventful life in an eventful age. Born in April 1564, he was the eldest son of John Shakespeare, a glove-maker who was prominent on the town council until he fell into financial difficulties. Young William was educated at the local grammar in Stratford-upon-Avon, Warwickshire, where he gained a thorough grounding in the Latin language, the art of rhetoric and classical poetry. He married Ann Hathaway and had three children (Susanna, then the twins Hamnet and Judith) before his twenty-first birthday: an exceptionally young age for the period. We do not know how he supported his family in the mid-1580s.

Like many clever country boys, he moved to the city in order to make his way in the world. Like many creative people, he found a career in the entertainment business. Public playhouses and professional full-time acting companies reliant on the market for their income were born in Shakespeare's childhood. When he arrived in London as a man, sometime in the late 1580s, a new phenomenon was in the making: the actor who is so successful that he becomes a 'star'. The word did not exist in its modern sense, but the pattern is recognizable: audiences went to the theatre not so much to see a particular show as to witness the comedian Richard Tarlton or the dramatic actor Edward Alleyn.

Shakespeare was an actor before he was a writer. It appears not to have been long before he realized that he was never going to grow into a great comedian like Tarlton or a great tragedian like Alleyn.

Instead, he found a role within his company as the man who patched up old plays, breathing new life, new dramatic twists, into tired repertory pieces. He paid close attention to the work of the university-educated dramatists who were writing history plays and tragedies for the public stage in a style more ambitious, sweeping and poetically grand than anything which had been seen before. But he may also have noted that what his friend and rival Ben Jonson would call 'Marlowe's mighty line' sometimes faltered in the mode of comedy. Going to university, as Christopher Marlowe did, was all well and good for honing the arts of rhetorical elaboration and classical allusion, but it could lead to a loss of the common touch. To stay close to a large segment of the potential audience for public theatre, it was necessary to write for clowns as well as kings and to intersperse the flights of poetry with the humour of the tavern, the privy and the brothel: Shakespeare was the first to establish himself early in his career as an equal master of tragedy, comedy and history. He realized that theatre could be the medium to make the national past available to a wider audience than the elite who could afford to read large history books: his signature early works include not only the classical tragedy *Titus Andronicus* but also the sequence of English historical plays on the Wars of the Roses.

He also invented a new role for himself, that of in-house company dramatist. Where his peers and predecessors had to sell their plays to the theatre managers on a poorly-paid piecework basis, Shakespeare took a percentage of the box-office income. The Lord Chamberlain's Men constituted themselves in 1594 as a joint stock company, with the profits being distributed among the core actors who had invested as sharers. Shakespeare acted himself – he appears in the cast lists of some of Ben Jonson's plays as well as the list of actors' names at the beginning of his own collected works – but his principal duty was to write two or three plays a year for the company. By holding shares, he was effectively earning himself a royalty on his work, something no author had ever done before in England. When the Lord Chamberlain's Men collected their fee for performance at court in the Christmas season of 1594, three of them went along to the Treasurer of the Chamber: not just Richard

Burbage the tragedian and Will Kempe the clown, but also Shakespeare the scriptwriter. That was something new.

The next four years were the golden period in Shakespeare's career, though overshadowed by the death of his only son Hamnet, aged eleven, in 1596. In his early thirties and in full command of both his poetic and his theatrical medium, he perfected his art of comedy, while also developing his tragic and historical writing in new ways. In 1598, Francis Meres, a Cambridge University graduate with his finger on the pulse of the London literary world, praised Shakespeare for his excellence across the genres:

> As Plautus and Seneca are accounted the best for comedy and tragedy among the Latins, so Shakespeare among the English is the most excellent in both kinds for the stage: for comedy, witness his *Gentlemen of Verona*, his *Errors*, his *Love Labours Lost*, his *Love Labours Won*, his *Midsummer Night Dream* and his *Merchant of Venice*: for tragedy his *Richard the 2*, *Richard the 3*, *Henry the 4*, *King John*, *Titus Andronicus* and his *Romeo and Juliet*.

For Meres, as for the many writers who praised the 'honey-flowing vein' of *Venus and Adonis* and *Lucrece*, narrative poems written when the theatres were closed due to plague in 1593–94, Shakespeare was marked above all by his linguistic skill, by the gift of turning elegant poetic phrases.

PLAYHOUSES

Elizabethan playhouses were 'thrust' or 'one-room' theatres. To understand Shakespeare's original theatrical life, we have to forget about the indoor theatre of later times, with its proscenium arch and curtain that would be opened at the beginning and closed at the end of each act. In the proscenium arch theatre, stage and auditorium are effectively two separate rooms: the audience looks from one world into another as if through the imaginary 'fourth wall' framed by the proscenium. The picture-frame stage, together with the elaborate scenic effects and backdrops beyond it, created the illusion of a self-contained world – especially once nineteenth-century developments in the control of artificial lighting meant that the auditorium could be darkened and the spectators made to focus on the lighted stage. Shakespeare, by contrast, wrote for a bare platform stage with a standing audience gathered around it in a courtyard in full daylight. The audience were always conscious of themselves and their fellow-spectators, and they shared the same 'room' as the actors. A sense of immediate presence and the creation of rapport with the audience were all-important. The actor could not afford to imagine he was in a closed world, with silent witnesses dutifully observing him from the darkness.

Shakespeare's theatrical career began at the Rose Theatre in Southwark. The stage was wide and shallow, trapezoid in shape, like a lozenge. This design had a great deal of potential for the theatrical equivalent of cinematic split-screen effects, whereby one group of characters would enter at the door at one end of the tiring-house wall at the back of the stage and another group through the door at the other end, thus creating two rival tableaux. Many of the battle-heavy and faction-filled plays that premiered at the Rose have scenes of just this sort.

At the rear of the Rose stage, there were three capacious exits, each over ten feet wide. Unfortunately, the very limited excavation of a fragmentary portion of the original Globe site, also in 1989, revealed nothing about the stage. The first Globe was built in 1599 with similar proportions to those of another theatre, the Fortune, albeit that the former was polygonal and looked circular, whereas the latter was rectangular. The building contract for the Fortune survives and allows us to infer that the stage of the Globe was probably substantially wider than it was deep (perhaps forty-three feet wide and twenty-seven feet deep). It may well have been tapered at the front, like that of the Rose.

The capacity of the Globe was said to have been enormous, perhaps in excess of three thousand. It has been conjectured that about eight hundred people may have stood in the yard, with two thousand or more in the three layers of covered galleries. The other 'public' playhouses were also of large capacity, whereas the indoor Blackfriars theatre that Shakespeare's company began using in

1608 – the former refectory of a monastery – had overall internal dimensions of a mere forty-six by sixty feet. It would have made for a much more intimate theatrical experience and had a much smaller capacity, probably of about six hundred people. Since they paid at least sixpence a head, the Blackfriars attracted a more select or 'private' audience. The atmosphere would have been closer to that of an indoor performance before the court in the Whitehall Palace or at Richmond. That Shakespeare always wrote for indoor production at court as well as outdoor performance in the public theatre should make us cautious about inferring, as some scholars have, that the opportunity provided by the intimacy of the Blackfriars led to a significant change towards a 'chamber' style in his last plays – which, besides, were performed at both the Globe and the Blackfriars. After the occupation of the Blackfriars a five-act structure seems to have become more important to Shakespeare. That was because of artificial lighting: there were musical interludes between the acts, while the candles were trimmed and replaced. Again, though, something similar must have been necessary for indoor court performances throughout his career.

Front of house there were the 'gatherers' who collected the money from audience members: a penny to stand in the open-air yard, another penny for a place in the covered galleries, sixpence for the prominent 'lord's rooms' to the side of the stage. In the indoor 'private' theatres, gallants from the audience who fancied making themselves part of the spectacle sat on stools on the edge of the stage itself. Scholars debate as to how widespread this practice was in the public theatres such as the Globe. Once the audience were in place and the money counted, the gatherers were available to be extras on stage. That is one reason why battles and crowd scenes often come later rather than early in Shakespeare's plays. There was no formal prohibition upon performance by women, and there certainly were women among the gatherers, so it is not beyond the bounds of possibility that female crowd members were played by females.

The play began at two o'clock in the afternoon and the theatre had to be cleared by five. After the main show, there would be a jig – which consisted not only of dancing, but also of knockabout comedy (it is the origin of the farcical 'afterpiece' in the eighteenth-century theatre). So the time available for a Shakespeare play was about two and a half hours, somewhere between the 'two hours' traffic' mentioned in the prologue to *Romeo and Juliet* and the 'three hours' spectacle' referred to in the preface to the 1647 Folio of Beaumont and Fletcher's plays. The prologue to a play by Thomas Middleton refers to a thousand lines as 'one hour's words', so the likelihood is that about two and a half thousand, or a maximum of three thousand lines made up the performed text. This is indeed the length of most of Shakespeare's comedies, whereas many of his tragedies and histories are much longer, raising the possibility that he wrote full scripts, possibly with eventual publication in mind, in the full knowledge that the stage version would be heavily cut. The short Quarto texts published in his lifetime – they used to be called 'Bad' Quartos – provide fascinating evidence as to the kind of cutting that probably took place. So, for instance, the First Quarto of *Hamlet* neatly merges two occasions when Hamlet is overheard, the 'Fishmonger' and the 'nunnery' scenes.

The social composition of the audience was mixed. The poet Sir John Davies wrote of 'A thousand townsmen, gentlemen and whores, / Porters and servingmen' who would 'together throng' at the public playhouses. Though moralists associated female play-going with adultery and the sex trade, many perfectly respectable citizens' wives were regular attendees. Some, no doubt, resembled the modern groupie: a story attested in two different sources has one citizen's wife making a post-show assignation with Richard Burbage and ending up in bed with Shakespeare – supposedly eliciting from the latter the quip that William the Conqueror was before Richard III. Defenders of theatre liked to say that by witnessing the comeuppance of villains on the stage, audience members would repent of their own wrongdoings, but the reality is that most people went to the theatre then, as they do now, for entertainment more than moral edification. Besides, it would be foolish to suppose that audiences behaved in a homogeneous way: a pamphlet of the 1630s tells of how two men went to see *Pericles* and one of them laughed while the other wept. Bishop John Hall complained that people went to church for the same reasons that they went to the theatre: 'for company, for custom, for recreation ... to feed his eyes or his ears ... or perhaps for sleep'.

Men-about-town and clever young lawyers went to be seen as much as to see. In the modern popular imagination, shaped not least by *Shakespeare in Love* and the opening sequence of Laurence Olivier's *Henry V* film, the penny-paying groundlings stand in the yard hurling abuse or encouragement and hazelnuts or orange peel at the actors, while the sophisticates in the covered galleries appreciate Shakespeare's soaring poetry. The reality was probably the other way round. A 'groundling' was a kind of fish, so the nickname suggests the penny audience standing below the level of the stage and gazing in silent open-mouthed wonder at the spectacle unfolding above them. The more difficult audience members, who kept up a running commentary of clever remarks on the performance and who occasionally got into quarrels with players, were the gallants. Like Hollywood movies in modern times, Elizabethan and Jacobean plays exercised a powerful influence on the fashion and behaviour of the young. John Marston mocks the lawyers who would open their lips, perhaps to court a girl, and out would 'flow / Naught but pure Juliet and Romeo'.

THE ENSEMBLE AT WORK

In the absence of typewriters and photocopying machines, reading aloud would have been the means by which the company got to know a new play. The tradition of the playwright reading his complete script to the assembled company endured for generations. A copy would then have been taken to the Master of the Revels for licensing. The theatre book-holder or prompter would then have copied the parts for distribution to the actors. A partbook consisted of the character's lines, with each speech preceded by the last three or four words of the speech before, the so-called 'cue'. These would have been taken away and studied or 'conned'. During this period of learning the parts, an actor might have had some one-to-one instruction, perhaps from the dramatist, perhaps from a senior actor who had played the same part before, and, in the case of an apprentice, from his master. A high percentage of Desdemona's lines

7. Hypothetical reconstruction of the interior of an Elizabethan playhouse during a performance.

occur in dialogue with Othello, of Lady Macbeth's with Macbeth, Cleopatra's with Antony and Volumnia's with Coriolanus. The roles would almost certainly have been taken by the apprentice of the lead actor, usually Burbage, who delivers the majority of the cues. Given that apprentices lodged with their masters, there would have been ample opportunity for personal instruction, which may be what made it possible for young men to play such demanding parts.

After the parts were learned, there may have been no more than a single rehearsal before the first performance. With six different plays to be put on every week, there was no time for more. Actors, then, would go into a show with a very limited sense of the whole. The notion of a collective rehearsal process that is itself a process of discovery for the actors is wholly modern and would have been incomprehensible to Shakespeare and his original ensemble. Given the number of parts an actor had to hold in his memory, the forgetting of lines was probably more frequent than in the modern theatre. The book-holder was on hand to prompt.

Backstage personnel included the property man, the tire-man who oversaw the costumes, call-boys, attendants and the musicians, who might play at various times from the main stage, the rooms above and within the tiring-house. Scriptwriters sometimes made a nuisance of themselves backstage. There was often tension between the acting companies and the freelance playwrights from whom they purchased scripts: it was a smart move on the part of Shakespeare and the Lord Chamberlain's Men to bring the writing process in-house.

Scenery was limited, though sometimes set-pieces were brought on (a bank of flowers, a bed, the mouth of hell). The trapdoor from below, the gallery stage above and the curtained discovery-space at the back allowed for an array of special effects: the rising of ghosts and apparitions, the descent of gods, dialogue between a character at a window and another at ground level, the revelation of a statue or a pair of lovers playing at chess. Ingenious use could be made of props, as with the ass's head in *A Midsummer Night's Dream*. In a theatre that does not clutter the stage with the material paraphernalia of everyday life, those objects that are deployed may take on powerful symbolic weight, as when Shylock bears his weighing scales in one hand and knife in the other, thus becoming a parody of the figure of Justice who traditionally bears a sword and a balance. Among the more significant items in the property cupboard of Shakespeare's company, there would have been a throne (the 'chair of state'), joint stools, books, bottles, coins, purses, letters (which are brought on stage, read or referred to on about eighty occasions in the complete works), maps, gloves, a set of stocks (in which Kent is put in *King Lear*), rings, rapiers, daggers, broadswords, staves, pistols, masks and vizards, heads and skulls, torches and tapers and lanterns which served to signal night scenes on the daylit stage, a buck's head, an ass's head, animal costumes. Live animals also put in appearances, most notably the dog Crab in *The Two Gentlemen of Verona* and possibly a young polar bear in *The Winter's Tale*.

The costumes were the most important visual dimension of the play. Playwrights were paid between £2 and £6 per script, whereas Alleyn was not averse to paying £20 for 'a black velvet cloak with sleeves embroidered all with silver and gold'. No matter the period of the play, actors always wore contemporary costume. The excitement for the audience came not from any impression of historical accuracy, but from the richness of the attire and perhaps the transgressive thrill of the knowledge that here were commoners like themselves strutting in the costumes of courtiers in effective defiance of the strict sumptuary laws whereby in real life people had to wear the clothes that befitted their social station.

To an even greater degree than props, costumes could carry symbolic importance. Racial characteristics could be suggested: a breastplate and helmet for a Roman soldier, a turban for a Turk, long robes for exotic characters such as Moors, a gabardine for a Jew. The figure of Time, as in *The Winter's Tale*, would be equipped with hourglass, scythe and wings; Rumour, who speaks the prologue of *2 Henry IV*, wore a costume adorned with a thousand tongues. The wardrobe in the tiring-house of the Globe would have contained much of the same stock as that of rival manager Philip Henslowe at the Rose: green gowns for outlaws and foresters, black for melancholy men such as Jaques and people in mourning such as the Countess in *All's Well that Ends Well* (at the beginning of *Hamlet*, the prince is still in mourning black when everyone else is in festive garb for the wedding of the new king), a gown and hood for a friar (or a feigned friar like the duke in *Measure for Measure*), blue coats and tawny to distinguish the followers of rival factions, a leather apron and ruler for a carpenter (as in the opening scene of *Julius Caesar* – and in *A Midsummer Night's Dream*, where this is the only sign that Peter Quince is a carpenter), a cockle hat with staff and a pair of sandals for a pilgrim or palmer (the disguise assumed by Helen in *All's Well*), bodices and kirtles with farthingales beneath for the boys who are to be dressed as girls. A gender switch such as that of Rosalind or Jessica seems to have taken between fifty and eighty lines of dialogue – Viola does not resume her 'maiden weeds', but remains in her boy's costume to the end of *Twelfth Night* because a change would have slowed down the action at just the moment it was speeding to a climax. Henslowe's inventory also included 'a robe for to go invisible': Oberon, Puck and Ariel must have had something similar.

As the costumes appealed to the eyes, so there was music for the ears. Comedies included many songs. Desdemona's willow song, perhaps a late addition to the text, is a rare and thus exceptionally poignant example from tragedy. Trumpets and tuckets sounded for ceremonial entrances, drums denoted an army on the march. Background music could create atmosphere, as at the beginning of *Twelfth Night*, during the lovers' dialogue near the end of *The Merchant of Venice*, when the statue seemingly comes to life in *The Winter's Tale*, and for the revival of Pericles and of Lear (in the Quarto text, but not the Folio). The haunting sound of the hautboy suggested a realm beyond the human, as when the god Hercules is imagined deserting Mark Antony. Dances symbolized the harmony of the end of a comedy – though in Shakespeare's world of mingled joy and sorrow, someone is usually left out of the circle.

The most important resource was, of course, the actors themselves. They needed many skills: in the words of one contemporary commentator, 'dancing, activity, music, song, elocution, ability of body, memory, skill of weapon, pregnancy of wit'. Their bodies were as significant as their voices. Hamlet tells the player to 'suit the action to the word, the word to the action': moments of strong emotion, known as 'passions', relied on a repertoire of dramatic gestures as well as a modulation of the voice. When Titus Andronicus has had his hand chopped off, he asks 'How can I grace my talk, / Wanting a hand to give it action?' A pen portrait of 'The Character of an Excellent Actor' by the dramatist John Webster is almost certainly based on his impression of Shakespeare's leading man, Richard Burbage: 'By a full and significant action of body, he charms our attention: sit in a full theatre, and you will think you see so many lines drawn from the circumference of so many ears, whiles the actor is the centre . . . .'

Though Burbage was admired above all others, praise was also heaped upon the apprentice players whose alto voices fitted them for the parts of women. A spectator at Oxford in 1610 records how the audience were reduced to tears by the pathos of Desdemona's death. The puritans who fumed about the biblical prohibition upon cross-dressing and the encouragement to sodomy constituted by the sight of an adult male kissing a teenage boy on stage were a small minority. Little is known, however, about the characteristics of the leading apprentices in Shakespeare's company. It may perhaps be inferred that one was a lot taller than the other, since Shakespeare often wrote for a pair of female friends, one tall and fair, the other short and dark (Helena and Hermia, Rosalind and Celia, Beatrice and Hero).

We know little about Shakespeare's own acting roles – an early allusion indicates that he often took royal parts, and a venerable tradition gives him old Adam in *As You Like It* and the ghost of old King Hamlet. Save for Burbage's lead roles and the generic part of the clown, all such castings are mere speculation. We do not even know for sure whether the original Falstaff was Will Kempe or another actor who specialized in comic roles, Thomas Pope.

Kempe left the company in early 1599. Tradition has it that he fell out with Shakespeare over the matter of excessive improvisation. He was replaced by Robert Armin, who was less of a clown and more of a cerebral wit: this explains the difference between such parts as Lancelet Gobbo and Dogberry, which were written for Kempe, and the more verbally sophisticated Feste and Lear's Fool, which were written for Armin.

One thing that is clear from surviving 'plots' or story-boards of plays from the period is that a degree of doubling was necessary. *2 Henry VI* has over sixty speaking parts, but more than half of the characters only appear in a single scene and most scenes have only six to eight speakers. At a stretch, the play could be performed by thirteen actors. When Thomas Platter saw *Julius Caesar* at the Globe in 1599, he noted that there were about fifteen. Why doesn't Paris go to the Capulet ball in *Romeo and Juliet*? Perhaps because he was doubled with Mercutio, who does. In *The Winter's Tale*, Mamillius might have come back as Perdita and Antigonus been doubled by Camillo, making the partnership with Paulina at the end a very neat touch. Titania and Oberon are often played by the same pair as Hippolyta and Theseus, suggesting a symbolic matching of the rulers of the worlds of night and day, but it is questionable whether there would have been time for the necessary costume changes. As so often, one is left in a realm of tantalizing speculation.

THE KING'S MAN

The new king, James I, who had held the Scottish throne as James VI since he had been an infant, immediately took the Lord Chamberlain's Men under his direct patronage. Henceforth they would be the King's Men, and for the rest of Shakespeare's career they were favoured with far more court performances than any of their rivals. There even seem to have been rumours early in the reign that Shakespeare and Burbage were being considered for knighthoods, an unprecedented honour for mere actors – and one that in the event was not accorded to a member of the profession for nearly three hundred years, when the title was bestowed upon Henry Irving, the leading Shakespearean actor of Queen Victoria's reign.

Shakespeare's productivity rate slowed in the Jacobean years, not because of age or some personal trauma, but because there were frequent outbreaks of plague, causing the theatres to be closed for long periods. The King's Men were forced to spend many months on the road. Between November 1603 and 1608, they were to be found at various towns in the south and Midlands, though Shakespeare probably did not tour with them by this time. He had bought a large house back home in Stratford and was accumulating other property. He may indeed have stopped acting soon after the new king took the throne. With the London theatres closed so much of the time and a large repertoire on the stocks, Shakespeare seems to have focused his energies on writing a few long and complex tragedies that could have been played on demand at court: *Othello*, *King Lear*, *Antony and Cleopatra*, *Coriolanus* and *Cymbeline* are among his longest and poetically grandest plays. *Macbeth* only survives in a shorter text, which shows signs of adaptation after Shakespeare's death. The bitterly satirical *Timon of Athens*, apparently a collaboration with Thomas Middleton that may have failed on the stage, also belongs to this period. In comedy, too, he wrote longer and morally darker works than in the Elizabethan period, pushing at the very bounds of the form in *Measure for Measure* and *All's Well that Ends Well*.

From 1608 onwards, when the King's Men began occupying the indoor Blackfriars playhouse (as a winter house, meaning that they only used the outdoor Globe in summer?), Shakespeare turned to a more romantic style. His company had a great success with a revived and altered version of an old pastoral play called *Mucedorus*. It even featured a bear. The younger dramatist John Fletcher, meanwhile, sometimes working in collaboration with Francis Beaumont, was pioneering a new style of tragicomedy, a mix of romance and royalism laced with intrigue and pastoral excursions. Shakespeare experimented with this idiom in *Cymbeline* and it was presumably with his blessing that Fletcher eventually took over as the King's Men's company dramatist. The two writers apparently collaborated on three plays in the years 1612–14: a lost romance called *Cardenio* (based on the love-madness of a character in Cervantes' *Don Quixote*), *Henry VIII* (originally staged with the title 'All is True'), and *The Two Noble Kinsmen*, a dramatization of Chaucer's 'Knight's Tale' These were written after Shakespeare's two final solo-authored plays, *The Winter's Tale*, a self-consciously old-fashioned work dramatizing the pastoral romance of his old enemy Robert Greene, and *The Tempest*, which at one and the same time drew together multiple theatrical traditions, diverse reading and contemporary interest in the fate of a ship that had been wrecked on the way to the New World.

The collaborations with Fletcher suggest that Shakespeare's career ended with a slow fade rather than the sudden retirement supposed by the nineteenth-century Romantic critics who read Prospero's epilogue to *The Tempest* as Shakespeare's personal farewell to his art. In the last few years of his life Shakespeare certainly spent more of his time in Stratford-upon-Avon, where he became further involved in property dealing and litigation. But his London life also continued. In 1613 he made his first major London property purchase: a freehold house in the Blackfriars district, close to his company's indoor theatre. *The Two Noble Kinsmen* may have been written as late as 1614, and Shakespeare was in London on business a little over a year before he died of an unknown cause at home in Stratford-upon-Avon in 1616, probably on his fifty-second birthday.

About half the sum of his works were published in his lifetime, in texts of variable quality. A few years after his death, his fellow-actors began putting together an authorized edition of his complete *Comedies, Histories and Tragedies*. It appeared in 1623, in large 'Folio' format. This collection of thirty-six plays gave Shakespeare his immortality. In the words of his fellow-dramatist Ben Jonson, who contributed two poems of praise at the start of the Folio, the body of his work made him 'a monument without a tomb':

> And art alive still while thy book doth live
> And we have wits to read and praise to give ...
> He was not of an age, but for all time!

SHAKESPEARE'S WORKS: A CHRONOLOGY

1589–91	*? Arden of Faversham* (possible part authorship)
1589–92	*The Taming of the Shrew*
1589–92	*? Edward the Third* (possible part authorship)
1591	*The Second Part of Henry the Sixth*, originally called *The First Part of the Contention betwixt the Two Famous Houses of York and Lancaster* (element of co-authorship possible)
1591	*The Third Part of Henry the Sixth*, originally called *The True Tragedy of Richard Duke of York* (element of co-authorship probable)
1591–92	*The Two Gentlemen of Verona*
1591–92 perhaps revised 1594	*The Lamentable Tragedy of Titus Andronicus* (probably co-written with, or revising an earlier version by, George Peele)
1592	*The First Part of Henry the Sixth*, probably with Thomas Nashe and others
1592/94	*King Richard the Third*
1593	*Venus and Adonis* (poem)
1593–94	*The Rape of Lucrece* (poem)
1593–1608	*Sonnets* (154 poems, published 1609 with *A Lover's Complaint*, a poem of disputed authorship)
1592–94/ 1600–03	*Sir Thomas More* (a single scene for a play originally by Anthony Munday, with other revisions by Henry Chettle, Thomas Dekker and Thomas Heywood)
1594	*The Comedy of Errors*
1595	*Love's Labour's Lost*

1595–97	*Love's Labour's Won* (a lost play, unless the original title for another comedy)
1595–96	*A Midsummer Night's Dream*
1595–96	*The Tragedy of Romeo and Juliet*
1595–96	*King Richard the Second*
1595–97	*The Life and Death of King John* (possibly earlier)
1596–97	*The Merchant of Venice*
1596–97	*The First Part of Henry the Fourth*
1597–98	*The Second Part of Henry the Fourth*
1598	*Much Ado about Nothing*
1598–99	*The Passionate Pilgrim* (20 poems, some not by Shakespeare)
1599	*The Life of Henry the Fifth*
1599	'To the Queen' (epilogue for a court performance)
1599	*As You Like It*
1599	*The Tragedy of Julius Caesar*
1600–01	*The Tragedy of Hamlet, Prince of Denmark* (perhaps revising an earlier version)
1600–01	*The Merry Wives of Windsor* (perhaps revising version of 1597–99)
1601	'Let the Bird of Loudest Lay' (poem, known since 1807 as 'The Phoenix and Turtle' (turtle-dove))
1601	*Twelfth Night, or What You Will*
1601–02	*The Tragedy of Troilus and Cressida*
1604	*The Tragedy of Othello, the Moor of Venice*
1604	*Measure for Measure*
1605	*All's Well that Ends Well*
1605	*The Life of Timon of Athens*, with Thomas Middleton
1605–06	*The Tragedy of King Lear*
1605–08	? contribution to *The Four Plays in One* (lost, except for *A Yorkshire Tragedy*, mostly by Thomas Middleton)
1606	*The Tragedy of Macbeth* (surviving text has additional scenes by Thomas Middleton)
1606–07	*The Tragedy of Antony and Cleopatra*
1608	*The Tragedy of Coriolanus*

1608	*Pericles, Prince of Tyre*, with George Wilkins
1610	*The Tragedy of Cymbeline*
1611	*The Winter's Tale*
1611	*The Tempest*
1612–13	*Cardenio*, with John Fletcher (survives only in later adaptation called *Double Falsehood* by Lewis Theobald)
1613	*Henry VIII (All is True)*, with John Fletcher
1613–14	*The Two Noble Kinsmen*, with John Fletcher

KINGS AND QUEENS OF ENGLAND: From the History Plays to Shakespeare's Lifetime

	Lifespan	Reign
Angevins:		
Henry II	1133–1189	1154–1189
Richard I	1157–1199	1189–1199
John	1166–1216	1199–1216
Henry III	1207–1272	1216–1272
Edward I	1239–1307	1272–1307
Edward II	1284–1327	1307–1327 deposed
Edward III	1312–1377	1327–1377
Richard II	1367–1400	1377–1399 deposed
Lancastrians:		
Henry IV	1367–1413	1399–1413
Henry V	1387–1422	1413–1422
Henry VI	1421–1471	1422–1461 and 1470–1471
Yorkists:		
Edward IV	1442–1483	1461–1470 and 1471–1483
Edward V	1470–1483	1483 not crowned: deposed and assassinated
Richard III	1452–1485	1483–1485
Tudors:		
Henry VII	1457–1509	1485–1509
Henry VIII	1491–1547	1509–1547
Edward VI	1537–1553	1547–1553

Jane	1537–1554	1553 not crowned: deposed and executed
Mary I	1516–1558	1553–1558
Philip of Spain	1527–1598	1554–1558 co-regent with Mary
Elizabeth I	1533–1603	1558–1603
Stuart:		
James I	1566–1625	1603–1625 James VI of Scotland (1567–1625)

THE HISTORY BEHIND THE HISTORIES: A Chronology

Square brackets indicate events that happen just outside a play's timescale but are mentioned in the play.

Date	Event	Location	Play
22 May 1200	Truce between King John and Philip Augustus	Le Goulet, Normandy	*King John*
Apr 1203	Death of Arthur	Rouen	*King John*
1209	Pope Innocent III excommunicates King John		*King John*
18/19 Oct 1216	Death of King John	Swineshead, Lincolnshire	*King John*
Apr–Sep 1398	Quarrel, duel and exile of Bolingbroke and Mowbray	Coventry	*Richard II*
3 Feb 1399	Death of John of Gaunt	Leicester	*Richard II*
Jul 1399	Bullingbrook lands in England	Ravenspur, Yorkshire	*Richard II*
Aug 1399	Richard II captured by Bullingbrook	Wales	*Richard II*
30 Sep 1399	Richard II abdicates	London	*Richard II*
13 Oct 1399	Coronation of Henry IV	London	*Richard II*
Jan–Feb 1400	Death of Richard II	Pontefract Castle	*Richard II*
22 Jun 1402	Owen Glendower captures Edmund Mortimer	Bryn Glas, Wales	*1 Henry IV*
14 Sep 1402	Henry Percy defeats Scottish army	Homildon Hill, Yorkshire	*1 Henry IV*

Date	Event	Location	Play
21 Jul 1403	Battle of Shrewsbury; death of Henry Percy (Hotspur)	Battlefield, near Shrewsbury, Shropshire	*1 & 2 Henry IV*
Feb 1405	Tripartite Indenture between Owen Glendower, Edmund Mortimer and Northumberland (Henry Percy)	Bangor	*Henry IV*
May–Jun 1405	Rebellion of Archbishop of York (Richard Scroop), Earl of Norfolk (Thomas Mowbray) and Lord Bardolph	Yorkshire	*2 Henry IV*
8 Jun 1405	Trial and execution of Archbishop of York and Earl of Norfolk	York	*2 Henry IV*
20 Mar 1413	Death of Henry IV	Westminster Abbey	*2 Henry IV*
9 Apr 1413	Coronation of Henry V	Westminster Abbey	*2 Henry IV*
c.1415–16?	Death of Owen Glendower	Wales?	*2 Henry IV*
Early Aug 1415	Execution of Earl of Cambridge, Lord Scroop and Sir Thomas Grey	Southampton	*Henry V*
14 Aug–22 Sep 1415	Siege of Harfleur	Harfleur, Normandy	*Henry V*
25 Oct 1415	Battle of Agincourt	Agincourt, Pas de Calais	*Henry V*
31 Aug 1422	Death of Henry V	Bois de Vincennes, near Paris	*1 Henry VI*
18 Jan 1425	Death of Edmund Mortimer	Ireland	*1 Henry VI*
Oct 1428–May 1429	Siege of Orléans	Orléans	*1 Henry VI*
17 Oct 1428	Death of Lord Salisbury	Orléans	*1 Henry VI*
18 Jun 1429	Capture of Lord Talbot at battle of Patay	Patay, near Orléans	*1 Henry VI*
18 Jul 1429	Coronation of Charles VII	Rheims Cathedral	*1 Henry VI*

6 Nov 1429	Coronation of Henry VI as King of England	Westminster Abbey	[1 Henry VI]
23 May 1430	Capture of Joan of Arc	Compiégne, near Soissons	1 Henry VI
30 May 1431	Execution of Joan of Arc	Saint-Ouen, near Paris	1 Henry VI
16 Dec 1431	Coronation of Henry VI as King of France	Notre Dame Cathedral, Paris	1 Henry VI
14 Sep 1435	Death of Duke of Bedford	Rouen	1 Henry VI
Summer–Autumn 1441	Arrest and trial of Eleanor Cobham and accomplices	London	2 Henry VI
20 May 1442	Lord Talbot created Earl of Shrewsbury	Paris	1 Henry VI
23 Apr 1445	Marriage of Henry VI and Margaret of Anjou	Titchfield, Hampshire	2 Henry VI
23 Feb 1447	Death of Humphrey, Duke of Gloucester	Bury St Edmunds	2 Henry VI
11 Apr 1447	Death of Cardinal Beaufort	Winchester	2 Henry VI
2 May 1450	Death of Earl of Suffolk	English Channel	2 Henry VI
Jun–Jul 1450	Rebellion of Jack Cade	Kent and London	2 Henry VI
Spring 1452	Richard, Duke of York, marches on London	London	2 Henry VI
17 Jul 1453	Death of Lord Talbot at battle of Cantillon	Cantillon, Gascony	1 Henry VI
22 May 1455	First battle of St Albans	St Albans, Hertfordshire	2 Henry VI
10 Jul 1460	Battle of Northampton	Northampton	[3 Henry VI]
Oct 1460	Richard, Duke of York, holds Parliament	London	3 Henry VI
30 Dec 1460	Battle of Wakefield	Wakefield, Yorkshire	3 Henry VI
2 Feb 1461	Battle of Mortimer's Cross	Near Wigmore, Herefordshire	3 Henry VI
29 Mar 1461	Battle of Towton	Near Tadcaster, Yorkshire	3 Henry VI

Date	Event	Location	Play
28 Jun 1461	Coronation of Edward IV	Westminster Abbey	*3 Henry VI*
1 May 1464	Marriage of Edward IV and Elizabeth Woodville	Northamptonshire	*3 Henry VI*
Jul 1465	Henry VI captured	Lancashire	*3 Henry VI*
26 Jul 1469	Battle of Edgecote Moor	Near Banbury, Oxfordshire	*3 Henry VI*
Oct 1470–Apr/May 1471	Readeption (restoration) of Henry VI	London	*3 Henry VI*
14 Apr 1471	Battle of Barnet; death of Warwick	Barnet, near London	*3 Henry VI*
4 May 1471	Battle of Tewkesbury; death of Edward, Prince of Wales	Tewkesbury, Gloucestershire	*3 Henry VI*
21 May 1471	Death of Henry VI	Tower of London	*3 Henry VI*
12 Jul 1472	Marriage of Richard, Duke of Gloucester, to Anne	Westminster Abbey	*Richard III*
18 Feb 1478	Death of Duke of Clarence	Tower of London	*Richard III*
9 Apr 1483	Death of Edward IV	Westminster	*Richard III*
Jun 1483	Death of Lord Hastings	Tower of London	*Richard III*
6 Jul 1483	Coronation of Richard III	Westminster Abbey	*Richard III*
2 Nov 1483	Death of Duke of Buckingham	Salisbury	*Richard III*
16 Mar 1485	Death of Queen Anne	Westminster	*Richard III*
22 Aug 1485	Battle of Bosworth Field	Leicestershire	*Richard III*
30 Oct 1485	Coronation of Henry VII	Westminster Abbey	[*Richard III*]
18 Jan 1486	Marriage of Henry VII and Elizabeth of York	Westminster Abbey	[*Richard III*]
Jun 1520	Meeting of Henry VIII and Francis I	'Field of the Cloth of Gold', near Calais, France	[*Henry VIII*]

17 May 1521	Death of Duke of Buckingham	Tower Hill, London	*Henry VIII*
29 Nov 1530	Death of Wolsey	Leicester	*Henry VIII*
25 Jan 1533	Marriage of Henry VIII and Anne Bullen (Boleyn)	Whitehall	*Henry VIII*
1 Jun 1533	Coronation of Anne Bullen (Boleyn)	Westminster Abbey	*Henry VIII*
7 Sep 1533	Birth of Princess Elizabeth	Greenwich Palace	*Henry VIII*
10 Sep 1533	Christening of Princess Elizabeth	Greenwich Palace	*Henry VIII*

FURTHER READING AND VIEWING

CRITICAL APPROACHES

Brooke, Nicholas, *Shakespeare's Early Tragedies* (1968). Strong on tragic structure.

Burns, Edward, *Richard III* (2001). Brief but stimulating study in series published for the British Council.

Clemen, Wolfgang, *A Commentary on Shakespeare's Richard III* (1957) trans. Jean Bonheim (1968). Good on language and imagery.

Marienstras, Richard, 'Of a Monstrous Body', in *French Essays on Shakespeare and His Contemporaries*, ed. Jean-Marie Maguin and Michèle Willems (1995), pp. 153–74. Cultural-historical analysis of significance of Richard's deformed body.

Moseley, Charles, *Shakespeare: Richard III. A Critical Study* (1989). High-class student guide.

Neill, Michael, 'Shakespeare's Halle of Mirrors: Play, Politics, and Psychology in *Richard III*', *Shakespeare Studies*, 8 (1975), pp. 99–129. From adaptation of sources to Richard's psychological complexity.

Rackin, Phyllis, *Stages of History: Shakespeare's English Chronicles* (1990). Particularly strong on the women.

Richmond, Hugh, '*Richard III* and the Reformation', *Journal of English and Germanic Philology*, 83 (1984), pp. 509–21. Examines religious vocabulary and debates.

Rossiter, A. P., *Angel with Horns and other Shakespeare Lectures* (1961). Sane, balanced.

Saccio, Peter, *Shakespeare's English Kings: History, Chronicle, and Drama* (1977). Handy comparison with sources and actual history.

THE PLAY IN PERFORMANCE

Brooke, Michael, '*Richard III* on Screen', www.screenonline.org.uk/
tv/id/1022653/index.html. Valuable overview of film and TV
versions.

Day, Gillian, *King Richard III*, Shakespeare at Stratford (2002).
Survey of productions.

Hankey, Julie, ed., *King Richard III*, Plays in Performance (1981).
Innovative edition annotated by means of reference to choices of
actors and productions down the ages.

Holland, Peter, *English Shakespeares: Shakespeare on the English Stage
in the 1990s* (1997). Discusses key modern productions.

Jackson, Russell and Robert Smallwood, eds, *Players of Shakespeare 3*
(1993). Includes interview with Penny Downie on playing
Margaret in the *Henry VI/Richard III* tetralogy.

O'Connor, John, *Shakespearean Afterlives: Ten Characters with a Life of
Their Own* (2003). Lively account of some historic Richards.

Richmond, Hugh M., *King Richard III*, Shakespeare in Performance
(1989). Useful overview.

Royal Shakespeare Company, 'Exploring Shakespeare: Richard III'
www.rsc.org.uk/explore/plays/richard3.htm. Rehearsal footage,
actor and director interviews, commentary on Michael Boyd's
2007 production.

Shakespeare Birthplace Trust Study Materials, *Richard III in
Performance* by Rebecca Brown, www.shakespeare.org.uk/
content/view/315/315/.

Sher, Antony, *Year of the King* (1985). Compelling diary of a great
actor describing what it is like to play the role of Richard.

Smallwood, Robert, ed., *Players of Shakespeare 4* (1998) and 6
(2004). Each volume contains an interview with an actor talking
about playing Richard.

For a more detailed Shakespeare bibliography and selections
from a wide range of critical accounts of the play, with linking
commentary, visit the edition website, www.rscshakespeare.co.uk.

AVAILABLE ON DVD

Richard III, directed by F. R. Benson (1911), on *Silent Shakespeare* (DVD 2004). Brief tableaux from a very early film version.

Richard III, directed by Laurence Olivier (1955, DVD 2006). Also starring Olivier. Shaped the image of Richard for two generations.

The Wars of the Roses (tx. 22 April 1965), directed by Peter Hall, with text adapted by John Barton. BBC television version of a highly influential project of the RSC in its early years, with Ian Holm as Richard and Peggy Ashcroft as Margaret. Only available in specialist archives such as the British Film Institute in London.

Richard III, directed by Jane Howell (BBC Television Shakespeare, 1983, DVD 2004). Nearly four hours long, due to a very full text, in contrast to the heavy cutting of all other filmed versions. Less successful than the three parts of *Henry VI* by the same director, which were an unexpected highlight of the BBC series.

Richard III in *Shakespeare: The Animated Tales* (joint BBC/Russian television production, 1994, DVD 2007). High-quality cartoon abbreviation, notable in that Richard is voiced by Antony Sher, whose legendary 1984 RSC stage production is not available on screen.

Richard III, directed by Richard Loncraine (1995, DVD 2000). Developed from the McKellen/Eyre National Theatre production. Brilliant transposition to Fascist 1930s setting: a definitive modern revisioning, rendering Olivier into a period piece.

Looking for Richard, directed by Al Pacino (1996, DVD 2005). Quirky but illuminating 'metaproduction' in which Pacino explores his fascination with the role and the play, assisted by actors and academics, including Kevin Spacey excellent as Buckingham.

REFERENCES

1 Quoted in E. K. Chambers, *William Shakespeare* (2 vols, 1930), Vol. 2, p. 212.
2 Stanley Wells, 'Television Shakespeare', *Shakespeare Quarterly*, 33 (1982), pp. 261–73 (p. 266).
3 Thomas Davies, *Dramatic Miscellanies* (3 vols, 1784), Vol. 3, pp. 440–2.
4 Thomas Davies, *Memoirs of the Life of David Garrick* (2 vols, 1780, repr. 1969), Vol. 1, p. 40.
5 Davies, 'Mr Garrick's First Appearance on a London Stage' in his *Life of David Garrick*, Vol. 1, pp. 37–50.
6 Julie Hankey, *Plays in Performance: Richard III* (1981), p. 42.
7 William Hazlitt, review in *A View of the English Stage; or, A Series of Dramatic Criticisms* (1818), pp. 5–9.
8 London Green, '"The Gaiety of Meditated Success": The Richard III of William Charles Macready', *Theatre Research International*, 10 (1985), pp. 107–28 (p. 125).
9 Review of *Richard III*, *Athenaeum*, 26 December 1896.
10 Review of *Richard III*, *The Times*, 3 November 1937.
11 Donald Wolfit, *First Interval: The Autobiography of Donald Wolfit* (1954), p. 205.
12 J. C. Trewin, review of *Richard III*, *Observer*, 17 September 1944.
13 Kenneth Tynan, 'Heroic Acting Since 1944', in *He That Plays the King: A View of the Theatre* (1950), pp. 32–113.
14 Sheridan Morley, 'A Breath of Fresh Air', *New Statesman*, 30 June 2003.
15 Hugh M. Richmond, *King Richard III*, Shakespeare in Performance (1989), p. 142.
16 Peter Hall, programme notes to *Edward IV* (second play of the trilogy, drawn from Parts 2 and 3 of *Henry VI*), RSC, 1963.
17 Milton Shulman, *Evening Standard*, 21 August 1963.
18 Ian Richardson on playing Richard III, in Judith Cook, *Shakespeare's Players* (1983).
19 Richardson on playing Richard III.
20 Benedict Nightingale, *New Statesman*, 24 April 1970.
21 S. P. Cerasano, *Shakespeare Quarterly*, 36 (1985).
22 John O'Connor, *Shakespearean Afterlives* (2003), p. 113.
23 John Peter, *Sunday Times*, 24 June 1984.
24 Interview with Simon Russell Beale by Peter Lewis, *Sunday Times*, 2 August 1992.
25 Irving Wardle, *Independent on Sunday*, 16 August 1992.
26 Paul Taylor, *Independent*, 13 August 1992.
27 Benedict Nightingale, *The Times*, 13 August 1992.
28 Irving Wardle, *The Times*, 5 November 1980.
29 Michael Billington, *Guardian*, 5 November 1980.
30 Julie Hankey, *Times Literary Supplement*, 14 November 1980.

31 David Troughton, 'Richard III', in *Players of Shakespeare 4*, ed. Robert Smallwood (1998).

32 Anton Lesser, 'Richard of Gloucester', in *Players of Shakespeare 3*, ed. Russell Jackson and Robert Smallwood (1993).

33 Henry Goodman, 'Richard III', in *Players of Shakespeare 6*, ed. Robert Smallwood (2004).

34 Goodman, 'Richard III'.

35 Benedict Nightingale, *New Statesman*, 24 April 1970.

36 D. A. N. Jones, *Listener*, 23 April 1970.

37 Irving Wardle, *Independent on Sunday*, 16 August 1992.

38 Henry Goodman on his portrayal of Richard III, *Richard III Online Playguide*, www.rsc.org.uk/richard/current/home.html.

39 Susannah Clapp, *Observer*, 27 July 2003.

40 Benedict Nightingale, *The Times*, 25 July 2003.

41 Troughton, 'Richard III'.

42 Cerasano, *Shakespeare Quarterly*, 36.

43 David Starkey, *Times Literary Supplement*, 28 August 1992.

44 Troughton, 'Richard III'.

45 Goodman, 'Richard III'.

46 Peter Holland, *English Shakespeares* (1997), p. 231.

47 Lesser, 'Richard of Gloucester'.

48 Hankey, *Times Literary Supplement*, 14 November 1980.

49 Lesser, 'Richard of Gloucester'.

50 Lisa Stevenson on playing Lady Anne, *Richard III Online Playguide*, www.rsc.org.uk/richard/current/home.html.

51 Katherine Duncan-Jones, *Times Literary Supplement*, 11 May 2001.

52 Taylor, *Independent*, 13 August 1992.

53 Wardle, *Times*, 5 November 1980.

54 B. A. Young, *Financial Times*, 5 November 1980.

55 Nightingale, *New Statesman*, 24 April 1970.

56 Katherine Duncan-Jones, *Times Literary Supplement*, 11 November 2001.

57 R. Chris Hassel Jr., *Shakespeare Quarterly*, 36 (1985).

58 Penny Downie, 'Queen Margaret', in *Players of Shakespeare 3*.

59 Andrew St George, *Financial Times*, 13 August 1992.

60 Taylor, *Independent*, 13 August 1992.

61 Taylor, *Independent*, 13 August 1992.

62 Sean Holmes on directing the RSC's 2003 production, *Richard III Online Playguide*, www.rsc.org.uk/richard/current/home.html.

63 Lesser, 'Richard of Gloucester'.

64 Troughton, 'Richard III'.

65 Hassel, Jr., *Shakespeare Quarterly*, 36.

66 Charles Spencer, *Daily Telegraph*, 27 April 2001.

67 Barbara Hodgdon, 'The RSC's "Long Sonata of the Dead": Shakespeare-history and Imagined Community', in *Re-visions of Shakespeare*, ed. Evelyn Gajowski (2004), p. 77.

68 Michael Billington, *Guardian*, 5 November 1980.

69 Paul Taylor, *Independent*, 30 October 1998.

70 Jones, *Listener*, 23 April 1970.

ACKNOWLEDGEMENTS AND PICTURE CREDITS

Preparation of 'Richard III in Performance' was assisted by a generous grant from the CAPITAL Centre (Creativity and Performance in Teaching and Learning) of the University of Warwick, for research in the RSC archive at the Shakespeare Birthplace Trust. The Arts and Humanities Research Council (AHRC) funded a term's research leave that enabled Jonathan Bate to work on 'Actor, Director and Designer'.

Picture research by Helen Robson and Jan Sewell. Grateful acknowledgement is made to the Shakespeare Birthplace Trust for assistance with picture research (special thanks to Helen Hargest) and reproduction fees.

Images of RSC productions are supplied by the Shakespeare Centre Library and Archive, Stratford-upon-Avon. This Library, maintained by the Shakespeare Birthplace Trust, holds the most important collection of Shakespeare material in the UK, including the Royal Shakespeare Company's official archives. It is open to the public free of charge.

For more information see www.shakespeare.org.uk.

1. Portrait of David Garrick (1745) Reproduced by permission of the Shakespeare Birthplace Trust
2. Directed by Bill Alexander (1984) Joe Cocks Studio Collection © Shakespeare Birthplace Trust
3. Directed by Sean Holmes (2003) Malcolm Davies © Shakespeare Birthplace Trust

4. Photograph of the set design for Richard III (2008) Lucy Barriball © Royal Shakespeare Company
5. Richard III Directed by Michael Boyd (2008) Ellie Kurttz © Royal Shakespeare Company
6. Directed by Sam Mendes (1992) © Michael Le Poer Trench
7. Reconstructed Elizabethan Playhouse © Charcoalblue

> **"Thanks to Bate and Rasmussen, we now have a rendering of the complete works that, in a rare publishing achievement, would also give complete satisfaction to the author himself."**
> *- Robert McCrum, The Observer*

Also Available:

A Midsummer Night's Dream	978-0-230-21789-8
Hamlet	978-0-230-21787-4
Love's Labour's Lost	978-0-230-21791-1
Richard III	978-0-230-22111-6
The Tempest	978-0-230-21785-0

The RSC Complete Works	
Hardback	978-0-230-00350-7
Paperback	978-0-230-20095-1
Leather-bound	978-0-230-00351-4

www.rscshakespeare.co.uk